D0000510

PROFIT LIKE THE PROS

PROFIT LIKE THE PROS

THE BEST

REAL ESTATE DEALS

THAT SHAPED

EXPERT INVESTORS

KEN CORSINI

BiggerPockets®
PUBLISHING
Denver, Colorado

This publication is protected under the U.S. Copyright Act of 1976 and all other applicable international, federal, state, and local laws, and all rights are reserved, including resale rights: You are not allowed to reproduce, transmit, or sell this book in part or in full without the written permission of the publisher.

Limit of Liability: Although the author and publisher have made reasonable efforts to ensure that the contents of this book were correct at press time, the author and publisher do not make, and hereby disclaim, any representations and warranties regarding the content of the book, whether express or implied, including implied warranties of merchantability or fitness for a particular purpose. You use the contents in this book at your own risk. Author and publisher hereby disclaim any liability to any other party for any loss, damage, or cost arising from or related to the accuracy or completeness of the contents of the book, including any errors or omissions in this book, regardless of the cause. Neither the author nor the publisher shall be held liable or responsible to any person or entity with respect to any loss or incidental, indirect, or consequential damages caused, or alleged to have been caused, directly or indirectly, by the contents contained herein. The contents of this book are informational in nature and are not legal or tax advice, and the authors and publishers are not engaged in the provision of legal, tax, or any other advice. You should seek your own advice from professional advisors, including lawyers and accountants, regarding the legal, tax, and financial implications of any real estate transaction you contemplate.

Profit like the Pros: The Best Real Estate Deals That Shaped Expert Investors
Ken Corsini
Published by BiggerPockets Publishing LLC, Denver, Colorado
Copyright © 2020 by Ken Corsini
All Rights Reserved.

Publisher's Cataloging-in-Publication Data
Names: Corsini, Ken, author.
Title: Profit like the pros: the best real estate deals that shaped expert investors / by Ken Corsini.
Description: Denver, CO: BiggerPockets Publishing, 2020.
Identifiers: LCCN: 2020936157 | ISBN: 9781947200319 (pbk.) | 9781947200326 (ebook)
Subjects: LCSH Real estate business. | Real estate investment. | Success in business. | Real estate developers--United States. | Real estate development--United States. | Wealth. | BISAC BUSINESS & ECONOMICS / Real Estate / General | BUSINESS & ECONOMICS / Investments & Securities / Real Estate | BUSINESS & ECONOMICS / Small Business | BUSINESS & ECONOMICS / Personal Success | BUSINESS & ECONOMICS / Real Estate / Buying & Selling Homes
Classification: LCC HD255 .C655 2020 | DDC 332.63/24--dc23

Printed on recycled paper in the United States of America
10 9 8 7 6 5 4 3 2 1

Dedication

This book is dedicated to my wonderful wife and partner, Anita. It would not have been a reality without your unwavering support and encouragement these last 20 years to take risks and chase my dreams (even the crazy ones).

TABLE OF CONTENTS

INTRODUCTION

I started flipping houses in 2005 at the ripe old age of 28—but I guess you could say I got my *real* start in middle school. It wasn't houses, though. It was candy.

I remember it clearly: I was 12 years old, and my parents were dragging me through the aisles of Sam's Club as I waited patiently for the bulk candy aisle. Surely they would let me spend my hard-earned allowance on a gigantic box of Jolly Ranchers—which in this instance, they did.

After that trip, I was stuffing my face with Jolly Ranchers when a lightbulb went off. My young, entrepreneurial mind launched into some quick mental arithmetic, and it hit me: I had purchased an entire bag of Jolly Ranchers for $10. If I resold each individually wrapped piece for 10 cents, I could make $20!

The profit spoke, and I answered—it was ingenious! The next day, I filled my backpack with candy, got to school, and started spreading the word: If you needed a fix, I was your dealer. Within days, I had sugar-addicted clients that needed my product, inventory that needed to move, and the promise of extravagant profits from my candy-selling enterprise.

Now, I was a pretty good student back then—solid grades, well-behaved, and liked by most of my teachers—but this new candy-dealing business was *technically* not allowed. For a good student like me, it was pushing the envelope, but I pushed on.

A week or two into my black-market candy biz, I started losing my stomach for deviousness. The under-the-desk exchange of money for candy and the close calls with teachers were simply too much stress for little Ken Corsini. With only $5 to go before reaching that $20 goal, I took my earnings, devoured the remaining inventory, and quit.

Looking back, however, it's clear that my little venture into the world of arbitrage was the first spark of my entrepreneurial wiring. This same wiring would manifest itself again and again over the next several years.

In college I started a business painting street addresses on curbs—an atypical endeavor, yes, but a surprisingly fruitful one. Driving through the neighborhood, I would tape a letter on each mailbox (my first foray into direct mail marketing) that announced I would return the next day, ready to paint an address on the curb for every accepted offer. At $15 a pop, I typically raked in a cool hundred bucks with just a few hours of work— definitely better than my friends making $7 an hour at Hamburger Joe's.

Luckily for me, my college sweetheart, Anita, had zero qualms with my entrepreneurial schemes. In fact, in our first year of marriage, just after college, I convinced her to let me sell her immaculate Nissan Maxima in hopes of taking the earnings to auction and "upgrading" to a nicer car.

Wouldn't you know, it worked! Over the next three years, that one car turned into fifteen cars, with profit building on profit each time. Since I was also working a full-time corporate job, the joke around the office was always "What's Ken driving to work today?"

That first corporate job was a lucrative opportunity as a client service rep for a risk management information system (RMIS) with a large insurance brokerage. For five years, I worked that 9-to-5, but I always maintained a side hustle and an aching ambition to be in business for myself. From flipping cars to selling on eBay, I was constantly in motion, always seeking a solid jumping-off point.

Enter: real estate.

About the fourth year into my corporate job, I found my future career in the most unlikely of places: a garage sale. Perusing the driveway full of old clothes, battered sports equipment, and outdated wall hangings, I happened upon a large binder, still wrapped in its original cellophane. On the cover was a picture of a dignified gentleman who sat beside the large, all-caps title: *NO DOWN PAYMENT*. The name at the bottom? Carleton H. Sheets.

Intrigued, I asked the seller how much he wanted for it, and he replied that even though he had paid hundreds for it, he'd let it go for $10. He also mentioned that the author was a legend in the real estate information marketing business. Smelling a deal, I forked over $10 and took it home for further inspection.

Inside that binder was a workbook and twelve CDs recorded by Sheets himself, and I spent the next year of my life listening to those CDs over and over again. If I was in my car, you better believe I was listening to the velvety voice of Sheets explaining the intricacies of lease options, assumable loans, and tax liens.

Anita, meanwhile, had zero interest in this newfound fountain of knowledge and was magically lulled to sleep whenever I popped in a CD. For whatever reason, she wasn't as captivated by the principles of real estate investing. I heard velvety, she heard *boooring*! Even today, it's one of our household's favorite ways to poke fun at our career path's origin.

Around this same time, I had a chance encounter with a gentleman who also changed the trajectory of my life. I met him only once, and to this day I couldn't even tell you his name, but his story left a lasting impression. He was semi-retired and working in a local home builder's showroom, though it seemed more for socializing than selling houses.

For no particular reason, I stopped by the showroom after work one day and ended up spending the next two hours captivated by story after story of this man's many real estate conquests. From buying pre-foreclosures at pennies on the dollar to sophisticated no-money-down deals, he had a story for every kind of deal under the sun. He also had an uncanny ability to speak without pausing, but I hung on to his every word, as if his next sentence might include the key to the secret of life.

When I left the showroom, having spoken maybe ten words throughout the conversation (mostly "Wow," "What!?" and "*Really?*"), I was completely enamored with the idea of following in this guy's footsteps. I even called my brother to tell him about the encounter and how I believed my life would be different as a result. I bet I know what my brother was thinking: "So Ken hears a few stories from a nameless showroom employee, and now he's planning to quit his job and change his life completely?"

Crazy, right? But within a year, that's exactly what happened.

After five years of faithful service in my corporate job, I walked into my boss's office one morning and told him I was leaving. I was 28 at the time, and I had to pursue my dream of being in business for myself. I knew that real estate was the vehicle that would propel me to success.

Fast-forward fifteen years: Anita and I have flipped more than 800 houses, bought and sold commercial and multifamily properties, built a construction company, started a brokerage with more than 200 agents and multiple franchisees along with a thriving mortgage company, hosted more than a hundred *Deal Farm* podcasts, formed a coaching program, spoken on stages around the country, and even starred in twenty-eight episodes of HGTV's *Flip or Flop Atlanta*.

It's been a whirlwind, but it all started with a little inspiration. While it was probably in my DNA to be an entrepreneur, a few fate-timed sparks finally lit the fire for good. Ultimately, those sparks came from listening to the stories of veteran real estate investors. The stories of deals—how they were acquired, how they were structured, how much money was made—inspired me like nothing else. With them came the ability to visualize myself doing the same things to create the same outcomes. Hearing firsthand accounts from other people made it *real*.

Today I still believe in the unparalleled power of a real estate investor's ability to inspire other investors. Sometimes it just takes hearing someone else's story to believe it can be yours as well. Sometimes a story from the front lines of real estate will spark a fire that goes on to change your life.

In 2019, I decided to begin collecting such stories from seasoned investors around the country that would inspire the next generation of real estate investors. That idea began with a BiggerPockets video series called *The Best Deal Ever Show*, and it soon morphed into the book you're reading now.

The opportunity to interview these investors has been one of the most rewarding experiences of my life. Amid conversations with some of the most talented, interesting, and courageous achievers in the industry, I've returned to that awestruck feeling where my vocabulary is whittled down to "Wow," "What!?" and "*Really?*" Upon realizing the value of this content, BiggerPockets and I agreed that it was important to take some of those interviews and distill them into a book that would inspire and educate beyond the original listening audience. I can picture the Ken Corsini from 2004—green, in a corporate job, and with an insatiable appetite for real-life entrepreneurship—devouring this book.

That said, I also selfishly wrote this book for the Ken Corsini of *today*. Admittedly, I'm not a voracious reader—I tend to *date* a lot of books but rarely agree to a full-blown commitment. While I'm great at starting to read books, I'm subpar on the follow-through. Most of the good stuff is packed into the first few chapters anyway, right?

Wrong. This book comes with the promise of each chapter being as distinctive and inspiring as the next; you won't find any frontloading here. Each interview is a bite-sized glimpse into an exceptional real estate mindset, but with thought processes broken down into steps and numbers any reader can understand.

There's no need to read it sequentially. Perhaps you want to read about someone in particular and skip to their chapter first—go for it! Or maybe there's a specific investment strategy you want to jump ahead to and explore—have at it! There are no rules when it comes to reading this book, and I'm betting that will suit most entrepreneurs perfectly. We hate rules!

When all is said and done, my only hope is that the stories herein inspire you to take action, and that in doing so you find success. Not just success, but *massive* success because, as you're about to read, your next payday might be waiting just down the street.

CHAPTER ONE

ANSON YOUNG

Mentoring Through an Inherited Mess

When Brandon Turner introduced me to Anson Young, it didn't take long for me to notice his unique way of thinking. Most investors tend to view value in monetary terms, but Anson is different. To him, a deal's human dynamic is just as valuable as the money everybody walks away with. Whether by mentoring an aspiring investor, helping a family in distress, or simply ensuring his deals are more than just transactions, Anson goes beyond monetary value every step of the way.

As founder and owner of Anson Property Group LLC, in Denver, Colorado, Anson focuses on helping off-market property owners sell quickly and seamlessly. In more than ten years of investing, he has closed more than 200 wholesale deals and one hundred fix-and-flips. Throughout it all, he's kept a healthy balance between hands-on deal management and investor outreach efforts, ensuring that he's always giving back amid growing success.

Networking has always been a key component in Anson's business model, whether it's through cultivating relationships with Denver agents or connecting with members of the real estate meetup he has run for nearly ten years. He started the meetup as a way for real estate junkies to simply hang out and talk shop, but it turned out to be a deal incubator too. Anson explains:

"When I started that meetup group, I didn't know how much real estate was about finding ways to add value for everybody. The fact is that truly caring and building rapport with people is not just enriching on a personal level—it also enables trust to be transferred to deals. It means referrals, repeat business, and more opportunities on so many levels."

As the de facto leader of Denver's social real estate network, Anson didn't take long to grasp the possibilities when presented with what turned out to be his best deal ever. Not only does it combine a unique partnership with an interesting inheritance, but it also illustrates the value in building strong personal connections—something we don't always see in real estate deals.

Insider Info Over Anson's ten years of real estate experience, he's accumulated a healthy mix of deal types. While he has purchased, renovated, and sold more than one hundred properties, he's also opted for a less risky approach on more than 200 deals. Wholesaling is different from a typical flip in that the investor doesn't buy the property but instead assigns his or her purchase contract to another investor for an assignment fee. Wholesaling is a great way for a new investor to break into the business without taking on the risk and financial responsibility of actually buying a property.

FINDING THE DEAL

Anson's checklist for finding deals is tried and true: driving for dollars, vacant property lists, and getting in front of the gatekeepers—agents, lawyers, and estate companies—for deals. Nevertheless, the big wins nearly always come from his network. Professional connections across Denver lead to countless client referrals, but those monthly meetups have turned out to be the unexpected golden ticket. Anson says:

"I just like to connect people and connect with people, especially those who are new to the business or trying things out. The whole premise of the meetup isn't just to snag deals, but that turns out to be one of the benefits of providing value."

A young man named John had been attending these meetups for months, but he hadn't yet scored a deal. For this married father of three, finding time to follow through on his dream of real estate investing wasn't easy. Nonetheless, he felt he had enough learning under his belt that he could be confident recognizing a good deal when he saw it.

When a thorny but possibly lucrative real estate situation arose in John's family, he found that he was first in line for an off-market deal with potential. His grandmother had recently moved into a nursing home, and the house she had lived in for forty years needed to be sold. This task fell to John's mom and aunt, but they were already overwhelmed before things had even started.

John felt that he could help his family find a solution, but he wasn't confident that he knew the best way to approach the situation. Of course, he could simply hand off the sale to a real estate agent and let them deal with everything, but that wouldn't further his goal of getting hands-on investing experience.

At every meetup John attended, Anson had let attendees know that he was available to provide mentorship if they hit a sticking point with things like title issues, legal problems, or tricky negotiations. This offer hadn't fallen on deaf ears, but John wouldn't just be asking for advice—he had a plan. If he could get Anson on board as an investor, he could work his first flip with a trusted mentor *and* create a fair sale for his family.

Ken's Take When leaders start networking groups, it can be a phenomenal opportunity not only to mentor new and aspiring investors but also to create partnerships and facilitate more opportunities. While Anson really does run his meetup from an altruistic perspective, I know other investors who do so primarily for deal flow.

On the other hand, if you're new to real estate and just looking to gain some experience, find a mentor. Working with a seasoned professional gives you access not only to their skill and authority but to their network (contractors, private lenders, etc.). This is especially true if you've already found a deal but don't feel confident about going it alone. Find a real estate veteran to team up with, offer a lucrative partnership, and get invaluable mentorship in the process.

✓ ASSESSMENT

After John filled him in on the details, Anson agreed that the home had the makings of a great deal. Built in 1945, it was a one-story brick ranch with a basement, four bedrooms, and two bathrooms. The home had great bones, but the problem was that it hadn't been updated since the '70s. Even if it didn't need any big-ticket repairs, a cosmetic overhaul would be crucial for a profitable flip.

Since it was ideally situated in a popular residential neighborhood near a well-rated elementary school, Anson knew the home's target market would be families with young children. He also knew that these families would want more space than its current 1,200 square feet. Finishing out the basement with two additional bedrooms and a bathroom—which would add about 1,100 livable square feet—would be a huge boost to the after-repair value (ARV).

There was also the issue of *stuff*. This house had accumulated lots of it—furniture, clothes, and other unwanted bric-a-brac. The grandmother, it turned out, had quietly become a hoarder in her later years. In some rooms, walking from one end to the other meant navigating through four-foot piles of hoarded junk. And not only that—a whopping fourteen cats lived in and around the property. Figuring out what to do with all the stuff was the family's most overwhelming issue.

Getting the house market-ready would probably cost around $40,000. Anson estimated the current value at around $215,000, and comparable renovated homes were selling for about $330,000. If he took on the project, he'd want at least a $50,000 profit, which meant there wouldn't be much of a margin for error. He'd be happy to offer mentorship if the numbers worked, but first he needed to decide on an offer that was fair for everybody's time and money.

 ## THE BREAKDOWN

Single-family home, 1,200 square feet
Denver, Colorado
Asking unknown

OFFER AND FUNDING

Even though Anson had a warm introduction to the "seller"—in this case, the rest of John's family—he still had to win them over. He and John organized a roundtable discussion to weigh options with John's parents and two aunts. They met several times over the following weeks, but it wasn't always about logistics. Often they didn't discuss the property at all.

"We would talk about our silly dogs or other random things, just to get to know each other. I enjoyed this at a personal level, but at an investor level, it had the extra benefit of really helping me understand where they were coming from. All this time with the family meant that I could sincerely base my offers around what they wanted."

Anson made no secret of the fact that they could ultimately get more money by renovating on their own and listing with an agent. However, that option would also involve managing contractors, as well as paying listing fees, commissions, appraisal and closing costs, and whatever else would arise in getting the house market-ready.

Though Anson's offer didn't provide the highest possible income for the family, it did provide a much higher level of simplicity. For a flat $215,000, the family could walk away from the burden of selling and simply move on. Above all, they wouldn't have to deal with emptying out all the *stuff*. When Anson assured them that they could simply take what they wanted and leave the rest, their relief was palpable. Ultimately, they opted to smash the easy button and accept his offer.

Insider Info Anson spent hours with this family not only building rapport but also gaining their trust. Over the course of multiple meetings, it became clear that Anson wasn't some greedy buyer trying to take advantage of them. As an investor, it's incredibly important to understand the needs and concerns of the seller *first*. By taking this approach, you will make sellers feel heard, understood, and confident that you genuinely want to help them. From there, you can develop a game plan that isn't solely about buying their house but about solving their specific needs.

Meanwhile, Anson and John established a partnership arrangement in which Anson would provide all the funding and project management and John would get 10 percent of the home's resale profit. Until then, through participation, John would "earn while he learned" about scheduling, budget planning, construction walk-throughs, marketing, design, and any other aspects of the project.

Another win for networking: A private lender Anson previously worked with agreed to fund 100 percent of the purchase and renovation. He lent $255,000 at 14 percent interest on a twelve-month balloon note. With none of his own money involved and plenty of upside potential, Anson was confident that the home's sale would cover all the accrued interest and net a profit of at least $50,000.

Insider Info Anson had been in the business long enough to know that the ideal way to structure a private loan is with a balloon note. Essentially, this just means the interest accrues until either the note matures or the property is sold. For investors juggling multiple projects, structuring their private loans this way alleviates the cash-flow burden that monthly interest payments can impose on a business.

TURNAROUND

Clearing out the house was the biggest task: It took three days and *five* forty-yard dumpsters filled with rejected miscellany, which was just what they couldn't resell or donate. As for the rest, they donated at least two pickup trucks full of items, caught most of the cats to "donate" to the seller's sister, and sold many of the older appliances at prices that were a steal for local buyers.

> *"This is one of my favorite examples of stacking the wins for the buyer, the seller, and the community. I was able to remove the burden of 'stuff' from the family's shoulders, on top of giving back to the community and creating a great overall partnership."*

From there, Anson hired a contractor to build out the basement and give the upper level a facelift, including kitchen updates, new bathrooms, carpet, and paint. They also replaced ceiling fans, lighting, and exterior doors, and repainted the outside trim.

Since the home hadn't been updated since the 1970s, all the floors were still carpeted, in the style of that era. When Anson peeked under a corner piece, he found pristine hardwood. Tearing out the carpet and refinishing the hardwood floors was the final big task, and they finished without a hitch.

AFTERMATH

Barely eight weeks after the start, the renovation came in at just less than $40,000. John had treated the project as an open book for real-life investing experience and finally felt like he'd gotten his start in the game. On top of that, he provided a low-cost extra hand for Anson's team. So far, it was a win-win—but they still had to sell the house.

They had started the job in autumn, so after finishing in early winter, they pulled the comps again to ensure the $330,000 projection still held. As it turned out, the market had changed—in their favor. With low supply and high demand for comparable houses, they pushed the odds with a top-of-the-market listing at $349,000.

Ken's Take Sometimes it makes sense to list a house higher than the comps would seem to indicate. In Anson's case, the house was move-in ready, looked nicer than comparable homes, and was the only ranch-style option within half a mile. If you wanted to live in that area—or two blocks away from the elementary school, where this was—it was the only game in town.

With the hot timing, they didn't even feel the need to stage the house. After listing on a Wednesday, they had five offers by Sunday. Two weeks later, they closed on one of those offers and received their asking price of $349,000—$20,000 more than Anson's initial prediction! He explains:

"One of the best parts of the deal was interacting not just with John but with his whole family. John's mom and her four siblings had been raised in that house—it wasn't just a home, it was a history. One particular memory I have was sitting at the closing table with the whole family before I purchased the house. Suddenly, John's mom said, 'I don't know if this is possible, but can you show us the house

when it's done? Our parents had always talked about doing updates and changes to the house but never did.'

"I said, 'Of course!' Right before hitting the market, when it was at its most pristine, I was able to watch them walk through the place they'd known so well. Some tears were shed amid gasps of 'Oh my gosh, this is my old bedroom!' and 'I couldn't imagine it turning out so well!' It was so rewarding to see how handling this home with kid gloves had paid off. I had 'taken care of Mom's house' and done it right. It was an amazing bonus."

This project was special not just because of its profitability but because of the solid relationship Anson had built with a family that was genuinely grateful for his help. Ultimately, the goal of keeping the interpersonal component strong while creating profit for everybody is what made this deal such a win-win.

TAKEAWAY

It's a People Business

Anson spent a month meeting with the family to discuss their goals and concerns before landing on an agreement. After that month, if another investor had come along with a better offer, I bet the family still would have stuck with Anson. The human component of real estate is so important because, frankly, sellers want to do business with people they feel they can trust.

This business is all about the people involved and how you can help them get through what can be one of the hardest times of their life. By being authentic, genuine, and caring, you offer a customer service component that a lot of investors simply ignore. They churn through houses and think it's a numbers game, but at the end of the day, it will always be a *people* game.

Be Solutions-Driven

Many distressed and motivated sellers have a pain point that needs to be relieved: overwhelming debt, frustrating tenants, or—in this case—an unexpected inheritance. Disentangling the underlying issues of a stressful situation means understanding a situation's dynamics at all levels.

Be a problem solver more than a home buyer. Whether it's moving stuff out of the house, taking over debt, or helping someone find a new place to live, honest work toward problem solving is what will make you stand out amid multiple potential buyers.

Look at the Footprint

Anson saw the whole home, not just what had already been finished. Building out a basement or attic is a great way to maximize square footage while avoiding the hefty costs of adding or constructing a second level. The cost to finish these already-encapsulated spaces can often run as low as one-third of the cost of a new addition. From a return on investment (ROI) standpoint, it's a no-brainer!

Focus Locally

As real estate businesses grow, some investors decide to expand outside of their local market. In Anson's case, rather than go wide, he chose to go deep. For Anson, this means concentrated effort on building a massive network of investors and industry professionals that help feed his pipeline.

It's hard to imagine outgrowing the opportunities within a large city like Denver. While competition may drive some investors to smaller markets, investors like Anson simply double down in their own backyard.

CHAPTER TWO

FRANK ROLFE

From Billboards to Trailer Parks

Billboards were the reason Frank Rolfe got into real estate, but that wouldn't happen until he finished his *first* career.

After getting his BA from Stanford a year early, he began preparing to enter an MBA program the following year. As a condition of entry, he was required to start a business over the summer, and somehow he landed on billboards.

The fledgling business did so well, however, that Frank never made it back to school. Instead, he ran the billboard company for the next fourteen years. After successfully selling it, he wanted to reinvent himself— he just didn't know how. It turns out that billboards came to the rescue again, but we'll get back to that later. For now, just know that he landed in mobile home parks, and did so with a bang.

Today Frank co-operates the fifth-largest mobile home park empire in the United States, staking claim on 20,000 lots within 200 parks in twenty-four states. It takes about 400 employees to run such a business, with most out in the field as property managers, maintenance, and rehab crews. The rest comprise the accounting, marketing, and legal teams. As Frank says, *"It's like running a city of 60,000 people—just spread out over the entire country."*

Although Frank's company owns many of the mobile homes in their parks, the business is based more on owning land rather than on owning the mobile homes themselves. The fact is renting out land is just easier—

there's less upkeep, turnover, utilities, and so on. Plus, liquidity potential is one of the company's criteria for making purchases, and land is much easier to get out of than a home.

Each possible park purchase is weighed with billionaire businessman Sam Zell's axiom of risk versus reward: Never buy when there's low reward and high risk, and always buy when there's high reward and low risk. With an easy exit strategy guiding their purchases, Frank's team never buys a property they can't immediately resell, and they target parks where mobile homes are owned with at least 70 percent equity, since mortgages put liquidity at risk. When all is said and done, their specific "buy box" dictates avoiding any purchase that won't get a 20 percent cash-on-cash return.

Insider Info Cash-on-cash return is simply a measure of the income earned for a given investment compared with the overall invested amount, expressed as a percentage and typically used with real estate or other cash-flow-producing assets.

Whether owning land or managing the units themselves, Frank focuses on making money as his primary goal. Once a park meets its initial purchase criteria, Frank's team further demands that parks have strength in four core areas: infrastructure, parcel density, location, and age of the mobile homes. Combining these factors with market trends provide a solid formula for whether or not to buy.

After acquiring a park, they first try to sell as many of the homes as possible for cash. Then they either rent out the remaining properties or offer rent-to-own, which gives people a path to ownership outside of owner financing. Frank explains:

> "In a mobile home park, the homes are just personal property, so we try to focus just on the land. We're always in acquisition mode, always selling and buying—it's been a common theme since we got in the business. Since we get a steady stream of offers on the properties we have, we follow the Warren Buffett rule of 'if you don't sell it, then you just bought it at the same price.' Whenever people offer more than what we would pay for it, we sell it."

FINDING THE DEAL

The funny thing about running a billboard company for fourteen years is that it puts you in touch with a wide range of business owners. Frank had built 300 different billboards for 300 different businesses, and he planned to leverage those connections to find a new venture for himself. He started off the hunt with a spin through his Rolodex.

"I was on a fact-finding tour to find what business was worth investing in. One project I remembered vividly was building two billboards for Glenhaven Mobile Home Park in Dallas, Texas. I called the owner, Ron, and asked if he would tell me a little bit about how things worked. His response: 'Why don't you see for yourself? I'll sell it to you right now for only $10,000 down on $400,000.'"

It was an unexpected offer, but Frank was interested in hearing more. He knew not to jump so easily, though. His first question hit the nail on the head: "So, how much are you losing a month, Ron?"

ASSESSMENT

Indeed, Ron was losing $2,000 monthly, but Frank had a hunch that the park was poorly managed—perhaps Ron was missing something that Frank could figure out. Getting eighty-three lots—even though only forty were occupied—for only $10,000 down seemed like an incredible deal.

When Glenhaven was built in the early 1950s, it was an upscale six-acre property with a whimsical Scottish theme, complete with Scottish-named roads like Glenfinnan and Dunrobin. At the time, everybody in the park seemed to drive British sports cars and attend law, medical, or dental school. Mobile home parks were new to America, and the cool cats were on the scene at Glenhaven.

But things had changed since then. As mobile home sizes increased over the years, density became an issue. Glenhaven's lot depth was around fifty feet, so homes were restricted to two bedrooms. Over time, use of the existing lots became like a game of chess, trying to match new home sizes to older lots. With new tenants sometimes needing to double up on lots or split an extra one in half, the total of usable lots declined to about seventy-five.

The park had also seen a significant demographic change, with the young professionals of the 1950s and '60s being slowly replaced by affordable-housing occupants. Current tenants were paying an insanely low price of $175 to $195 per month, and even Frank knew that market rents were closer to $400. The price was actually working *against* occupancy. Any renter who didn't pass muster elsewhere could easily find a home at Glenhaven; the number of rough-edged tenants was likely turning ideal clients away.

When he visited the park, Frank immediately saw the pluses: direct highway frontage, a decent adjacent single-family neighborhood, and large shade trees and a creek providing a quasi–nature preserve feel. But he also noticed the "no-tell" hotel next door and its questionable guests milling about the park's entrance.

A closer look at the park itself confirmed his suspicions about poor management:

> "One of the first things I noticed was that the tenants had built a sort of amateur wrestling facility out of plywood and particle board. There were even makeshift concession stands. The park had a kind of 'Keep Glenhaven Weird' theme, which was the culture Ron had created with no rules and no management. 'If you can't live anywhere else, you can live at Glenhaven! No credit screening, no criminal screening, just come on over and enjoy our wrestling ring!'"

Frank's vision was to turn the park into a high-quality version of itself, cleaning up the landscape, implementing more screening checks, and eventually attracting top-tier tenants. Raising occupancy and rental prices seemed like an easy way to generate $16,000 per month. If he could fix the negative cash flow, he could worry about capital outlay later. Since he'd put only $10,000 down, if he couldn't resolve what seemed like an easily fixable problem, he would just bail.

> "It's important to approach each deal from the perspective of a lender. Since all real estate is about leverage, you are making a mistake if you don't look at every property from a banker's perspective. With mobile home parks, that means counting only lot rent and not

mobile home rent, putting greater importance on infrastructure and location, and shying away from the states and markets that lenders hate. I'm also a huge believer in the importance of good due diligence. Benjamin Franklin said that 'diligence is the mother of good luck,' and he was 100 percent correct.

"Of course, with Glenhaven I did absolutely none of these things—I had no idea what I was doing and had not yet learned through trial and error!"

 # THE BREAKDOWN

Mobile home park, seventy-five lots, six acres
Dallas, Texas
Asking $400,000

OFFER AND FUNDING

Accepting Ron's offer would risk only $10,000 and some time and effort. If he could remedy the $2,000 loss per month, he figured he could clear even more hurdles after that. With one phone call, Frank was now in the mobile home industry. He transferred the $10,000 to Ron, signed owner-finance terms on a thirty-year seller-financed note at 6 percent, and moved into an on-site single wide to get down to business.

Insider Info Frank pointed out that he wouldn't advise people to jump into a deal as quickly as he did back when he "knew nothing about real estate." These days, before making a purchase, he ensures that all the right pieces are in place: a Phase I environmental assessment, land surveys, inspections, financial analysis, the works. To make sure you're covering all your bases, always use mentors, education, and online resources before investing. For more information, you can check out the mobile home category of the BiggerPockets Blog at www.biggerpockets.com/mobile-homes.

TURNAROUND

Frank's plan was to live and work in Glenhaven for about a year and learn the business from the ground up. First, he needed to root out the $2,000 monthly loss. After poring over the financial statements, he saw the problem as clear as day: Ron had been providing free cable to all residents. The price tag? Two thousand dollars per month!

The cable went to all the lots, which meant nearly half of that payment provided cable to nobody. Adding insult to injury was the obvious fact that most of the tenants used satellite dishes anyway. Since the cable contract was month to month, Frank promptly canceled it. A letter to tenants informing them of the change received almost zero pushback. With that one simple move, he'd solved the negative cash flow.

Next, Frank began a quest to return Glenhaven to its former glory, hoping that this would be the key to attracting more tenants. Those existing tenants who wanted to keep things just as they were resisted nearly every attempt to raise cleanliness standards. The first six months were nothing but abject misery, but Frank persisted: He renovated empty units, spruced up the common areas, designated a home for the future park manager's residence and office, and cleaned up trash, dead trees, and other debris.

"The big trick to Glenhaven was bringing back the residents' sense of pride in living there. One of the first people I met there was an old man who lived at the back of the property. He'd grafted two single wides together into an L shape with a professional-looking landscaped garden in the pocket of the L. He was a super-classy guy—always wearing a blazer around—a former engineer and holdover from the 1950s and '60s era of Glenhaven glamour. I knew the best thing I could do was to make the other residents as proud of their home as he was."

After putting nearly $40,000 into cosmetic improvements with little growth in occupancy, Frank finally got a windfall. A nearby mobile home park was slated for demolition, and knowing that its residents would need a new place to stay, Frank called the owner to offer his vacant lots. It was a match made in heaven, and the other park owner wanted to make things happen fast.

The incoming tenants were used to paying well over $300 per month, which made raising Glenhaven's rents incredibly easy. Their arrival changed the park's entire demographic and vision overnight. Before, the residents had been mostly carnival workers and itinerants, but now the park was filled with families with reliable jobs and track records.

Suddenly, all the tenants who hated rules and community living standards were outnumbered. It was the best thing that could've happened: Instead of Frank having to fight them tooth and nail on every change, the troublesome tenants now *wanted* to leave. Whenever one moved out, Frank renovated their property for a sale, often to the friends and families of the new transplants.

After the exodus of old tenants, Frank renovated all the vacated properties and set a new rent of $300 across the board. But just as he was hitting his stride, Frank experienced the most terrifying moment of his career: The property lost all natural gas.

It was a twenty-degree winter day and the residents were up in arms—seventy-five families with no heat, cooking gas, or warm showers. Frank was out of town, but he started frantically making calls. Apparently, hidden gas leaks had led to colossal waste, so the provider had shut off the entire system.

Getting the gas turned back on required pressure testing, and the lines failed. Fixing them would require tearing up the park grounds, adding new lines, and spending up to $400,000—as much as Frank had paid for the whole park! If that was his only option, it made more sense to shut the whole thing down and just sell the raw land.

> "After all I'd accomplished, I thought, 'This is the moment where I need to just give up.' At that point, I thought I was done with the turnaround and had moved on to buy more parks. Being sucked back into a Glenhaven disaster was very disheartening. The situation looked hopeless, and I was not sure the park could be saved—I figured I would have to give the park back to Ron."

Frank called Ron to say he was ready to throw in the towel, but to his surprise, Ron responded that he'd been waiting for a call like this. He'd known about the leaks all along! They'd have to deal with the lack of disclosure later. For now, families were freezing and Frank had to act fast.

Since Ron had been worrying about this impending catastrophe for years, he'd already worked out a solution: Simply install one propane tank per home at a cost of $1,000 per lot. It was the only viable option, and Frank scheduled the installations immediately.

The city caught wind of the plan, though, and as workers were getting ready to unload the tanks, city officials showed up to claim it was illegal to use propane when natural gas was available. Frank called his lawyer, who reminded the officials of a pending court rule over their attempt to unfairly dictate the use of natural gas service throughout the city. Not wanting Glenhaven to be an example of their tyranny, the city backed down.

The propane tanks were a small, expensive victory. Since Ron had been caught withholding obligatory sales information and knew he had to make things right, he agreed to deduct half the cost of the retrofit from the outstanding loan balance. With the biggest hurdle hopefully behind him, Frank was back on track.

"Ron's offer was more than fair, as the changeover was a huge improvement to the park's value. Now, instead of master-metered gas, each resident had their own propane tank, which they had to pay directly to refill. I was out of the gas business entirely."

AFTERMATH

By the end of year two, Frank wasn't visiting his property to see what sort of hang-ups the tenants had created, but to marvel at all the changes that seemed to happen through magic. The filled lots were bringing in nearly $300,000 in annual revenue. He was netting $100,000 with practically zero threat to cash flow, and still had miles to go if he chose to raise rents. Though he literally could have lived off just the yearly profit from Glenhaven, Frank's success motivated him to start buying more parks instead.

"Not a day went by that I did not learn something new, either about the park business or human nature. The big lesson learned was that the entire stigma against mobile home parks and their residents is completely false. I had been duped like all Americans who watch TV or movies—mobile home parks are the original 'fake news' victim. Perhaps one day they'll shed the unfair stigma, but until then, the fact that most investors will not even consider a 'trailer park' is what creates some degree of the opportunity."

Ken's Take True, Frank got some lucky breaks on his first park, but the turnaround wasn't just magic. The fact that he lived on-site that first year was possibly the most important decision Frank made toward guaranteeing the park's future success. I'm not suggesting that investors should always move into their properties, but it often takes a high level of commitment to really turn a property around. Moving into the mobile home park was about as committed as it gets!

TAKEAWAY

Learn What You're Doing

Frank knew billboards. After fourteen years of successfully building his billboard business, he sold it and began researching his next niche. Even though he jumped into mobile home parks, he was fully cognizant that he didn't know what he didn't know. Instead of assuming he had hit yet another home run, he rolled up his sleeves and dove headfirst into the project to learn everything he could. Frank put it this way:

> *"As with any hobby, you're never going to be good at what you're doing unless you know how to realize what is an opportunity and what isn't. You can't just jump into it and think, 'I'm gonna be the trailer park king.'"*

Like any niche investor, you'll become wildly profitable in a specific area or business strategy when you've truly become an expert. For Frank, learning the ins and outs of mobile home parks has allowed him to scale his company to the size it is today—but it all started when he fully committed to learning the business.

Location Is Key

Profound, right? Who knew that location was key for real estate investing? (Sarcasm intended.) You can find mobile home parks in a lot of different locations, and believe me, they're not all created equal.

Not everybody will have the same criteria, but most mobile home park investors would agree that location dictates the chances for success. Decent growth potential, employment opportunities, and nearby shopping should be your starting criteria when evaluating a location—basically the same characteristics you'd want in any residential investment.

Interestingly, mobile home parks are one of those asset classes you can find in areas that seem to make very little economic sense. Those are the parks that Frank suggests investors avoid. He's learned to target certain parks over the years, saying:

> *"I drive by parks all the time that nobody should touch—there's no rental or purchase market because there's nothing going on in those areas! Location is key: We seek nice suburban areas near nice schools, shops, and so on. People in mobile home parks are no different than anybody else."*

One Man's Trash...

Frank's story is the perfect example of how what appeared to be a losing real estate venture actually had tons of upside potential—it just needed to be in the right hands. The seller was losing $2,000 a month due to a veritable circus of management issues (including the makeshift wrestling ring). He gave Frank a heck of a deal, even holding back the note to get out from under the property.

Before long, Frank was able to generate more than $100,000 in yearly profit. This is a perfect illustration of how smart investors profit in real estate by rescuing underperforming properties from burnt-out owners and transforming those properties into cash cows.

> *"When I started cleaning up the common areas and the most offensive homes, I started noticing things that Glenhaven had not seen in a long time: people painting their porch, picking up trash off the road, or sweeping their driveway. We've seen that over and over during the past twenty-five years of bringing old parks back to life, and that's the moment that residents start pitching in and making things better. It's kind of like empowering people to improve their lives, and it's extremely gratifying to see."*

Never assume that the current owner of your next purchase has maximized the property's value or even understood its potential. What they consider trash might just become your treasure!

CHAPTER THREE

COREY PETERSON

Life-Changing Multifamily Deal

I f Corey Peterson's then girlfriend (now wife of eighteen years) had never told him she "couldn't marry a car guy," he might still be selling used cars somewhere. Instead, he's running and operating $95 million in real estate, hosting the influential *Multifamily Legacy Podcast*, and speaking around the country on multifamily investing.

After leaving the car business, Corey bounced around between a few careers—restaurant manager, financial advisor—until he discovered fix-and-flips in 2005. By 2011, he was a full-time real estate investor, operating as the "Big Kahuna" for his company Kahuna Investments.

These days, Corey is based in Gilbert, Arizona, owning and managing about 2,500 units across the country from the comfort of his home. He keeps things simple with a core four-person team that's so well defined it's worth breaking down here:

- **The acquisition manager** typically underwrites 300 to 400 deals a year just to find one to three great ones. His philosophy is that you "have to kiss a lot of frogs to find a prince or princess."
- **The client relations manager** simply "loves on our people," keeping investors happy by paying attention to birthdays, anniversaries, and life events, and adding other human touches.

- **The lead generator** (who happens to be Corey's wife) uses her pharmaceutical industry experience to call on dentists, doctors, and chiropractors to tell Kahuna's story and get people into their investment funnel.
- **The asset manager** creates the plans and systems necessary for running their multi-million-dollar business, working directly with management companies to ensure comprehensive maintenance of company standards.

Which leaves us with Corey's role: building upon the team's cumulative efforts to seal the deal with investors. In light of his strong focus on building an investor base that's founded on relationships, it's no surprise that many of these investors have become an extension of Corey's team. (The stable cash-flow returns and long-term capital appreciation they get doesn't hurt either!) Corey states:

"I still prefer sales the old-fashioned way: one on one. I feel like this is the highest and best use of my time. I like to understand the deal holistically, see the vision to success, know how our team can execute it, and lead our investors through this process."

Like many investors, Corey started out with single-family homes. And like many investors, he soon wanted more. With a typical Kahuna mindset, he figured he should "go big or go home" and began searching for his first multifamily property.

FINDING THE DEAL

It was 2011, and Corey had just made it through his first six years of investing during one of the biggest economic downturns in recent history. He not only survived but also squirreled away a sizable chunk of cash from single-family success while building several strong investor relationships. With nowhere to go but up, he set his sights on multifamily investing.

Delving into at-home studies, online courses, and local real estate events, Corey planned to educate and network himself into finding a good deal. A year of this went by, and he had yet to find anything. Desperate for the right partners or the right deal, he signed up for a pricey weeklong multifamily seminar and hoped it would be worth the expense.

As the seminar's director welcomed the audience on day one, she asked if there were any announcements from the audience. Corey recognized his golden opportunity, raised his hand, and stood up to declare:

"Hey, listen, I have a crap-ton of money, and I'm looking for some deals. If you have a deal, I would love to look at it and see if it meets my criteria."

It was a genius move, and Corey didn't have to buy lunch or dinner for the rest of the week! Of course, he didn't *technically* have the money, but with several investors waiting in the wings, he figured he could put them to good use.

Of the many who subsequently approached Corey, a two-person team stood out. They had acquired a 144-unit $3.4 million apartment complex under contract with $150,000 down as earnest money. They needed an additional $1.5 million in equity and had to close on the purchase in less than a month. With $150,000 on the line, they were financially drained and out of prospects, and they hoped Corey could float them through to a successful deal.

ASSESSMENT

Corey flew down to Greenville, South Carolina, to check out the property. It was a 1970s Class C garden-style complex with ten brick buildings, a quaint pitched roof, a community clubhouse, and a pool. The location had lots of green space and a satisfying residential vibe, but it was only three miles away from convenient big-box stores like Lowe's and Best Buy.

Insider Info Multifamily properties are often loosely classified into A-class, B-class and C-class categories based on factors such as income levels, crime rates, vacancy, rent amounts, age, condition, and so on. While A properties are newer and will likely perform better in terms of expected occupancy levels and rents, B and C class properties are typically purchased because of the opportunity to renovate and increase overall revenues and financial performance.

However, things were downhill from there: Occupancy was at a low 79 percent with not exactly high-caliber tenants. A few of them were selling and producing drugs, and the corruption permeated the entire community. Ample foot traffic and shady loitering accompanied the drug activity, and the situation wasn't helped by taciturn property management and countless cases of deferred maintenance.

The entire property was an overgrown mess—physically and metaphorically—but all Corey saw was opportunity:

"If someone had told me, 'Buy this property, and in five years, you'll be a multi-millionaire,' I would have said, 'I sure hope so!' What's scary is that I actually believed it, while other investors would have run away. It was in a great area, but it was a beat-down dog. Fact is, I was ready to buy in. I saw the vision, I underwrote it, and I knew it could work."

Corey decided that the core issue was that the property was poorly run. It needed discipline and reliable management. If he could provide a safe, stable, and attractive place to live, then he could turn the complex into a cash-flowing machine.

His vision was to first eradicate the drug problem, then renovate the units to enhance tenant criteria and slowly drive up rental prices. With higher-quality tenants and living conditions, Corey wagered that those who appreciated the progress wouldn't mind paying a little extra for it. Since it would take around two years to turn the property around and at least $500,000 in capital expenditures, he worked out a partnership offer.

Insider Info Corey could have come into the deal as a limited partner and have left the management and operations to the two other general partners. However, this being his first deal, he had no interest in leaving the success of the project in the hands of two men whom he barely knew—and who had limited experience themselves. It made sense for him to roll up his sleeves as a general partner and help control the day-to-day processes and decisions needed to turn this property around.

THE BREAKDOWN

Multifamily, 144 units
Greenville, South Carolina
Asking $3.4 million

OFFER AND FUNDING

Confident that the deal had all the right ingredients for success, Corey offered to raise the $1.5 million in equity required to close the deal. The three men would work together as general partners syndicating a limited partnership deal for Corey's pool of investors.

Access to Corey's lenders would come at a cost: He asked for 75 percent ownership within the general partnership. It was an incredibly high percentage, but the others needed his money and, as it turned out, his leadership.

Ken's Take When people ask how a typical multifamily deal is structured, my response is always: There is no "typical." Every sponsor has their own way of syndicating a deal and structuring equity and debt. In Corey's case, he was in a strong position to negotiate the lion's share of the deal because the initial two partners couldn't have pulled it together otherwise. Since he stepped into the driver's seat to raise the private equity, secure the debt, and oversee the rehab and management of the property, it wasn't a far stretch for him to take majority interest.

Corey secured a two-year bridge loan for $2.4 million at 6.5 percent interest. The interest rate stung, but he planned to refinance after turning the property around. For the down payment, projected operating expenses, and renovation costs, he leaned on his private investors for $1.5 million in equity, broken down as an $800,000 down payment, $200,000 for closing costs and acquisition fees, and $500,000 for renovations. Although it would take some time to turn this property into a profitable venture, he structured the deal as a 50/50 profit split between the general and limited partners.

Insider Info One notable way Corey made money in this deal was through an acquisition fee. Taking a fee from the initial equity to compensate himself for putting the deal together was a bright way to get paid on the front end while also taking part in ownership and asset management. Most acquisition fees are between 1 and 4 percent. For example, if a property is purchased for $1 million and the acquisition fee is 2 percent, the syndicator will collect $20,000 at the time of acquisition.

TURNAROUND

All of Corey's hopes hinged on fixing the drug problem, but he couldn't just kick people out or search the units without a warrant. Acting on a lightbulb moment, he realized he could make it the troublesome tenants' *own* idea to vacate the premises. When he called up the local police and offered the apartment complex as training grounds for their K9 drug dog unit, they loved the idea. After scheduling a visit, Corey posted signs all around the property announcing the impending K9 training.

The following morning, Corey learned that two renters had moved out in the middle of the night—a vanishing act that cleared up most of the drug problem! Numerous renters who had been too afraid to say anything before came forward to express their gratitude. To let tenants know he was serious about keeping the area clean, he then hired local police to keep a nightly watch on the property.

"This is what we found: No matter what class of building you're buying—Class C, B, or A—there's always the crème de la crème of that tenant class. We run our properties militantly in what we expect, and there are great Class C people with great credit who seek us out for a clean, safe, and disciplined place to live."

With the drug problem on the mend, Corey could focus on the renovation. Each building got a new roof, refreshed landscaping, and a revamped parking lot. Interiors received fresh coats of two-tone paint, modernized cabinets and appliances, and new countertops with a chic epoxy finish.

Everything was going according to plan until Corey learned a painful lesson: *Know thy operating agreement.* The other two partners had been showing themselves to be more hindrance than help with even simple decisions, but things came to a head when Corey discovered they'd surreptitiously altered the operating agreement, which outlined the terms of their three-person general partnership. Instead of the 75 percent voting rights that should have come with 75 percent ownership, his voting rights were demoted to only 33 percent thanks to how they'd altered the text. Now, despite nominal majority ownership, his vote counted for less than his partners' combined votes.

Although Corey had hired a trustworthy lawyer to write and review the operating agreement, neither he nor Corey had noticed this modification. In most cases, any person with a conscience would point out a revision that huge, and Corey just hadn't been looking for the deceit. With trust completely broken, he'd had enough—he bought out his partners for $650,000, taking a colossal hit to his bank account but washing his hands of the clown investors.

Ken's Take The partnership structure and operating agreement are key in outlining *who's* doing *what*. Corey had worked hard on both of these components but accidentally overlooked a colossal revision. Luckily, his rude awakening happened early enough that the deal worked out in his favor. By buying out his partners, he likely saved the project before the weight of their ignorance could ruin everything. Not only that—he learned an invaluable lesson that made him a smarter operator and a better partner for every deal that followed.

Now that Corey could call the shots without hindrance, he proceeded to secure new property management and renovate the units with each move-out. After renovating, he could ask for a higher and more competitive rental price than what the previous tenant had paid.

Insofar as the quality tenants who wished to remain, he didn't want to push them out with a sudden price hike—even if the improved living conditions merited it. Instead, he implemented a monthly rental increase of about $4. Keeping property income steady would be a delicate balance between maintaining yearly rental renewals at 65 percent while doing his best to recoup the unanticipated cost of buying out the two partners.

Insider Info Steady rental renewal rates are a multifamily property's bread and butter. High turnover can be a huge profit buster, since lost rent and turnover costs can absolutely eat away at cash flow. It's important to find harmony between increasing rents at the rate originally estimated in your financial projections (and justified by improvements) but not so quickly that you lose tenants.

Securing strong rental income also meant curbing delinquent payments, so Corey introduced an online payment system using Automated Clearing House (ACH) drafts. Getting rental payments on time wasn't just about avoiding the annoyance of late fees and chasing people down; it would boost the odds of a strong refinance and prove to the limited partners that he meant business. Eventually, if Corey chose to sell, having an automated system for rent collection would be incredibly alluring for buyers.

Implementing the ACH requirement (combined with increasing rents) was at first "like ripping off a Band-Aid." Over time, though, these changes attracted the right renters and filtered out the people who didn't want to deal with improvements. Here's how Corey describes it:

"In the beginning, occupancy went down before it went up. We trained tenants on the new payment system, but many kept coming up with excuses why they couldn't use the online payment portal. They'd say, 'Well, I don't have a way to log in at home,' and we would invite them to use the community center's computer. Then they'd say, 'Well, I don't have an account,' and we'd respond that in that case, they'd have to send a check to corporate by the twenty-fifth of each month. If it wasn't sent by the twenty-fifth, though, it would arrive late and their account would get dinged. Setting boundaries and repercussions eventually led most to decide that paying on the portal was their easiest option."

AFTERMATH

The renovation took about a year longer than Corey had predicted, but over that time, occupancy rose to 98 percent. Every time someone moved out, he stepped in to renovate the unit so it would bring in peak rental income. Over three years, he raised rents from about $475 to $675 per month. The limited partners got 50 percent of net cash flow along the way, but for those first three years, Corey just funneled his own share of the profit right back into the venture.

He spent nearly $700,000 getting everything fixed up—which was $200,000 over the original budget—but by the end of year three, the property was a smooth-running machine earning positive returns for all the partners. By the third of every month, 99 percent of rent collections were in the bank (largely due to the ACH drafts). Plus, the property was earning $95,000 in monthly income—an extra $324,000 yearly compared with the beginning!

Corey's first multifamily investment had been a resounding success: He had resolved countless deferred maintenance issues and fixed the social problems, and he was earning consistent returns. After five years, he was ready to cash out on his masterpiece. Rather than list it traditionally, though, he wanted to see if there was a better way to sell.

"I may have grown up poor, but I was always resourceful. I never said I was the smartest kid in the room, but I've always said, 'Let me find smart people, help them, and bring them together to solve problems.' My team got together and said, 'There has to be a lot of broken 1031 exchange people out there—how do we market to them? Sometimes, they just want to place their money somewhere headache-free and avoid inflation. Let's put the property up for sale for a ridiculous price and see what happens.'"

Insider Info A 1031 exchange enables those who've recently sold an investment property to reinvest those earnings into a similarly priced property, deferring taxes on that profit. Since the sale of multifamily or commercial properties can create a large tax burden, it's not uncommon for investors to utilize the 1031 exchange to roll profits into another multifamily or commercial property.

Despite all its benefits, there's a downside to the 1031 exchange: Investors looking to roll profits into a 1031 must identify the new investment within forty-five days of selling the original property and must *close* within 180 days. As with any real estate transaction, there's always the possibility that a deal will fall through for some reason. A failed, or "broken," 1031 exchange can have huge tax implications and leave investors desperate to quickly find another project into which they can roll their earnings.

Corey understood the dynamics of broken 1031s, and hoping to sell at a premium, he set out to find buyers in that exact predicament. He presented the property as a "dream package" where investors could simply place their money into a profit-generating machine.

As it turns out, there were plenty of investors who just wanted to press the easy button on Corey's offer. He sold it for $8.8 million at a 4 percent cap rate, walking away with a net profit of $4.7 million for himself and the investors.

Insider Info The cap rate (or capitalization rate) is the most common way to measure the performance of a particular investment property. It's calculated by dividing the net operating income, not including financing costs, by the purchase price. Cap rates typically reflect the inherent level of risk for a property. A lower cap rate indicates more stability—for example, a Class A property in a strong location. A higher cap rate indicates more risk—for example, a Class C property in a less-desirable neighborhood.

Using a 1031 exchange himself, Corey reinvested his earnings and bought another multifamily property for $12.7 million. Today it pays him about $450,000 in yearly cash flow. Corey's team has gone on to purchase eleven more multifamily properties and is continually on the hunt for more.

TAKEAWAY

Multifamily Pays in Multiple Ways

One reason investors flock to multifamily deals is because of the multiple ways you can get paid as a syndicator. Here's how Corey explains it:

"Multifamily can pay you up front, it can pay cash flow, and if you can do it right, there's room for a huge win—sunsets and palm trees!"

Again, the sky's the limit when structuring multifamily ventures. There is no right or wrong way to do it, but I will say this: Savvy operators incorporate acquisition fees up front, they take part in the property's monthly cash flow, and they structure their ownership so that they'll cash in on the lion's share of back-end profit when the deal is exited.

Watch Your Multifamily Like a Hawk

While not every operator stays intimately involved in stabilizing a property, it's vitally important to do so early in your multifamily investing career. This is especially true if you haven't already established a solid working relationship with an asset manager and/or a property manager you trust. This having been Corey's first deal, he would not leave things up to chance. He says:

> *"On that first deal, I was pretty active—more in the asset manager role. I had third-party management running the property, but I was heavily involved in the decision-making process."*

Nobody will care about the success of your property as much as you. In addition, you'll probably have investors you fiercely want to protect. From watching over contractors, to removing problem tenants, to implementing new systems and increasing rents, turning a property around takes major effort and commitment. Unless you've built an unbelievable team that you implicitly trust, you're likely better off in the trenches to ensure a successful property transition.

Have a Disposition Strategy

Most investors don't have a real strategy for selling a property, be it single-family, multifamily, or commercial. Because real estate agents and brokers dominate the industry, many investors don't know any better than to list a property on the local MLS or commercial listing site.

Whereas most people assume that they can achieve top dollar through a standard listing service, Corey bucked that notion and strived to achieve a premium profit. He believed that if he could target a buyer who needed to close quickly because of a broken 1031 exchange, he could sell for even more than what a typical broker would get.

This kind of strategy should resonate with sellers in any property category. Who is your ideal buyer? How do you take a more *proactive*—not *reactive*—marketing approach? Identifying this target market and executing a plan to sell direct on your next project could make the difference between an average deal and a home run.

CHAPTER FOUR

STACY ROSSETTI

Negotiating 50 Percent Off a Storage Facility

Don't let the isolated tiny home atop one of Georgia's tallest mountains fool you—Stacy Rossetti is a mover and shaker. She and her family left the Atlanta suburbs in 2019 to get a "breath of fresh air" up in North Georgia, but the truth is they could have moved anywhere they wanted. When your real estate empire is built on the ability to work remotely, you can do things like that—and you might as well make a vacation out of it, because Stacy also set things up so she barely has to do any work at all.

Ten years earlier, Stacy's first career was traveling the world selling wind turbines. When the company she worked for started going downhill, she began looking for a second career. After seeing her husband, Pete, flourish in the home inspection company he'd recently built, she wanted a piece of the entrepreneurial pie. His business turned her attention to real estate, so she got a coach and started educating herself on investing.

It was 2010, and houses were still relatively cheap after the Great Recession. Stacy quickly snagged her first wholesale deal and kept them coming after that. From there, she started flipping, and it wasn't long before one rehab turned into thirteen, which turned into twenty-three, then thirty-six. Pete's home inspection business was a huge boost to her operation, and eventually they started investing as an official partnership.

By 2016, they had built an investor base, owned a few buy and holds, and had completed hundreds of transactions. However, in the midst of running that year's twenty rehabs all at once, Stacy discovered she was pregnant. Realizing there was no way to continue with such a workload in post-baby life, she started looking for a passive income solution.

> *"I was asking myself, 'How am I going to have a little baby and run twenty rehabs at a time? There's no way.' So, I stopped buying houses and told everyone I knew that I was looking for passive income. I looked at portfolios of houses. I looked at multifamily. I looked at commercial buildings. Then one of the best things in my life happened—my Realtor sent me the listing for an ugly, dumpy, but most beautiful storage facility."*

It's been four years since Stacy followed that lead, and today she and Pete own upwards of 500 self-storage units. They have only two employees: an office manager for administration and a property manager who typically works only one day a week. Stacy's self-proclaimed philosophy is to *"make as much money as I can with as little work as I can."*

Although Stacy still makes treks to the city to serve as a teacher, leader, and mentor for Atlanta investors, particularly in her role as founding president of the South Atlanta Real Estate Investors Association (REIA). She's also taken much of her work remote by offering online workshops and coaching. Thousands of students have benefited from her teaching on managing multiple rehabs through automation and systematization, finding private money, online marketing, and, of course, investing in self-storage.

> *"We're building a portfolio of facilities we can manage from anywhere. We want to be able to travel whenever we want, wherever we want. The thing is, comparatively speaking, there aren't a lot of storage facility owners in the world, and a lot of them just don't seem to think this way. They have one or two and stop there.*
>
> *"I love storage facilities because not only do you create passive income, but you are also building passive wealth. Everybody gets into*

real estate investing because they want to know how to make lots of money without doing lots of work. They end up doing wholesaling and rehabs, which I totally understand, but that's active income— you have to work your butt off!"

Insider Info Successful real estate investors around the country have found tremendous success through running their local REIA. Sometimes it's the ability to sell education and coaching to members that lures leaders into the space, but usually it's the network of other industry professionals—from private lenders to bird dogs to potential partners—that provides the biggest return on investment. Running an REIA can be a great side project to fuel your investing business with both motivation and connections.

FINDING THE DEAL

Stacy had just three essential investing criteria: The property had to be close to Atlanta, be easy to manage, and have a clear path toward generating passive income. When she saw the self-storage listing for $500,000, she made an appointment to view it immediately.

"It was a match made in heaven. As a rehabber, when I see an ugly building, my heart just flutters and skips a beat! I drove over to take a look and I knew this was the one. Now, to only convince my husband and lender..."

ASSESSMENT

The owner of the storage space, Big John, was a commercial HVAC engineer with an office right around the corner. The facility had been for sale for five years, and though several offers had come in, he never accepted one. By the time Stacy showed up, though, he had come to realize three things: The place was a dump, he was bored, and his wife wanted to move to Florida. In other words, he was motivated to sell.

Five years seems like an incredibly long time for a property to sit on the market. In most cases, you would assume the property is overpriced and has some sort of hair on it that nobody wants to touch. However, a savvy investor should dig deeper to see whether the owner's patience has begun to wear thin and a lowball offer might be warranted. As with any other kind of property, the longer it sits, the more likely the buyer will negotiate.

You've probably seen the exact property that this one resembled: a long strip of sixty-four 10' × 10' units surrounded by ample parking and other industrial buildings. Built in the '80s, the building stood on a three-acre lot with about fifty parking spaces surrounding the units. Stacy expected it to be dumpy from the photos, but it turned out to be more of an actual dump: Along with abandoned-unit leftovers and trash, hundreds of tires had been discarded all around the property, which taught people over the years that they could just leave their junk wherever they wanted.

As they walked and talked, Big John proudly proclaimed that all the units were full. But when he noted the profit they were bringing in, Stacy nearly jumped out of her skin—the number was a mere $2,000 per month. Even with no experience in self-storage, Stacy knew something wasn't adding up. She figured that renting fifty parking spaces and sixty-four units for at least $60 each should work out to almost $7,000 per month.

Finally, she had to ask what was wrong—were people not paying? Big John laughed, explaining that although it was 100 percent full, it wasn't filled with *paying* customers. Many of the tenants had stopped paying ages ago. He just hadn't cleared their stuff out. Plus, he wasn't using the parking spaces as rentals. People parked wherever they wanted, whenever they wanted. Stacy explains the dire situation:

"Literally, if someone left, moved out, or stopped paying, he would just leave their unit as-is. After a while, he had no space left to rent out. And I'm telling you, a lot of storage facility owners are just like him. When you buy a mismanaged property, you'll meet people like this guy, who had no P&L statement, no balance sheet, and no numbers to show me. Adding insult to injury, he only took cash. To prove that he was making $2,000, he opened an office drawer and pulled out a handwritten ledger of who paid and how much. That's all he had! But this has turned out to be the type of property I like to buy."

It was a storage facility of almost entirely wasted space, and Stacy's wheels were spinning. If she could reorganize and restripe the parking lot, clear out the trash and abandoned units, and get everything generating income, she hoped to bring in at least $60 per month for each unit and parking space. The estimated $10,000 it would take to get things up and running seemed like nothing compared to the huge profit potential.

THE BREAKDOWN

Self-storage facility, 64 units, 50 parking spaces
South Atlanta, Georgia
Asking $500,000

OFFER AND FUNDING

Had the property been occupied by paying tenants and had accurate accounting to show to lenders, Stacy would have been able to take the records to a bank and get a reasonable long-term loan. Then the property would've easily been worth the $500,000 asking price, but that wasn't the case. Using this as negotiating leverage, Stacy turned to Big John and broke it down:

> *"I know you have this on the market for $500,000, but unfortunately, that's the price it would be worth if, and only if, you had run this thing properly. Banks need a record of income, expenses, and occupancy, so I won't be able to get a bank loan and neither will anyone else. I'll need to use private money, which means I'll have to pay double what I'd pay with a bank loan. Because of that, I'm going to have to offer very low. I don't mean to hurt your feelings—it just is what it is. My offer is $200,000 and I can close fast."*

You read that right—Stacy offered $200,000 on $500,000 asking. As you might guess, Big John bluntly responded that he would never accept such a low number. However, her detailed explanation had got him thinking, and after a few days, he called her up with a $250,000 counteroffer. In truth, she'd been willing to go with that all along. They got the property under contract, and Stacy called one of her private lenders, who gave her a loan for $260,000 at 9 percent interest for five years.

Ken's Take I'm not the first to say it: There's an art to negotiation. Big John probably had no intention of ever cutting his sale price in half. Stacy did a phenomenal job of educating him on the reality of the situation for not just herself but for *any* potential buyer. Big John probably didn't realize how many buyers he'd lost over that five years, not just because his price was too high, but because they wouldn't be able to get financing based on the property's performance. When Stacy's explanation finally settled in, he was willing to be more realistic. Sometimes negotiation just boils down to education.

TURNAROUND

Big John cleaned up the property a bit before handing over the keys, but he left plenty of work for Stacy and her husband to bring it up to par. There were also more than fifty vehicles strewn about the parking lot, some paying, some not, and some abandoned. Cleaning out the units and tracking down vehicle owners was more time-consuming than expensive, but they eventually got everything in order.

Being lax with rules and turnover had likely cost Big John tens (if not hundreds) of thousands of dollars over the years. Tenants took advantage of him all over the place—first by not paying, then by disappearing without clearing out the units. Rules vary from state to state, but Stacy stayed on top of truancy with strict contracts:

"We invested in a great software system that we could manage from anywhere. The problem was that everyone was so accustomed to paying cash whenever they wanted that most tenants were affronted by the idea of going online to pay. The cash payment 'system' was pretty shady, and our job was to create a viable business that we could sell down the road. I wasn't taking any you-know-what! The first rule when running a facility that actually makes money is 'train your tenants,' and that's exactly what I had to do. Rent was due on the first, late by the fourth, and you were overlocked on the fifteenth. If you didn't pay by the twenty-fifth, we started the auction process."

As Stacy and Pete got all the new rules in place, the rebellious tenants started leaving, conveniently making space for new tenants whom they could actually train. Parking spaces and units began filling up through Stacy's use of online marketing. Meanwhile, they renamed the facility Ms. Lillian's Self-Storage after their newborn daughter, who'd inspired the purchase.

AFTERMATH

The original Ms. Lillian's Self-Storage has now been nearly 100 percent full for two years, with a current value of around $550,000. Not only did Stacy buy the facility for $250,000 below asking price, she also created nearly $300,000 in equity! On top of that, the facility is bringing in about $6,500 in monthly rents. With total monthly expenses at $2,500, that's a cash flow of $4,000 per month.

It took about a year to set up the management software, find the right tenants, and get the property fully cleaned up, but it was a year of education that would pay itself forward. Stacy and Pete managed the property during that time to learn the process from the inside out, but even then, they only checked on it about once a month.

Insider Info Here's how Stacy breaks down her operational expenses: $100 for pest control and lawn care, $150 for software, and $200 per week to their employee who serves as boots on the ground (but since he's paid to check on *all* their properties, the cost per property is actually less than that). It's hardly anything, especially considering you often get to skip climate-control costs in storage facilities.

As Stacy approaches the five-year mark on her loan, she'll refinance with a bank and reduce her monthly payment by approximately $500. Not only that—with the property's increased valuation, she'll be able to score a huge cash-out option on the refinance. Of course, she plans to take that money and buy yet another storage facility, using her favorite method of finding properties: "#drivingforstoragefacilities."

Since this deal, Stacy and Pete have ditched all their residential rental properties and abandoned the flipping business. At the time of this writing, they have six locations under the Ms. Lillian's brand and three more under contract between South Atlanta and North Georgia. It all started with an intention to reach financial freedom through passive income, something they've managed to accomplish in less than five years. As Stacy puts it:

> *"How many residential rental properties do you need in order to make $4,000 a month? Eight? Ten? Why would I manage that many when I can manage one storage facility for the same income? I haven't been to any of my facilities in the past six months. Before we got the property manager, my husband would go check on them once or twice a month, but that's it. The only thing you really have to do is make sure the units are cleaned out when somebody moves out and overlock them when necessary. But even doing that—and even now, with 500 doors—takes no more than one day a month."*

TAKEAWAY

Do Your Own Math

While Stacy didn't find this facility off market (as she does most of her properties), she still smelled opportunity upon discovering how long it'd been for sale. Any property listed for that amount of time is 100 percent overpriced. Plus, the seller has probably had the chance to marinate on about five years of negative feedback from all those lost buyers.

No matter what a seller claims they're making, the claim *always* requires additional digging to truly interpret what the word "making" means. Big John's handwritten ledger likely didn't account for taxes, insurance, maintenance, capital expenses, salaries, and so on. And who can say whether that handwritten ledger was even accurate?

Some fast mental math showed Stacy that nothing about the numbers made sense, and further due diligence proved her point. In this case, she was able to educate the investor that he simply didn't have what he thought he had. No bank would lend based on a $500,000 sale price with no real accounting and lackluster performance.

By respectfully educating Big John on the reality of his property's financeability, Stacy got him to drop his price by a full 50 percent. Ultimately, it was her willingness to get to the bottom of the bogus numbers that ensured she didn't overpay and enabled her to negotiate the *right* price for amazing upside potential.

Mom and Pop Are Probably Tired of Their Poorly Run Shop

Stacy has developed a model hinging on an ability to buy self-storage properties with cap rates well into the teens. Were she targeting high-profile properties that regularly trade through commercial brokerages—the large, on-site-managed properties on main roads with climate control and several stories—this couldn't happen. Not a chance.

By targeting off-market properties on back roads with little curb appeal, Stacy discovered an entire world of mom-and-pop self-storage facilities that few people even consider targeting. Small, local-owner properties not only lend themselves to remote management (which saves a ton on expenses), they also tend to be better candidates for price negotiation. A 50 percent price drop can only happen when you operate beneath the fray of commercially traded offerings and focus your efforts on smaller mom-and-pops.

Find the Value-Add Opportunities

By now, you've probably noticed that this is a recurring theme. *Value-add* means looking for ways to increase revenue or sales price based on creatively adding to or changing a property. This is true even when it comes to basic storage facilities.

I actually bought a distressed eight-acre boat and RV storage facility from a bank several years ago. While there wasn't an opportunity to add to the lot, we figured out how to maximize revenue by reconfiguring the spaces based on demand for various needs. Just the simple act of optimizing the lot increased our occupancy and revenue, and ultimately the property's value. We ended up selling it for a million dollars more than the purchase price in just two short years.

Similarly, Stacy immediately saw that the seller was missing out on a huge opportunity to rent the parking spaces. It's hard to understand how he didn't see the additional rental revenue staring him in the face, but not every property owner looks at maximizing profit potential through the same lens. Sometimes it just takes a fresh set of eyes. As investors, we can create significant wealth simply by understanding when and how to unlock that potential.

CHAPTER FIVE

KRYSTAL AND DEDRIC POLITE

The Polite Way to Virtual Wholesale

When Krystal and Dedric Polite decided to go into real estate full-time, they jumped from zero to one hundred in more ways than one. They had both held successful corporate jobs in their ten years since college, but they always dabbled in various side hustles—from e-commerce to writing and directing plays to even running a successful mall scooter franchise. When real estate investing became a recurring topic of conversation, Krystal finally said, *"Let's stop talking and actually do it."*

They dove into education and landed on an initial model of targeting wholesales. The plan was to build up cash reserves through assignment fees, then funnel the money into purchasing multifamily rentals for building long-term wealth and passive income. They started by targeting their local region of Burlington, North Carolina, and their hometown of Boston, Massachusetts; and it was only months before they scaled nationwide with a virtual model.

It's been less than two years since they took the plunge, and today Krystal and Dedric have closed more than sixty wholesale deals and own twenty-four rental units valued at more than $2.5 million. They find off-market properties the way most of us do: through direct mail, text messaging, cold-calling, ringless voicemail, and referrals. The difference, however, is that instead of limiting their territory, they snag deals wherever they want—often without even glimpsing the property's interior.

Whether it's a cash purchase, subject-to, wholesale, or owner finance, the Polites do nearly all negotiating through phone or email from the comfort of their home. When necessary, they pay local companies or reach out to online real estate groups for boots-on-the-ground photos or assessment. From there, locating attorneys, contractors, or other local services simply boils down to asking their large network of social media followers and fellow investors for recommendations.

Insider Info Dedric and Krystal found an ingenious way to build their boots-on-the-ground network with an online program that teaches investors how to drive for dollars "the Polite way." Building relationships with students across the nation has also led to their participating in deals where students needed a leg up. By being entrepreneurs who provide value, they fortify and encourage others while creating a deal-funneling system for themselves.

The Polites are an authentic example of a power couple, with Krystal bringing the marketing savvy, people skills, and serial entrepreneur attitude while Dedric focuses on sales, acquisitions, finances, and business development. It's been a winning combination from the start, as Dedric explains:

> *"I always wanted to be a real estate investor, especially after purchasing a successful house hack when I was 25 years old. But I'm the analytical type, and after that first deal, I got stuck in analysis paralysis until I met Krystal. She's a serial entrepreneur who just pushed us out the door saying, 'Hey, stop talking about real estate and let's actually get educated and do it.'"*

FINDING THE DEAL

They decided to pursue real estate in 2017, and in the year that followed, Krystal and Dedric spent nearly $100,000 on mentors, masterminds, coaches, consultants, and courses. By the time they were confident enough to start chasing a deal together, Krystal had officially quit her day job to focus fully on direct-to-seller marketing. Dedric, meanwhile, kept his corporate day job and spent evenings following up on leads.

Heeding the time-tested advice of numerous investors, Krystal began searching for that first wholesale in her own backyard. Only, instead of North Carolina, she chose the backyard of her youth and college years: Boston. Not only did she know it like the back of her hand—she also knew the market was booming.

Ken's Take A lot of people think that investing in their own town is the only option—particularly when starting out—but that's not the case. It's not a bad idea to target deals close to home, but sometimes that's just not where the deals are. The Polites were not only acutely familiar with the Boston housing market, but they also knew that most deals just had bigger numbers there. With a network already established and confidence in their ability to know a deal from a dud, they made a great decision to go virtual.

Using a list-building website, Krystal filtered a niche list targeting absentee multifamily owners in a specific Boston county who owned the property outright and had purchased it prior to 1985. They loaded the sixty-nine resulting addresses into a driving-for-dollars app, and it sent out a direct mail piece to all the owners. In the meantime, they continued the grind and crossed their fingers for a call.

Amazingly, Krystal would receive responses from seventeen owners over the next few months, but a woman named Betsy stood out. She and her husband, Gerard, were living in New Jersey and had completely forgot that his Boston triplex even existed—the mail piece had jogged their memory! Since only her husband's name was on the deed, Betsy promised to have him follow up soon.

In the meantime, Krystal passed the baton to Dedric, emailing him notes from the call so he could run the numbers. Minutes later, her phone rang. Dedric was on the line, rushing to ask, *"Do you realize where this is? I think we just hit the mother lode—it's in a red zone where people are flipping houses like hotcakes!"*

ASSESSMENT

They spent the next few days waiting for the follow-up call, but it never came. In the span of a month, Krystal called Betsy back once, twice, then a third time—to no avail. Not yet willing to give up, she made a final call from Dedric's phone so that a new number would show up. This time, Betsy answered, sounding delighted and slightly embarrassed that Gerard hadn't got in touch. She passed the phone off to him with a mild reprimand while Dedric hopped on to talk numbers.

Gerard was a successful business executive who had inherited the property from his uncle in the mid-'80s. The stately, 3,150 square-foot Victorian triplex was built in 1900 with three floors, five bedrooms, and three bathrooms. Each level served as a single-unit rental, but in Gerard's thirty-plus years of ownership, he had neglected the property, eventually forgetting that it even existed.

When Dedric asked when they could do a walk-through, Gerard replied that he didn't have a key. Not only that—he didn't even know whether the property was occupied. If it was, he wasn't sure if the residents were sending rent somewhere or just squatting. Assuming there were occupants, he wouldn't know how to get in touch with them, and he didn't seem keen on figuring out how.

Gerard was interested in selling, sure, but he admittedly had no idea what he wanted for the property. After fumbling around with the idea for a while, he figured he'd be happy with $500,000.

Since it had taken over a month to get Gerard on the line, Krystal and Dedric spent that time undertaking thorough online research. Not only that, they were able to get one of their Boston-based investor friends to snap some photos and do a quick exterior assessment. With the information they'd gathered, they were willing to bet that the property's ARV was an easy $1.5 million. Since they were looking at a million-dollar spread, the only question was whether they should flip it themselves or wholesale.

THE BREAKDOWN

Triplex, 3,150 square feet
Boston, Massachusetts
Asking $500,000

OFFER AND FUNDING

Given the likely squatter situation, there was definitely hair on the deal. But with an ARV of triple the purchase price, this was one of those jackpots where the seller just didn't know (or care) about what they had. Still, Dedric wanted to play hardball: He offered $375,000 to Gerard's $500,000. Gerard didn't bite, but he did go down to $475,000. Accepting that number with a virtual handshake, the Polites promised a cash payment and a sixty-day close.

They immediately followed up with an email contract and form for Gerard to sign that gave them authorization to notify the occupants they would need to vacate the premises. But for the second time, Gerard disappeared. Weeks followed, with Dedric following up through email and phone calls, but he didn't hear a peep. After a month, Krystal decided to have a look at their email correspondence.

"I took one look at their emails and knew the reason Gerard had ghosted us: He didn't want to deal with tenant issues. Even though he'd never mentioned this directly, I could just tell that it was the sticking point. Boston is tenant-friendly and it can take up to a year to go through the eviction process. I realized, 'He's not going to deal with that. We have to take that burden on ourselves.'"

Krystal knew exactly what to do. She talked with Dedric and suggested he write a final email that simply said:

"We're going to go ahead and take care of the tenant issues and get the squatters out. All we need from you is to sign the contract, send

it back, and let us know where you would like us to send the money. We're ready to close this week if that works for you."

One minute later, Gerard emailed them back with a signed contract and his banking information. Krystal was right—he just didn't want to deal with eviction issues. With the property under contract, they planned to use transactional funding to purchase it for $475,000, then double close to a secondary buyer at a number hopefully much higher than their purchase price. However, before anything, they needed to find that buyer.

Insider Info Wholesale contracts typically allow the wholesaler to assign the original purchase agreement to an end buyer and earn an assignment fee in the process. However, sometimes assignments are frowned upon or simply aren't practical, especially if the wholesaler is making a nice spread and doesn't want the buyer to know. In such cases, you need two separate closings: one to purchase the property from the seller and a second to turn and sell to the end buyer. When these transactions happen back-to-back, it's typically referred to as a *double close*. If an investor doesn't have the liquidity needed for the initial purchase, they can use transactional funding, a very short-term loan engaging the lender's funds just long enough to purchase and sell the property within a few days (if not hours).

TURNAROUND

During the months they'd spent waiting through Gerard's ghosting episodes, Dedric had been making connections with Boston brokers and investors. He offered them the opportunity to share the deal with their cash-buyer lists in exchange for an acquisition fee of their own. Once he and Krystal got the signed contract, they sent out information about the triplex, including photos of the exterior. But of course, every time an interested buyer called, the first question was "When can I get in?"

Krystal and Dedric still didn't have access, and just like Gerard, they were passing that hot potato to the next person. Even if the inside was a mess or the tenants were difficult to evict, they were confident that someone would realize the property was a no-fail opportunity. Although most potential buyers wouldn't want to take on such a headache, it would take only one willing buyer to close. The Polites explain:

"The play on such properties is to gut them, then turn each of the triplex units into separate condos. Investors will spend $100,000 per unit on the rehab, then sell each one for $500,000. If we decided to wholesale, the price for buyers would be about $150 per square foot. Their post-renovation sale price would likely be $475 per square foot. There was so much meat on the bone! We spent a long time considering whether or not to take it down ourselves, but being a thousand miles away, we didn't want to manage a virtual rehab and knew there would be plenty of profit with a wholesale."

They found their willing buyer within a week and closed just thirty days later. Dedric and Krystal opted for a double close, and transactional funding at 1 percent covered their purchase from Gerard. An hour later, their end buyer purchased the property for $580,000, a whopping $105,000 above what they had paid just minutes before!

Ken's Take Krystal and Dedric didn't have a cash-buyer list and still managed to pull down more than $100,000 on an out-of-state wholesale deal. Lacking a buyer list might keep some people from nailing down that wholesale contract, but the Polites were convinced that a good deal would sell itself. They knew they could leverage online outreach and their existing Boston relationships to find the right investor to take down the deal. This is the entrepreneur mindset at its finest.

AFTERMATH

Although Betsy had called in July and the closing wasn't finalized until October, Krystal and Dedric hadn't let the interim go to waste. On the contrary, they'd spent that time refining their marketing process and managed to close their first wholesale deal in August for an $11,000 profit. The following month, they turned a second contract for $5,000. By October, they'd corralled Gerard and closed on this third deal for a $105,000 profit.

The triplex brought in just the right amount of cash to enable Krystal and Dedric to start buying up multifamily rentals of their own. Confident that he was ready to take the leap, Dedric quit his job and went into real estate full-time. Just like they'd planned, they used the money to purchase their first few buy and holds, catapulting themselves to where they are today. It might still be early in their career, but they've already hit their stride.

"We only started wholesaling to buy and hold. We always wanted passive income, but we didn't start off with a ton of savings to buy multifamilies. When we found out about wholesaling, we said, 'Let's use this to get capital and start buying rental property.' And that's exactly what we've been able to do. We've replaced our income from corporate America and make well more than six figures as full-time real estate investors and entrepreneurs."

 ## TAKEAWAY

Wholesaling Can Be a Virtual Business

I've found that wholesalers are split when it comes to acquiring deals in person versus over the phone. With the wealth of information and data on the internet, you can make fairly accurate offers without the benefit of personally walking a property. In fact, my own team puts 95 percent of our properties under contract before ever seeing them.

The Polites are proof that you don't have to be physically present to have investing success. Not only that, you don't even have to start off with a strong network where you're looking. With today's access to a thriving online world of real estate resources, it's surprisingly easy to find boots on the ground.

Ultimately, success in virtual wholesaling comes down to systems: sourcing motivated sellers, honing negotiating skills, and staying organized. Krystal and Dedric figured out their strengths in this space and quickly found ways to put them to use:

"Whether it's texting, cold-calling, or direct mail, Krystal is a master marketing ninja. She looks at it like a puzzle, teeing up the leads to motivate sellers for that call. From there, I talk to owners, work the numbers, and get the properties under contract."

If you've really landed a solid deal, finding local real estate professionals to market it isn't rocket science either. Virtual wholesaling really does afford you the freedom and flexibility to work from anywhere.

Invest in Yourself

In one transaction, Krystal and Dedric made more than what most people make in a year. You might think it was this specific deal that got them where they are today, but they had laid the path to success much earlier.

> "Leading up to this, we spent upwards of $100,000 on education—masterminds, mentors, courses, and coaches. When it came down to really getting into it, we easily saw the benefits of our investment. We were seeing things played out that the coaches and masterminds had all talked about. Investing in education helped us elevate our business rapidly—and from there, it afforded us the ability to start purchasing, which was our goal from the start. By that point, we knew that with the right systems and tools, this was definitely possible."

This deal didn't fall into their lap—Krystal and Dedric *made* it happen, generating life-changing money in the process. Of course, opinions differ when it comes to paying for education in this industry. The tens of thousands I myself have spent on training and masterminds over the years have come back to me a hundredfold. I often tell my students that the right training and mentoring can pay for itself with only one deal, and the long-term dividends typically produce a yield far and above what you'd typically achieve by figuring it out on your own.

What's Your Endgame?

One of the things I love about the Polites is their clarity on the purpose of their business. When they got into real estate, their sole focus was (and continues to be) building wealth through acquiring rentals. As a result, they have amassed a portfolio of twenty-four rental units in just three years.

There have been years in my career when I've been so distracted running my "business" that I lost sight of long-term goals. How many investors get into flipping and wholesaling for the sole purpose of generating a nice paycheck, completely missing the opportunity to create lasting wealth?

The Polites have known from the get-go that you don't get wealthy working on what you *make*, but by what you *own*. For now, they spend hours grinding to ultimately build a portfolio of appreciating, cash-flowing properties that will carry them into a comfortable (and probably early) retirement. The potential to build wealth in real estate is unlike that in any other industry. You can spin wheels fixing, flipping, and wholesaling houses, but don't forget your endgame.

CHAPTER SIX

BRANDON TURNER

Fourplex Makeover

Brandon Turner discovered how to live for free when he was only 21 years old. Finished with college and recently married, he and his wife Heather moved to the small town of Grays Harbor, Washington. A friend and mentor had already introduced Brandon to the idea of real estate investing, so instead of a house, he and Heather purchased a small apartment complex at a great price. After experiencing the blissful satisfaction of using rental income to cover their entire mortgage payment, they were hooked on real estate.

Ten years later, they've traded the West Coast for the Island Coast, calling Hawaii home while renting more than one hundred doors across single-family and multifamily homes and mobile home parks. Brandon's current focus is larger commercial investments throughout the Midwest, particularly mobile home communities. His strategy is simple: Flip houses to generate income, then use that income to hire employees to grow his burgeoning mobile home park business.

"I'm taking active income, turning it into passive income, and over time, turning that into massive income."

Four full-time employees and several partners make up Brandon's real estate team. The key to their success is extreme lead generation through online list-building resources and leveraging personal networks. After aggregating tons of initial leads, they filter them through a process Brandon calls the LAPS funnel.

The LAPS funnel:
1. Leads—Create incoming *leads*.
2. Analyze—Accurately *analyze* the leads to determine value.
3. Pursue—When appropriate, *pursue* the leads.
4. Success—If you follow the funnel, you'll achieve *success*!

Following the LAPS funnel helps Brandon ensure that his team pursues only the truly worthwhile leads. This commitment to process has resulted in a homemade brand of success that's hard to deny—by 2021, he expects to own at least eight mobile home parks and more than 1,000 doors!

FINDING THE DEAL

Before Brandon began building a mobile home empire, his bread and butter came from steadily acquiring two to six rentals or flips per year. Back in 2016, six successful years of investing had led to some disposable income burning a hole in his pocket. While still in Grays Harbor, he opted to invest locally by trying to find a new multifamily buy-and-hold property.

Using a list-building website, Brandon sourced a list of 300 absentee-owned small multifamily properties that had been owned for at least five years. For each address, he printed a simple letter from home with a computer font he'd created to resemble his own handwriting. Next to the closing signature was a smiling photo of himself and Heather. By his logic, people want to sell to people they like, and who doesn't like a friendly local couple? The letter read:

> *Hi, my name is Brandon. My wife Heather and I buy a lot of properties in Grays Harbor. We're looking to buy another one, and we came across yours. We'd love to talk about it, so if you want to sell, give us a call.*
> *—Brandon and Heather Turner*

P.S. We can buy it for cash, even if it's in bad condition or has tenants. We've dealt with it all.

Note the postscript! According to studies by Professor Siegfried Vögele, author of the *Handbook of Direct Mail: The Dialogue Method of Direct Written Sales Communication*, the most-read part of a letter is the postscript. Knowing this, Brandon put the most crucial information in the P.S., which he felt "gave the 'sales-y' part without sounding sales-y."

From the 300 direct mailings, Brandon received a stellar response of forty calls. Some called only to say, "Take me off your list!" But a handful had some level of motivation and were intrigued by the unexpected offer on their home.

Ken's Take A 13 percent response rate on a direct mail campaign is incredible. At my company, we're lucky to get *1* percent, which is why we typically send out thousands of letters instead of hundreds. Brandon's success demonstrates two key points:

1. A well-written, personalized letter can go far.
2. Booming areas usually bring bigger paychecks, which means rural or blue-collar towns are often forgotten by investors. What that means for *you* is reduced investor competition. As Brandon says: *"There are areas within driving distance of pretty much every major city in America—no matter how expensive—where you can buy cash-flowing deals. They do exist."*

Of the forty callbacks, roughly twelve turned out to be viable investments. Brandon made twelve offers, and every single one was rejected—*including* his offer on the fourplex that would go on to become his best deal ever.

ASSESSMENT

The property was technically a fourplex, but at first glance, you'd probably just see four very similar side-by-side homes. Two units were empty, one had squatters, and one had a garbage hoarder. That's right—not just a hoarder but a *garbage* hoarder. And since none of the occupants were paying rent, getting them out could get sticky (literally).

Each stand-alone unit was 700 square feet with two bedrooms and one bath. The front yards were patchy and overgrown, and the wooden posts holding up the front-door awnings were half-painted. Overall, the property could best be described as depressing. Inside, though, the condition was surprisingly acceptable. The biggest-ticket items would be new appliances, siding, landscaping, and two new roofs.

As Brandon describes it, the neighborhood wasn't somewhere you'd want your kid playing alone out front, but he had a vision to redefine things. A better-than-average renovation—essentially an *over*improvement—might not just boost the area's appearance but also attract higher-quality tenants. If the property had consisted of only one home, there would have been little potential for changing the street's dynamic, but with four individual units, Brandon believed he could make a significant impact.

Brandon suspected that the total renovation would cost about $110,000. He was happy to invest in a quality rehab up front, since this would minimize repair costs in later years. If the numbers held, he'd follow the BRRRR (buy, rehab, rent, refinance, repeat) method toward what would be a notably higher appraisal value.

THE BREAKDOWN

Fourplex: four stand-alone units, 700 square feet each
Grays Harbor, Washington
Asking $90,000

OFFER AND FUNDING

The owner, Henry, wanted to sell for $90,000, but with the estimated $110,000 rehab, Brandon didn't think it made sense to pay more than $40,000. Henry laughed outright at this offer, simply saying, "No way." Brandon figured that was that, but a month later, Henry called out of the blue to ask if Brandon could do $45,000. They had a deal.

Ken's Take Too many investors assume no means no, when in reality, *no* often just means *not right now.* Seasoned investors know that most deals come in the follow-up. Just because a seller says no to your "lowball" offer today doesn't mean that the situation won't change later. In fact, I find that most of our deals go under contract *months* after the initial contact. That's why it's crucial for investors to have a thorough follow-up system for seller leads.

Like most savvy investors, Brandon prefers using other people's money to fund his deals. After Brandon posted about this deal on BiggerPockets.com, a private lender stepped up to loan him $100,000 with 10 percent monthly interest and one point at the end of twelve months. For the remaining $55,000, Brandon got an unsecured line of credit from his bank, figuring that the refinance would quickly cover his expenditures.

TURNAROUND

With the closing contract signed and lending arranged, Brandon was ready to bring his vision to life. Predicting that rental income from just one of the units would fully cover the interest payments across all four, he would focus on renovating one at a time. That way, he'd start bringing in rental income as soon as possible to minimize out-of-pocket holding costs.

He knew he needed a special design to achieve the neighborhood impact he sought, so Brandon hired a friend, designer Krister Lyle, to draw up a dynamic plan for the units. The $1,500 investment wasn't cheap, but Krister came through with a detailed vision of bold-colored exteriors (red, green, blue, and teal), window boxes for flowers, front yard fences, and new trim and landscaping.

The rest of the renovation mostly called for standard-finished and identical building materials for each unit—which is a huge benefit of multifamily renovation projects. Brandon hired a contractor to get started on one of the empty units. Meanwhile, he turned his attention to the squatters and trash hoarders. The former were easy to clear out, but the trash hoarders were a different story. According to Brandon:

"That house was the worst thing I have ever been in—ever. They just wouldn't take their trash out. Oh, and there were rats. Hundreds of rats living in the garbage. You walked through and they would just casually climb around. The garbage was piled up to the ceiling,

and in some spots I effectively had to sift through it. The toilet was unbelievable."

On top of that, they hadn't paid rent in years and didn't plan to start. Henry had let this slide because he simply didn't know how to handle it, but Brandon did: *eviction*. He got the legal process started, and trusting that the hoarders would be gone within a few months, he focused on the other units.

The first unit was fixed up after three months, so Brandon hired a local property manager to rent out and manage it. She quickly secured renters for $675 monthly, which—as predicted—paid the fourplex's entire monthly interest payment. The second unit was rented three months later, and over the remaining year, a new unit was generating rental income every three months. Since two of the units had a slightly bigger feel, the property manager got them rented at $750 monthly.

Insider Info One of the benefits of investing in multifamilies is the ability to renovate one unit at a time. In many cases, existing tenants continue paying rent for their unrenovated units while the investor renovates the vacant ones. This way, rental income keeps flowing in while individual units are strategically improved for higher rents.

Brandon ended up putting $120,000 into renovation, financing, and holding costs. With the $45,000 purchase, he was all-in at $165,000— essentially $41,000 per unit. The four units were bringing in a total of $2,850 in rent a month, for a yearly total of $34,200. All this on a total investment of only $165,000!

AFTERMATH

With the fourplex finished, it was time to refinance. A local bank appraised the property at $220,000 and promised a 70 percent cash-out refinance of $154,000, which would cover nearly everything invested! But the day before signing, the bank mysteriously decided to finance only a 55 percent cash-out at $120,000. It was a take-it-or-leave-it option, so Brandon took it. It would still cover the loan and then some. Plus, he knew he could refinance again later if he wanted a higher loan from a different bank.

Brandon opted for a thirty-year mortgage, but he set up a plan to have it paid off in only eighteen years using rental income alone. Why? Because four days after he purchased the fourplex, his daughter Rosie was born. (In fact, her very first outing into the world was to the title company while Brandon signed closing papers.)

Maybe you see where this is going—the property is Rosie's college fund! Here's how it will work: Based on normal appreciation, the fourplex will be worth around $300,000 to $350,000 in eighteen years, right when Rosie will be preparing for college. Since the property will be paid off, Brandon will refinance again to pull out $225,000 to $250,000 (70 percent of the appraised value) in *tax-free* cash for Rosie's education. That being said, Brandon assures me that if Rosie opts to skip college and go straight into entrepreneurship or real estate investing, he'll be overjoyed. Whatever she chooses, he'll still have more than $200,000 to help further her goals.

Then comes the final step in the BRRRR process: repeat. After the eighteen years are up, Brandon will take out a new mortgage on the property, again using rental income to pay it off over the fifteen to twenty years that follow. When *that* mortgage is paid off—long after Rosie has finished college and maybe has kids of her own—Brandon can repeat the process a third time (and so on).

Insider Info A successful BRRRR process is like creating a beefed-up personal bank account. You can earn a much higher return, your tenants invest in *your* account every month, and it's appreciating faster than money invested in any bank account out there.

Once Rosie is old enough, Brandon will task her with running the profit and loss statements and fielding phone calls. By managing "her own" property, she'll learn about real estate investing while staving off the burden of student loan debt. Heck, it may even provide a more lucrative education than college!

Although Brandon could sell the property down the road, opting for tax-free refinancing has the same profit potential in the long run (after considering fees and taxes, and recapturing depreciation). Don't forget cash flow: Even after mortgages, property management, and holding costs, he still averages more than $1,000 a month.

And that vision to redefine the neighborhood? It worked. The fourplex turned into the nicest property around, so it attracted great tenants, which in turn made the area a better place to live. When he bought them, they were just four dilapidated units. Now Brandon hears things like "Oh, you own those properties over on First Street? Wow, they look so good—that really turned around the neighborhood!"

TAKEAWAY

Get Personal

No matter the market, direct mail has always been one of the frontrunners for generating motivated seller leads. But even with direct mail, most real estate investors get only a 1 percent response rate on a *good* day. Brandon's 13 percent rate was higher than average due to a great letter that stood out thanks to two very specific bits of personalization:

1. A "handwritten" font
2. A photo of himself and his wife

These personal touches enabled Brandon to connect with the recipients on a level that made him more tangible and relatable than if he'd written a standard prefab letter. At my own company, we've also found that we get a better response rate when our outreach includes a picture of ourselves. It all goes to show that personalized letters—particularly in smaller markets—can be incredibly effective.

The same goes for your in-person interaction with potential sellers. I find that the best approach is to immediately build rapport through genuine, empathetic interaction. This isn't something you can fake, so if your interpersonal skills need some work, don't wait to start polishing them! Ultimately, sellers want to do business with people they know, like, and trust. People simply feel more comfortable dealing with a real, likable person than with a corporate stiff.

The HGTV Factor

Everybody deserves a quality build—period. As Brandon says:

> *"The biggest takeaway from this deal was realizing the HGTV factor! Which is to say: Do a good job. There are really good people who want beautiful, quality homes even if their price point is lower. Don't*

judge tenants by their economic place in life. A lot of rehabbers and landlords say, 'This is a Class D property in a Class D area, so I'm going to give you a Class D product.' And you know what? They attract only Class D people."

Too often I see investors make the mistake of assuming that low-income tenants or buyers won't mind a lower-quality product. The fact is that a person's income has nothing to do with whether or not they prefer comfortable, quality, attractive surroundings. Nearly everybody wants the highest level of comfort their money can buy, so creating as nice a place as possible will always attract the highest-quality tenants within a given income range.

In Brandon's case, aiming higher than the neighborhood "class" not only turned the entire street around, it also enabled him to attract more tenant applications overall. More applications meant that he could be more selective about who he approved, thus decreasing the likelihood of delinquency and other problems that arise from lower-quality tenants.

Real Estate Can Reach Across Generations

Using a property to provide for your children and your children's children can play a pivotal role in your financial legacy. Brandon didn't buy some multi-million-dollar property in order to set up his children and grandchildren for success. He just made a smart, simple investment for less than $165,000.

"Every month, Rosie and I will sit down and go over the numbers— what was income, what was expenses—and that'll be a thing we just do together. I think that experience will make a bigger impact than even the $250,000 [from the refinance]."

Don't lose sight of the opportunities available to you today that can impact the future in ways that most people simply can't imagine. Just one good investment today can be a total game changer for your family— twenty, fifty, or even one hundred years from now. In addition to using investments as instruments to pay for your children's future, you can use them as a tool to teach them about real estate, business, management, and investing. Even a degree in real estate seldom offers that type of hands-on experience!

CHAPTER SEVEN

OLA DANTIS

The Perfect FHA House Hack

Ola Dantis is the founder and CEO of Dwellynn, a real estate syndication group that has sourced more than $40 million in multifamily deals across the country. They focus on acquisition, repositioning, development, and management of affordable, quality residences for passive investors. Impressive, right? But how about this: Ola reached this level with only *four years* of real estate investing experience under his belt.

Leading a multifamily syndication firm after a mere four years of working in real estate is no small feat, but Ola won't take all the credit. He nods first to his wife, Weona, and his real estate mentor, Joe Fairless. At Dwellynn, he counts on two partners and three local team members to help find and structure deals, and an offshore team to manage administrative tasks.

Born and raised in Nigeria, Ola attended the University of Birmingham in England to earn his bachelor's and master's degrees in strategic marketing and consulting. Once finished, he returned to Nigeria to launch a consulting firm for small businesses and work pro bono for a startup nonprofit—his first tastes of entrepreneurship.

Around this time, his then girlfriend Weona got an internship in Florida. Ola flew out to visit her, and as the plane descended, he couldn't help but notice the "beautifully symmetrical streets and homes of suburban America." Gazing down from the window, he was already imagining the opportunities that the country had to offer.

However, he wasn't yet thinking of real estate. A few years after that first visit, Ola and Weona married and moved to the United States, and he ended up working as a business analyst in Baltimore. Then came a fateful consulting job for a friend in Dubai who happened to be working on a multifamily syndication deal.

You've probably heard how accountants for real estate investors quickly become investors themselves—they see their clients' winnings and want a piece of the pie. Similarly, Ola arrived in Dubai wearing his business analyst hat, but once he saw the ins and outs of the real estate deal, he realized he should switch professions.

He didn't waste any time. Since that trip, Ola has worked on everything from single-family units to big apartment complexes. But his best deal ever might come as a surprise: a house hack! Well, it's *more* than a house hack, but we'll get to that later.

FINDING THE DEAL

Before diving into real estate, Ola and Weona had been renting a luxury apartment in suburban Baltimore and commuting to their standard 9-to-5s in the city. However, luxury had a price, and it wasn't long before Ola noticed a pattern—sit in traffic, go to work, sit in traffic, get home, eat dinner, go to bed, repeat. He kept wondering: *Is this all there is?*

After observing his friend's real estate deal in Dubai, Ola spent the entire flight home thinking, *Hey, I might be able to do this in the United States—a much larger real estate market.* Now that he'd seen the syndication concept from an insider's perspective, he knew he could translate that experience into investing for himself.

Unable to let go of this new idea (and with Weona's blessing), he started seeking his first investment. The end goal was syndications, he knew that much, so he figured he would start small and scale up from there. While educating himself on real estate as quickly as possible, he scanned listings and built connections with brokers and wholesalers. A few months in, while perusing the downtown Baltimore MLS, he came across a duplex for $299,000. Ola knew exactly what to do.

"The reason I always mention Dubai is because some people get opportunities but miss the mark when the opportunity doesn't come

in an expected package—something that's been tied up with a ribbon. When my friend called seeking help on some of the pain points in his business structure, the easy thing to say was 'Sorry, no, I can't. I'm busy with work.'

"Instead, I thought, 'What if I go on this trip and learn something new that can help my young family?' Of course, had I turned down his offer, I wouldn't be here having this conversation about real estate and how to achieve financial freedom with one of the surest assets in the world."

ASSESSMENT

The duplex was a three-story brick row house from the 1920s with a quaint backyard patio. The upstairs unit had two levels, two bedrooms, and one bath, and it was being rented to a couple who hoped to continue their lease after the owners sold it. Meanwhile, the vacant lower unit had one bedroom and one bath. Both units had private entrances and a washer and dryer.

The surrounding Class A neighborhood was situated near pubs, restaurants, and a beautiful six-acre park. With downtown and bustling Johns Hopkins Hospital barely two miles away, finding buyers or renters should have been easy. Unfortunately, classy as the neighborhood was, the duplex stood out like a sore thumb. The roof desperately needed replacing, the original cast-iron bathtubs would have to go, and the Formica kitchen countertops would be a turnoff to anybody living in the twenty-first century.

Ola projected that renovating the duplex to bring it up to the neighborhood's competitive standards would cost at least $50,000. However, he had an idea: If he and Weona moved into the downstairs unit, the upstairs renters would likely cover the whole mortgage. Not only that—if they renovated to raise the property value, the investment had double-play potential: house hack and live-in flip!

THE BREAKDOWN

Three-story duplex row house, 1,980 square feet
Downtown Baltimore, Maryland
Asking $299,000

OFFER AND FUNDING

Knowing that the property had been sitting on the MLS for well over four months, Ola figured the sellers might be willing to accept a lower offer. He crossed his fingers and offered $220,000. After some negotiation, they settled on $240,000, with a new roof to be provided by the sellers.

For the funding, Ola scored a Federal Housing Administration (FHA) loan and had to put down only 3.5 percent ($8,400) on a thirty-year fixed mortgage with 3.5 percent interest. Given the low rates, he and Weona aimed to cover the $50,000 renovation cost with earnings they had been setting aside from their day jobs. It didn't hurt that the upstairs renters were paying $1,200 monthly, which already covered the mortgage.

Ken's Take   Not only does an FHA loan offer a low down payment and great interest rates, it also offers renovation assistance through its 203k program. I won't lie—there's tons of paperwork involved (typical for the government), but it also allows homeowners to borrow funds for the renovation.

While the 203k program is a bit cumbersome, we have worked it with several clients and it's certainly doable. Combining reduced-down-payment loans with house-hack savings makes a great real estate investment that much better—at least once you get done with the paperwork!

TURNAROUND

The fact that Ola had never sold, renovated, or even *owned* a home before didn't slow him down. He and Weona settled into the new digs for a few months; then they got started with a contractor. First, the messy stuff—ripping out piping, faucets, kitchen countertops, and the entire bathroom, especially the rusting cast-iron tubs.

Since they were planning to buy and hold rather than flip and sell, standard mid-range finishes would fit the bill (enter Ikea). All appliances were replaced and updated with chic stainless steel, the walls were repainted, and the old hardwood floors were covered with durable, renter-friendly laminate flooring.

Ken's Take Renovating to buy and hold does not typically demand the same standards as renovating to flip. While you want to make a nice product for your renter, it's important to be practical in your selections and finishes. In most cases, basic builder-grade finishes will more than suffice.

After six weeks of work, *voilà*—their first live-in flip was complete! One night over dinner, Ola commented to Weona that despite the out-of-pocket renovation investment, their bank accounts seemed to be growing faster than ever. They were discovering the power of having renters pay the mortgage, and none too soon, since the upstairs renters were ready to move out.

The timing was perfect for another reason—in just a few months, they'd have a newborn daughter, Temi, and she would need that second upstairs bedroom. With the downstairs remodeled, they found renters for a competitive rate of $1,200 a month and moved upstairs to rinse and repeat.

There's nothing like a newborn baby as motivation to finish a live-in flip. Luckily, they had already purchased the necessary materials when they renovated the first level, so most of the job was copy and paste. They wrapped up construction in only three weeks—two weeks after Temi was born!

AFTERMATH

As predicted, the rehab cost about $50,000 total, so Ola was all-in at $290,000. The renovated duplex now easily surpassed market standards, but did the investment pay off? You bet it did. In fact, a new appraisal came in at $375,000—an $85,000 equity gain.

Insider Info Remember the BRRRR strategy—buy, rehab, rent, refinance, and repeat. When you refinance a property at its higher value, you can pull out a portion of the equity as a bank loan. It's tax-free funding for new projects.

Ola was even more struck by the money he *didn't* have to spend to realize that gain. By maintaining renters throughout the flip, he drastically reduced out-of-pocket costs. After fully grasping the potential of infusing these savings into new projects, they found renters for the upstairs unit for $1,400 per month. With $2,600 in total rental income, Ola and Weona were left with nearly $1,600 in monthly cash flow after expenses.

Meanwhile, Ola and Weona found another nearby property for $75,000 to start the process all over again. After putting $75,000 into the renovation, they sold the property for $245,000—a $95,000 payday. They were most certainly off to the races! Of course, Ola then leveraged *those* earnings into another great deal, aiming to scale each time.

Each deal—and all the grit, focus, and hard work that went with it—was a step toward his current level of multifamily commercial syndication. While other deals would go on to earn him fatter paychecks, the duplex was the catalyst for all the successes to follow. In fact, just weeks before our interview, he closed on a 160-unit cash-flowing commercial property in Texas.

TAKEAWAY
Pay Attention to Days on Market

When Ola saw that the property had been on the local MLS for more than four months, he also saw an opportunity—savvy investors pay attention to these things. An owner whose property has been on the market for a long time is usually more motivated to negotiate, and with every passing day, that motivation typically increases. For a list price of $299,000, Ola's first offer of $220,000 was certainly a lowball, but through negotiation, he was still able to get the seller to agree to $240,000—which is a $60,000 reduction. Plus, he got them to install a new roof!

Real estate is often just a numbers game. Make enough lowball offers and you *will* find a buyer willing to bite. Some of our coaching students focus their entire acquisition strategy on MLS properties that have been listed for more than 120 days and have had good success. Again, make enough offers and some percentage of them are bound to get accepted.

Question Comfort

As Ola says, "If real estate had a gateway drug, house hacks would be it." Before the duplex investment, Ola and Weona rented in a luxury apartment building. It was convenient and comfortable, but once they were willing to get *uncomfortable*, they realized they'd been settling for less all along.

> *"Before living in the duplex, I never had to worry about property taxes, never had to worry about when the trash goes out, never had to worry about parking. But when you change your life and get a little uncomfortable, you start to see some real change.*
>
> *"In fact, for us, just getting rental income was a big game changer. After that first rent check, I turned to Weona and exclaimed, 'Somebody's actually paying us to live here!'"*

That's when the switch flipped in his mindset. Through the experience of house hacking inside a live-in flip, they found that financial freedom far outweighed any of the inconveniences. Plus, they created a domino effect: The profit from each new property fell into the next, creating generations of profit-producing homes.

The First One Typically Leads to More

Many people would be slowed down by full-time jobs and a comfortable living situation—not to mention a baby on the way. It's the cautious, traditional idea of stability that usually wins versus building a future amid transformation.

Ola and Weona embraced the idea of changing things in order to change things, and the payoff has given them more fulfillment and freedom than they ever imagined. Ola recently moved his young family from Baltimore to Houston—the fourth-largest city in America—to build and scale Dwellynn even more. And it all started with just one great deal!

CHAPTER EIGHT

ANNA MYERS

From Data Analytics to Airbnb Investing

Nobody in this book works with data quite the same way Anna Myers does, but she didn't always apply those skills to real estate. Though both her father and grandfather were real estate investors, Anna opted out of the succession, instead choosing a career in computer programming and data analysis.

Anna eventually began putting money into a few residential real estate investments, even if it was only to write off income that was being eaten up by taxes. However, in doing so, she began seeing just how scalable real estate really is. With the family gene activated, she created a five-year plan to switch her career to full-time real estate investing.

> *"I spent those first few years diving deep into education, and I have to admit that I probably listened to all the BiggerPockets podcasts while jogging or driving. I also attended seminars and read so many books."*

No matter what Anna learned in her studies, data analysis remained the bedrock of her education. After attending a multifamily boot camp led by Neal Bawa, she scored a position volunteering for his company, Grocapitus Investments, as an analyst. Eventually, all her effort paid off: Anna is now the vice president of that very organization.

She is also an active general partner on their nearly 2,000 residential multifamily units and 780 self-storage units. In keeping with its approach to multifamily as a team sport, the company has numerous limited-equity partners and about twenty-five employees working remotely—eighteen of whom are virtual assistants—to manage their $265 million in assets.

Insider Info Outsourcing staff as virtual assistants (VAs) can be a smart way to scale at a low cost. When your operations are highly systematized, like Anna's, it's that much easier to bring VAs on to "plug and play" without extensive training.

Focusing on the Southeast and the Sun Belt, Anna's company approaches investments with a data science lens, homing in on hot investment zones with hyperlocal analyses of demographic and market trends. This way, they boost the odds of success before even finding a single property.

The numbers they use aren't top secret—often, they're just government data that cities and counties are required to make publicly accessible. They typically look at data from 2000 to 2017, and their main criteria for metropolitan areas and cities are:

1. Population growth of 20 percent or more
2. Median household income growth of 30 percent or more
3. Median property value growth of 40 percent or more
4. Job growth above 2 percent annualized (or 1.5 percent for megacities)
5. Crime rates no greater than 500 and trending downward based on information from www.city-data.com
6. Landlord-friendly states

After finding ideal investment zones, Anna's team then uses a suite of metrics to analyze the *micro*-neighborhoods therein, looking for the following:

1. Median household income between $40,000 and $70,000
2. Median contract rent between $700 and $1,000
3. Unemployment rate no higher than 2 percentage points past the overall area rate
4. A poverty level under 20 percent (although 15 percent is strongly preferred)
5. Diverse micro-neighborhoods to mix up the potential tenant pool

Anna explains, "We are literally that specific. We turn away deals every week. People might come to us with a deal that screams profit, but if it doesn't meet our demographics, we don't bring it to our investors. As data geeks, we use all our tools to help us place our money and our investors' money in the best locations. We are also true scientists—always testing and tweaking our methods. Markets will go up and down, and things will happen to all investments, but we believe that if the market and the micro-neighborhood have strong fundamentals, there's much more cushion for corrections or errors."

FINDING THE DEAL

When Anna and her husband's last child left home for college, they decided to sell their Bay Area home and downsize to a rental. They'd purchased it eighteen years earlier, in 1998, and anybody who knows the Bay Area won't be surprised that the home's value had increased by more than 300 percent.

Because they understood the opportunity that a 1031 could offer, they didn't immediately put the home up for sale. First, they rented it out for two years, which was a genius 1031 move that enabled them to sell their long-term asset as a hybrid. The IRS would still regard it as their primary household, but it also counted as an investment property.

After a profitable sale, Anna began the hunt for a multifamily rental into which she could invest the earnings with a 1031 exchange.

Insider Info The IRC 121 exclusion—otherwise known as the home sale gain exclusion—allows for a married couple filing jointly to avoid capital gains on the sale of a primary residence if they've lived in the property for two of the previous five years. However, this exclusion applies only up to the first $500,000 ($250,000 for a single taxpayer) in profit. Any amount of profit higher than $500,000 is susceptible to a capital gains tax, unless a 1031 exchange (which you'll remember from Corey Peterson's chapter) is used. Because the sale of Anna's home resulted in a profit well above $500,000, they wisely opted to reinvest those earnings through a 1031 exchange.

Anna planned to use the same techniques that work so well in her multi-million-dollar investment company to find a buy-and-hold property for herself. In addition to the usual metrics, she wanted a market that was Airbnb-friendly and strong with short-term rentals. Using the BiggerPockets forums to network, Anna connected with longtime member and investor Jay Hinrichs, who pointed her to Charleston, South Carolina.

Charleston indeed seemed to check all the boxes, so Anna and her husband flew in to meet with some of Jay's brokers there. They saw thirteen MLS properties in two days, but an $855,000 property Anna had found on LoopNet seemed most promising.

ASSESSMENT

The historic 1850s duplex was a classic Charleston-style double house designed to face the street at full length. It reigned in the Upper King district, the heart of Charleston's food and bar scene at the corner of King and Cannon Streets. The property's two levels were each 750 square feet with two bedrooms, one bath, and a colonial-style covered porch that ran the length of the property's facade.

The forest-green columns and window trim against the white-painted siding gave the property a charmingly classic feel, but the charm stopped there. Inside, the decor was hideous and run-down—from the paint to the popcorn-style ceilings to the Formica countertops, everything was as dated as it looked. On top of that, the foundation was in poor shape, there was no crawl space, and there were dry-rot issues in the walls.

Charleston being an old city, there are countless historic properties with foundations so badly shifted over time that they have gained the affectionately titled "Charleston lean." You practically have to hold on to the walls for balance while walking through some of them. As Anna describes it:

"This one could certainly get a marble rolling without effort, but it at least had less of a lean than others I'd visited. It was 1850—they didn't understand the meaning of the word 'foundation' back then—and fixing the lean would mean tearing up the gorgeous heart pine floors."

Nonetheless, the area's investment and tourism potential were quickly developing, with hip eateries and bars sprinkled everywhere. Three nearby colleges added a steady stream of students to the already bustling scene, which would bode well for Anna if she needed to fall back on long-term renters. Even better, the property was already zoned for short-term rentals.

While the duplex came with the typical noise of a busy neighborhood, it was also next door to a fire station. Replacing the historic single-pane windows wouldn't be cheap, and even then, the noise would not be attractive to renters. Nonetheless, the seller had been running a real estate office downstairs and a lucrative Airbnb upstairs. The fact that he was already getting customers despite the appearance, the lean, *and* the fire station was a solid enough proof of concept for Anna.

She envisioned transforming the home's two levels into separate Airbnbs for tourists and other short-term renters. If the numbers were right, short-term rentals could bring in up to $4,000 in total monthly cash flow. If that didn't work, long-term student rentals at $1,000 per room would be a simple plan B.

First, Anna would address items that needed immediate repair— namely the dry rot and the cosmetic renovation—in order to get the Airbnb up and running as quickly as possible. Assessing the short-term budget needs at $35,000, she would tackle larger projects (like installing a new roof) after seeing some cash flow.

THE BREAKDOWN

Two-story duplex, 1,500 square feet
Upper King district, Charleston, South Carolina
Asking $855,000

OFFER AND FUNDING

Anna negotiated the seller down to $835,000 from the $855,000 asking price, but funding the deal turned out to be more challenging than expected. Even though the property had commercial zoning, Anna was aiming to lock in a thirty-year *residential* loan to avoid working with a commercial lender. The multiple conventional lenders she tried wouldn't recognize the income the property could generate as a short-term rental, though, and loan appraisals kept coming in short.

The loan delay meant Anna had to ask the seller to extend the closing date. To keep him from looking for other buyers, she agreed to pay him rent and take over running the Airbnb. The seller was a real estate investor and entrepreneur himself, so he was willing to agree instead of falling out of contract.

Ken's Take To keep the seller on the line while she shopped around for financing, Anna had the clever idea of incorporating a "rent and re-rent"-style Airbnb agreement. This can be a fantastic Airbnb strategy in and of itself: Get a master lease and turn the property into an Airbnb that generates more revenue through short-term rentals than the underlying master lease payment.

After struggling through multiple lenders, Anna finally found a conventional thirty-year fixed Fannie Mae loan for $533,850 amortized at 4.6 percent interest. The only catch was that, in addition to her 1031 exchange funds, she would need to bring an extra $78,000 from her savings to close on the loan. While the situation was not ideal, she believed the house would be worth it in the long run.

TURNAROUND

With the closing papers signed, Anna's first job was getting rid of the dry rot. Like securing the loan, this turned out to be more difficult than anticipated; the rot was more extensive than anybody had realized. Four-fifths of the building's exterior had to be replaced, including two of the columns, most of the upstairs porch, the entire set of back stairs, and much of the entry facade. As the dry-rot problem revealed its hidden extent, Anna had to re-allocate much of her predicted renovation cost.

With dry rot devouring her bank account, Anna opted not to gut the inside. Instead, she gussied it up with new paint and hip decor. The kitchens—a key rental appeal factor—received special attention with refinished cabinets, undermount sinks, and new granite countertops. As for the original pine floors, she opted to let the home keep its lean rather than rip them out to correct the foundation.

Anna was living in the Bay Area and trying to manage the renovation remotely, which—surprise, surprise—*also* turned out to be more difficult than expected. Contractors are notoriously hard to nail down in Charleston (and nearly everywhere else, for that matter), and as for the one Anna found...

> *"He had a wonderful personality but a terrible problem of always being late. He would claim that he'd be there the next day and then not show up, so I spent a lot of time and anxious moments trying to get his crew back on my site. This is probably a familiar story for many readers. It was especially nerve-racking when I had guests booked and the unit was still a mess three days prior to their arrival. I can turn into quite the squeaky wheel when I need to, though, so we finally got the job done."*

Because Anna had refurnished the units and had been running them as Airbnbs before actually closing on the property, workers had to move the furnishings to non-construction areas while working through the property's various rooms. Piling everything together in a corner, they would do their best to protect the furnishings from construction debris and try to put them back when finished. Though some things got broken and a few small items went "missing" along the way, the job eventually came together. Anna explains one pleasant surprise:

> *"There was an odd wall in the upstairs living room that jutted out. Our contractor, who was very experienced with these old buildings, was convinced there was a fireplace underneath. His company specialized in masonry, but we had no idea what we would find behind the walls. We agreed to have him take down the walls, not knowing if we would just find rubble. Right after the wall came down, he FaceTimed me to show the INCREDIBLE original 1850s fireplace he'd exposed underneath—and it was still functional! I had them seal it off and spruce up the grout and masonry for a beautiful accent piece."*

As far as the neighborhood noise, the home's structure and its status in a historic district wouldn't allow for double-pane windows, so Anna eventually found a company to create custom inserts to buffer the sound. The price tag was hefty, but the difference in noise level and the energy savings were worth every penny.

It took four months to go from contract to completed renovation to Airbnb listing. Another three months of mildly tricky rentals passed as

Anna nailed down a boots-on-the-ground team that included an amazing turnover assistant and key vendors for HVAC, plumbing, maintenance, and pest control.

A solid team was crucial for seamless remote management, but the real key to pulling it all together was developing automated systems and processes to manage the guest experience online. After seven months of in-depth engagement, Anna could finally step away and let the property churn on its own. The price tag during that entire process? A hefty $95,000—which was $60,000 over budget, due almost entirely to the surprise dry-rot issue.

AFTERMATH

Going over budget was painful, but the rental thrived from the start. It brought in $10,000 monthly, with $4,000 of that as pure profit. After a purchase price of $835,000 in 2016, the property now has an estimated value well over $1.2 million! On top of the cash flow, Anna has created a vacation home for her family—they visit the Airbnb twice a year for several weeks to enjoy the city.

Ken's Take One of the benefits of taking on a large renovation project like this is the opportunity to create a significant equity leap. Increasing the value of a high-dollar property means a difference of hundreds of thousands of dollars versus the tens of thousands of dollars you'd get from renovating lower-priced homes. Anna did a phenomenal job researching the right location to make sure she would be in a position to capture appreciation through strong short-term rental demand, all while harnessing the tax benefits of the 1031 exchange. With big risk comes big reward—at least if you know what you're doing!

The city of Charleston has since designated the duplex's neighborhood as an Opportunity Zone (OZ), meaning that investors have a tax incentive to come in and renovate more properties in the area. They've also clamped down on short-term rentals, but the new law doesn't apply to Anna's property since it was grandfathered in with its pre-existing zoning before the law took effect.

"There are many older buildings being bought up and fully renovated because of the Opportunity Zone, so my property value is increasing due to the 'rising tide' effect with the rest of the neighborhood. And old houses are like boats—they need constant work, but at least this one is in an awesome location and is always working for us."

TAKEAWAY

It's All About the Data

When you know how to work with data, the data will work for you. Anna has honed her data skills throughout her career to make brilliant investment decisions. After leveraging this experience in the multifamily space, she was ready to apply those time-tested concepts in pursuit of a huge equity opportunity.

As with nearly any investment, you should analyze local markets carefully to make sure both monthly rental rates and property values will stay steady and appreciate. If nothing else, you should research at *least* basic demographic and real estate trends (which you can easily find online) before investing in any project.

"We share our methods for how we choose cities and neighborhoods on our education platform, www.multifamilyu.com. We believe all investors should be empowered with data to make good decisions when investing, and our methods use only free tools available on the internet to everyone."

Anna is not shy in turning down a deal that doesn't fit perfectly into the data "buy box," nor is she shy about sharing her buying criteria. There are several websites for data on specific locations, but three of her go-tos are www.city-data.com, www.neighborhoodscout.com, and www.localmarketmonitor.com.

Find the Opportunity... Zones

Opportunity Zones are typically in distressed or low-income areas and offer various tax incentives to lure investment dollars for development. While the district where Anna's building is located wasn't designated as an OZ at the time of purchase, she now benefits from the vast amount of investment dollars being poured into the area.

"Charleston's Upper King is one of those OZs that has people raising their eyebrows and saying, 'Really? That's an Opportunity Zone?' But again, data helps in selecting the right OZs. They're not all what one would typically consider distressed or low-income, but the tax incentives are the same across the board."

As investors, we should approach OZs from multiple angles. For example, owning property that's near an area where investment dollars are pouring in will likely mean you'll reap an increase in value. As another angle, we can look at utilizing attractive opportunities to wipe out tax liability by investing in an OZ fund, or even by *creating* the fund and managing projects that other investors can take advantage of.

Harness the Power of the 1031 Exchange

While most people don't think about using a 1031 exchange on a primary residence, living in the Bay Area for eighteen years created so much equity for Anna and her husband that when they sold their home, it was a taxable event. Luckily, by understanding the power of the 1031 exchange, Anna knew to use this tool to roll her gains of over $500,000 into a cash-flowing asset in Charleston.

Here's the deal, though: Anna will likely sell this Charleston house one day, and my hunch is that once again she'll roll those earnings into another cash-flowing asset via a 1031 exchange. Theoretically, she could continue rolling equity gained from these projects into the next (and the next, and so on), never paying any capital gains but snowballing the equity value each time. This cycle of rolling equity into the next asset over and over is how you really harness the power of the 1031 exchange.

There are even opportunities to roll 1031 exchange money into an OZ fund. Leaving these funds alone for at least ten years can completely wipe out any capital gains tax on those invested dollars.

CHAPTER NINE

SEAN CONLON

A Bet on Ralph Lauren

Sean Conlon and his four siblings were raised in a two-bedroom home in a little village in County Kildare, Ireland. Home life was crowded and money was scarce, so he sought refuge in the local library. There he found free entertainment, spending hours reading about legendary avatars of the American dream—Carnegie, Rockefeller, Getty—among other "useless things" like fly-fishing and falconry. (By the way, Sean's now a successful fly fisherman *and* falconer.)

At age 17, Sean was at the top of his class, but he dropped out of college to start bringing in income for his struggling family. He became a low-level banker for Lehman Brothers by day and loaded mail trains by night. Life became work; no more hours at the library, and certainly no time for dreams.

Four years later, while standing on the train platform awaiting the next haul, Sean was hit with a realization: *"I'm going to be average for the rest of my life."* That hadn't been the plan. According to Carnegie, Rockefeller, and Getty, he had greatness within him—He just had to find it. *"Fine,"* he thought, *"I might be average in Ireland, but in America, I can be* anything."

Within days, Sean had packed his belongings and set off for the United States with fifty bucks to his name. Promising his family that they'd soon be receiving riches from his pursuit of the American dream, he landed in Chicago in the middle of winter.

The streets were not, as he'd predicted, paved with gold. It was snow that covered the streets, cold and uncomfortable. But like the Vikings, who burned their boats upon reaching a new land, Sean had no intention of returning to Ireland.

He soon found work as an assistant janitor, but his head was in the clouds—he was doing more dreaming than cleaning. After three years of proving himself to be *"the worst assistant janitor ever,"* Sean decided it was time to become one of those real estate moguls he grew up reading about. By day, he would continue working as an assistant janitor, but by night, he would chase his dreams. With a massive phone book on his desk, he began a campaign of one hundred nightly cold calls. He explains:

> *"I was tenacious because I was afraid. I had nothing else I was qualified for, and I was an incredible dreamer. I really thought I could make something of myself in real estate, and it was tangible—I could see and touch what I wanted to sell by simply walking down the street."*

Six months of rejection ensued. On the verge of giving up, Sean finally caught a break when a woman let him sell her condo for $23,000. He pocketed a meager $300 in commission, but that was all the momentum he needed.

Four years later, Sean was one of the top-selling real estate brokers in North America. In those early years, he had spotted something in Chicago that nobody else had—multifamily new-construction condominiums, and the lack thereof—and created a system around it. Sean says:

> *"I wasn't reinventing the wheel, but they hadn't done many multifamily condo conversions in the neighborhoods around Wrigley Field and several others. I convinced a couple other investors to go in on this with me, and we were immediately successful. From there, I put contracts under every single door I could find."*

Eventually, Sean could afford to rent out a small office, and there he became a one-stop shop for anybody interested in developing real estate. He had in-house development plans, properties, and closing attorneys, so you could enter the office as one thing and leave as a real estate developer. It was a great time for investing, and in those years, Sean probably created a thousand Chicago multimillionaires.

Though he started out with boots on the ground, Sean eventually became the lender for all the investors he'd created. Today he owns properties all over the country while running a merchant bank and commercial brokerage for custom client requests. But the real bread and butter centers on leveraging his network, which, as he says, is the most valuable asset he has.

Sean's work is essentially a scaled-up model of what he did in the '90s, just with bigger figures and broader territory. It boils down to taking his global network (with a net worth of trillions of dollars) and introducing key investors to real estate operations in need of capital. Simply put, he is paid to connect the dots—the very, very valuable dots, with entry prices generally ranging from $10 million to $500 million. He explains:

> *"I drop on the ground wherever it is—India, Italy, Spain, the UK, and so on—then I introduce everybody and connect the dots. Local financing, land finding, et cetera. I put the pieces together."*

These days, Sean is mainly involved in million- and *billion*-dollar deals, but his best deal ever came when he had yet to make more than $200,000 on a single investment. Let's see how it all began.

FINDING THE DEAL

It sounds like an oversimplification, but Sean found this deal by, well, looking. It was still early in his career, in the mid-'90s, and he was hungry for a game-changing deal. The internet wasn't yet doing its thing, so like most Chicago investors, Sean found new listings through a booklet delivered every night at midnight. Arriving early to the office each morning, he would underline the hot properties and steal away when he found time to check them out.

On his way to visit one of the listings, Sean happened to notice an unlisted mixed-use building with retail on the first floor and apartments above. He became fixated on it. Nearly every morning after that, he sat on a doorstep across the street, drinking coffee, and stalking his prey.

✅ ASSESSMENT

The beautiful brick-and-stone building dated back to 1895 and sat on a street corner covering 20,000 square feet. The retail space, totaling about 2,600 square feet, was accessible from two separate street entrances. Below it was a spacious basement, and above were three additional stories housing sixteen residential units.

The historic building was in the heart of Lincoln Park, a tree-lined neighborhood known for diverse nightlife, dining, and entertainment. A train station buzzed nearby, pouring out a steady stream of commuters and tourists. With all that lucrative foot traffic, Sean couldn't understand why the first floor was occupied by a humdrum cowboy boot store.

In fact, the building seemed out of sync with the entire area; it was shabby and languishing, but the neighborhood seemed affluent and robust. A nicer building might have caught some eyes, but this one was a drain on its own existence.

After months of rumination, Sean devised a plan: Ralph Lauren didn't know it yet, but this building would be the future home of one of his retail stores. Having heard rumors that the fashion mogul was looking for a new Chicago location, Sean was confident that the luxury brand would be a much-needed upgrade from the cowboy boot store.

The passersby were the right demographic, and the location itself would ensure brand marketing to the train station's abundant foot traffic. Having Ralph Lauren as a tenant would also raise the building's value, bringing in new customers not only for retail but also for the sixteen apartments above.

The thing was, the property wasn't for sale—and, true, Sean hadn't spoken to a single Ralph Lauren representative. However, he'd watched the people walking by, counting their numbers, and he knew the area was thriving. All he had to do was convince Ralph Lauren.

Scratch that. *First*, he had to convince someone to sell him the building.

THE BREAKDOWN

Mixed-use building, 20,000 square feet
Lincoln Park, Chicago, Illinois
Not for sale

OFFER AND FUNDING

Putting his plan to action, Sean entered the boot store to ask its manager for the property owner's information. Smelling trouble, the cowboy turned him away. However, it was no use: Sean tracked down the owner and quickly discovered that he wasn't looking to sell. As Sean describes it:

> *"The owner was completely, completely dismissive—in fact, he was quite rude initially. I stayed on him, politely pushy. That's the thing about consistency. One day, the seller's whole world changed, and he became ready to make a deal."*

Confident that everybody has their number, Sean followed up with the owner a whopping twenty-five times before he finally agreed to sell. Although market value was likely around $2 million, Sean offered $2.4 million to get the owner's attention. It was undoubtedly risky paying that much over market, but he knew he'd recoup the overpayment by snagging his star tenant.

Then Sean took it a giant step further by offering to take a nearby vacant building off the owner's hands for $1 million. With that, he finally got the main property under contract for $2.9 million while his real estate peers chided him for overpaying.

Their objections weren't unfounded, particularly since Sean still hadn't secured (or even spoken to anybody at) Ralph Lauren. If he couldn't get them to sign on, he would have paid way too much for a building that might not even earn a profit. But he had faith in his intuition, and he knew that overpaying now was the only way to achieve a bigger payday later.

Sean found a partner who understood construction and financing but brought a different skill set than his own—one of his fundamental partnership rules is complementary skill sets. They put up 30 percent of their own money to secure traditional bank financing and set aside $300,000 for the turnaround.

Insider Info Today Sean notes that *"a smarter person would do five or six deals [adding up to a similar amount], own 20 percent, and get the capital from somewhere else. Better to own 20 percent of a deal like that than go all-in."* His point is well taken—it's typically better to spread your risk around by taking small portions of multiple deals. Seasoned investors understand the risk of being a majority stakeholder in a large deal like this. If the project goes south, the lender can go after the assets of the primary guarantor. Depending on the size of the project, taking on most of the risk can even result in bankruptcy for the owner.

TURNAROUND

Sean had caught his prey, and now it was time to make the building fit for an American fashion icon. He put $300,000 into cleaning it up, mostly increasing the building's curb appeal with new windows, tuckpointing, and fresh paint.

Meanwhile, he cold-called Ralph Lauren's real estate department and charmed his way into getting their attention. (The Irish accent may have helped.) As it turned out, they didn't care much about potential sales figures. A store in that location, they quickly realized, would be a huge billboard aimed at the area's plentiful foot traffic. They signed a lease at $82 per square foot—well above the $30-per-square-foot average market price—and opened a new Rugby Ralph Lauren store in the retail space within six months.

Ken's Take The right anchor tenant in a retail property can often make or break an investment. How many times have you seen a shopping center die because the large anchor store moved out? Or how about the shopping center that is revived when a new anchor tenant moves in? That said, while it's generally not advisable to purchase a property based on the assumption that you'll land your dream tenant, Sean has a knack for being the exception to the rule. He knew the neighborhood inside out, he developed a strong intuition, and he was willing to take a huge risk.

AFTERMATH

The unbelievable rent hike was like a catapult for the property's value. With investors enamored of the enviable rents and high-profile tenant, Sean had no problem flipping just one year later at more than three times his total investment. After the $2.9 million purchase and $300,000 facelift, he sold his dream property for $10.4 million, clearing more than $7 million!

Insider Info Commercial properties are valued based on the amount of income they generate. Sean did an amazing job convincing Ralph Lauren to pay above-market rent to establish a presence in this bustling location, which served as a direct multiplier on the property's value. The high rent translated to higher overall income, which translated to a higher overall sale price. Kudos to Mr. Conlon on selling everybody on his dream!

TAKEAWAY

Wait for That Step-Up Opportunity

Sean went from deals earning $200,000 in profit to one with a $7 million payday. What did he do differently? Not much—he just used his ever-growing experience and kept his eyes open. He explains:

> "The CIA knows it: You pick up intelligence on the street. In reality, what made me different or 'better' was that I worked hard, I walked the streets, I talked to everybody, and I studied. Common sense is not that common. People wouldn't think the key to success on that deal was sitting on a doorstep, drinking coffee, and watching that property every morning. But that's what it was."

As investors, most of us are far more capable than we give ourselves credit for. The investors who make the leap from Little League to the majors don't typically have some inherent advantage over everyone else. Like Sean, they lean on their experience, wait for the right opportunity to come along, study it carefully, then take a calculated risk.

Intuition Is a Real Thing

Sean bought a property that he studied carefully based on what I would call intuition. Does that mean he made a hasty investment decision or one without sound fundamentals? Some of his colleagues thought so. But did those colleagues also take the time to carefully observe traffic patterns and study the potential of this particular property? Probably not.

I think investors need to give themselves more credit when it comes to using intuition and making real estate investment decisions. Sometimes the available data just doesn't provide the complete picture. Maybe there aren't enough *good* comps to paint a realistic picture of value.

Those moments of intuition aren't random. They are usually based on foundational experiences, and whether conscious or not, your brain is likely computing more bits of information than you can even comprehend. Always be prudent when making a high-stakes decision, but don't be afraid to listen to your gut either. The best decisions are often made when you're striking a good balance between the two.

Know When to Exit

Sean had a vision for where he believed this property would take him. Multiple things had to happen in order for him to achieve his goal, among them the owner agreeing to sell and Ralph Lauren agreeing to move in at above-market rents. Amazingly, Sean was able to buy the property, make some renovations, and place Ralph Lauren as the anchor tenant. The stars had aligned, but the next question was, what now?

Sean did as many seasoned investors would do—he took the money and ran! This property was firing on all cylinders and Sean had an opportunity to cash out $7 million within one year of owning the property. Why wait for a market correction? Why wait to see if Ralph Lauren decides to move out at the end of their lease? The $7 million could be immediately invested in *multiple* other projects to exponentially increase Sean's net worth.

Interestingly, just a few years after Sean sold the property, Ralph Lauren did in fact move out and the value of the property took a hit as a result. (Luckily, the new owners were able to re-tenant the property.) It goes to show that timing can be everything in a real estate transaction. I hate to compare real estate investing to gambling, but sometimes you have to know when to walk with your winnings.

CHAPTER TEN
LEE ARNOLD
Code Enforcement Meth House

Lee Arnold is one of the few investors I know who can say he got started in real estate as a teenager. Before that, he was a grocery store bag boy working the night shift and making minimum wage. Late at night after one of his shifts, he was decompressing in front of the TV and saw an infomercial for an upcoming local real estate event. The tune was the same then as it is now: "Come to our free seminar and we'll teach you how to get rich in real estate!"

The thing is, Lee believed it—at least enough to show up. And as it turned out, the three-hour seminar was surprisingly informative. Still, he knew it was just the tip of the iceberg. To learn more, the organizers said he'd have to attend their three-day boot camp the following weekend. That one *wouldn't* be free, though. Lee would need to come up with a cool $1,500.

He didn't have the money, but he *did* have faith that he could figure out where to get it. First, he asked his family for a loan. No dice. Lee then made the rounds at the grocery store, asking everybody up to the store managers and pharmacists for their investment. No luck there either.

Finally, Lee tried the local bank, where he was able to refinance his truck loan and pull out just enough to cover the $1,500. It was the biggest check Lee had ever written, but the boot camp training gave him the confidence he needed to start looking for deals. Within weeks, he found a single-family residence that he thought could make a great flip, but now he had even *less* money than when he'd started.

There would be no truck refinance this time, so Lee circled back to one of the grocery store's pharmacists, who'd playfully hinted at providing a loan if Lee ever found a worthwhile investment. Turns out, he'd been speaking the truth—the pharmacist bankrolled the single-family flip as a hard-money lender, and Lee ended up creating a profit for both of them. After Lee took that profit from one deal to the next, it wasn't long before he could bankroll himself. He explains:

> *"This pharmacist was really important to my journey. He became my first hard-money lender, so I learned early on that the pathway to wealth in this business is getting to a place as quickly as possible where you become the bank."*

There have been stops and starts along Lee's twenty-plus year career, but overall he's traveled a storybook path from bag boy to real estate virtuoso. Today he lives in the pristine mountain town of Coeur d'Alene, Idaho, where he enjoys the best of two worlds: quiet Idaho living paired with easy access to the hot metro market of Spokane, Washington, only thirty miles away.

Lee employs more than a hundred people across several real estate branches: construction, brokerage, investment education seminars, and private money lending (particularly to students he's trained in his seminars). With such diversification, it's no surprise that he turns up to a hundred deals a year.

My favorite part of Lee's investment strategy is what he dubs the "six-point process." It's a decision-making funnel that analyzes a deal's best turnaround from most ideal option to least. After finding a property, here's how he winnows down the options:

1. Wholesale
2. Wholetail
3. Retail strategy
4. Seller finance
5. Lease option
6. Rent

Insider Info It might surprise you to see renting as Lee's least-favorable option. Positive cash flow through rentals is usually touted as a great investment model, right? But there's a good reason for his avoidance: Because he predicts an impending market downturn, focusing on accumulating cash reserves *now* means he's situated to buy up as many properties as possible when (and if) property values drop. That's why he's careful not to buy anything he can't get into and out of in under ninety days.

"Now is the time to be stockpiling cash to be ready for the next [market] correction. There's not a single one of us who was in the business in 2008 to 2010 who didn't say, 'I wish I would've had a couple million dollars coming into that turn.' We were buying houses and paying 40 to 50 cents on the dollar compared to today!"

About 60 percent of Lee's deals come from direct mail or cold calls to addresses sourced from pre-foreclosure and code-enforcement lists. The rest mostly come from word of mouth, whether through networking, internet and radio ads, or "whatever else it takes to get in front of sellers." His far-reaching efforts have even led to deals brought to him by his local government—but more on that later.

FINDING THE DEAL

Lee understands one of the most underrated advertising rules out there: Use what you have. A company of his uses vans and trucks for construction, so why waste all that blank space when it can be wrapped with ads? Vehicle marketing is mobile, far-reaching, and even works while stationary.

Case in point: One of Lee's vans wrapped in standard "We Buy Houses!" advertising was parked beside his Spokane office when a passerby named Jeanette noticed it. She walked in, asked the receptionist if they would buy her house, and just like that, Lee found a deal that would change everything.

ASSESSMENT

While a seller walking into the palm of your hand is an investor's dream, there were still some logistics to figure out. Lee ushered her into his office to learn more.

Jeanette had retired from the Air Force a few years prior and fallen in love with a man who had an affinity for crystal meth. They moved in together, and it wasn't long before Jeanette started using drugs as well. The home quickly fell into disrepair, and within three years, code enforcement had received more than 200 complaints about the house. The yard was always covered in trash, people were loud at all hours, and there were innumerable signs of drug use in and around the home.

Countless code violation notices were issued and ignored. The city followed up with fines and ultimately liens, which of course went unpaid. Finally, they arrested Jeanette and boarded up the home, labeling it a drug nuisance property and taking the first step toward what looked like a long and red-tape-ridden foreclosure.

By the time Jeanette entered Lee's office, she owed more than $25,000 in liens and had two upside-down mortgages totaling around $60,000. Having just been released from jail, she was on the edge of homelessness and had more debts than she could dream of paying. Jeannette was ready to start over; she hoped to somehow sell the home and walk away with a $10,000 nest egg—just enough to get sober and back on her feet.

The property was an 850-square-foot two-bedroom, one-bathroom home with an unfinished basement and attic. Large windows looked out at sweeping views of the downtown Spokane skyline just two miles away, and a quick stroll led to eateries, pubs, and nature trails along the Spokane River.

Since the house hadn't yet been foreclosed on, Lee was able to have a look inside. Jeanette's description hadn't quite prepared him for what he saw: Graffiti lined the walls, furniture had been tossed around and left to lie wherever it fell, the basement was filled with trash and mattresses, and water damage covered the ceilings. Used syringes littered the floors; Lee even found a box of at least a hundred behind one of the toilets.

Lee knew that the consequences of meth use—not unlike a mold problem—could cost anywhere from $2,500 to $8,500 to remediate. From there, he estimated spending about $50,000 to clear the home out, gut it, then proceed with a full renovation. With $85,000 owed against a house that likely wouldn't have an ARV much higher than $100,000, buying the property seemed like a losing proposition.

Most investors would take a hard pass at this point, but not Lee—he knew the power of short sales. The advantage of distressed properties like these is that cities are often ready to wash their hands of them, liens included. Knowing this, Lee created an offer that could help the neighbors, help the city, and hopefully even help Jeanette. If he could convince them all to sign on to his plan, he'd even make a profit.

THE BREAKDOWN

Single-family home, 850 square feet
Spokane, Washington
Asking $10,000 to owner; more than $85,000 debt

OFFER AND FUNDING

You might be wondering why Jeanette expected any money from the sale when she owed more than $85,000 on the house. Simply put, she had an ace in the hole. Since her name was on the title, she was in control of the property until she either signed away her rights or lost them. No doubt she'd eventually lose those rights through foreclosure, but that could take up to one year.

What did one to three more years mean for the city? More calls from angry neighbors. More cleanup. More paperwork. As Lee explains it:

> "If they don't work with a short sale, the problem won't get any better. Cities can go after the banks [with fines and litigation] if they don't manage to get the homeowner to do what is right by the city. Meanwhile, the city has to deal with the repercussions of the 'zombie' property, dealing with complaints and eventually foreclosure. If they can all get out from under the troubled property, the city and the lienholders are willing to take a loss—even if it means the homeowner gets to walk out with cash."

If Jeanette didn't agree to sell, the city would have to foreclose—something municipalities always prefer to avoid. Knowing this, Lee offered Jeanette $26,000, promising to figure out a way for her to keep $10,000 of it while he used the rest to pay off the remaining debt.

Insider Info Government officials don't enjoy foreclosures. In most cases, they take at *least* a year of city resources, with neighbor complaints and paperwork mounting all the while. On top of that, they're missing out on valuable tax revenue that the property could be generating. Cities *want* investors to buy the property before foreclosure papers are served. This means that a clued-in investor has a unique opportunity to work with a municipality before a distressed seller loses their home completely.

With his promise to Jeanette in mind, Lee met with city officials and the mortgage lenders to suggest that they forgive the debt and let Jeanette walk away with some cash. The sooner they reached an agreement, the sooner Lee could begin transforming the property into something positive for the neighborhood.

The city agreed to forgive $18,500 worth of liens as long as Lee signed a performance guarantee promising to bring the property back to life within nine months. The lenders were willing to take a reduced payoff of only $8,500 to get the hopeless asset off their balance sheets. With $7,500 going to the city and $8,500 to the lenders, Jeanette would exit the closing with the $10,000 she'd hoped for.

Using the lending branch of his own investment company, Lee got a loan for 90 percent of the acquisition cost and 100 percent of the renovation. This came out to only $2,600 down, with the rest financed at 8 percent interest and one origination point.

Ken's Take As a high-volume flipper, Lee understands the value of good lending terms. Like many investors around the country, he has accumulated a strong pool of private lenders for his business—so much so that he has created his own company and lends to other investors as well. Whereas some investors don't take the time to build relationships and drive down lending costs, Lee has made it a priority and therefore benefits from reduced interest expenses. Imagine the difference in interest paid on one hundred houses at 8 percent versus 12 percent—it adds up to hundreds of thousands of dollars in savings!

TURNAROUND

Squalor was too kind a word for the home's pathetic state, but Lee had nine months to get it up to snuff. He started with the exterior, installing new vinyl siding, a new front porch, and clean, simple landscaping.

"You always want to start with the exterior so the neighbors and city can see immediate improvement. We went from boarded up to beautiful, immediately getting a buzz in the neighborhood. Neighbors were elated!"

From there, they reconnected the gas, heating, and power (which had been disconnected during the drug-complaint days) and got to work on the interior. The cleaning alone was a mammoth job—furniture, trash, and used syringes kept them busy for days. Then they repaired the roof and water damage, gutted the kitchen and bathrooms, redid all the electrical, and put in new textured drywall.

They converted the attic into a master suite—adding a bedroom, a bathroom, and an extra 500 square feet to the home. Finally, new flooring and coat of paint inside and out finished the job. At four months in with only $52,000 spent on the renovation, they were ready to put the home back on the market. Lee explains:

"You want to improve the property to the level of the community in order to gain maximum return on the investment. The goal of your rehab is to maximize profit, not to maximize the amount of rehab you accomplish."

AFTERMATH

Listing through his own brokerage, Lee quickly sold the home for $139,500. He had spent $26,000 on the purchase, $52,000 on the renovation, and $18,000 on closing, holding, and interest costs. At $96,000 all-in, you can't argue with a $43,500 profit.

Ken's Take Remember, Lee used the lending and listing services of his *own* companies on this property, which funneled much of that $18,000 expense back into his other entities. Having several different real estate–related businesses myself, I can certainly appreciate the power of keeping these expenses "in-house."

However, this isn't one of Lee's best deals because of profit—it's because of what the deal inspired in his investing model. Nearly every large housing market in America is rampant with nuisance and lien abatement properties—boarded-up, blighted homes with owners owing far more than the property is worth. Before Jeanette, Lee wasn't aware of the problem, but targeting homes with code enforcement issues is now one of his primary acquisition strategies. In his words:

"There's a huge opportunity for investors to align with metropolitan areas in order to clean up blight and make it safer for kids to walk to school. It's one of my favorite strategies because I haven't seen a lot of people utilizing it. It's a tremendous value for the community: It helps the homeowner, it helps the neighbors, and it enables us as investors to find good, clean profitable deals."

Lee also points out that many investors using code enforcement lists tend to prioritize based on high homeowner equity. Instead, he encourages people to work every lead the same way. If a property is on a code enforcement list, there could be a strong argument for a short sale—especially if the home is distressed. When lenders and lienholders recognize the low likelihood of ever getting their money back, you have a tremendous opportunity to negotiate those liens down and get the property priced to where you can buy and still make a profit.

Insider Info Code enforcement notices are accessible through public records in nearly every U.S. municipality. The way each city provides this information varies, but you can usually access the records with a little research. Some municipalities post the information online; others may require that you investigate a bit more. Some even have monthly or weekly code enforcement hearings that you can attend to get the scoop in real time.

There's an even better reason to focus on short-sale nuisance properties: When you do great work for the city, guess who they'll call when another such property pops up? The *city itself* becomes a lead generator! In the years since this deal, Lee has obtained multiple investments through his relationship with the local government.

TAKEAWAY

Advertise Everywhere

While this deal introduced Lee to a new acquisition strategy, targeting code violations, it's interesting that he didn't actually acquire the property by using that strategy. The deal simply came to him through signage on a parked company vehicle.

Find any successful investor with more than five years in the game, and I'll almost guarantee that they use numerous marketing channels. You can typically spot the top dogs in any market from seeing their advertising everywhere—on billboards, at bus stops, at the top of a Google search, on postcards, and even wrapped on the side of a van. Never put all your marketing eggs in one basket; as an investor and a business owner, it's crucial to attack your marketing efforts from all angles.

No Equity, Yes Opportunity

Lee discovered that code violations can be a great acquisition channel not simply because of the correlation between distressed homes and motivated sellers, but also because other investors don't understand the opportunity they represent. A typical investor would talk to the seller, find out that the city liens and debt add up to more than the house is worth, and move on to the next lead without giving it a second thought.

But as Lee points out, that is *exactly* why there is opportunity: The competition simply doesn't know how to take advantage of these situations to make such properties worth buying. With just a touch of salesmanship and negotiating prowess, a savvy buyer can negotiate liens down or eliminate them altogether. That may seem crazy, but it makes sense—why *wouldn't* a municipality be motivated to see a blighted property renovated, thereby increasing the area's value (and tax revenue)?

The same is true for mortgage debt. As a potential short sale buyer, you must paint the complete picture for the lender, educating them on the poor condition of the property, the code enforcement liens, and the home's reduced value. You're not just making it *seem* hopeless, you're letting them know how hopeless it really is. All the information you provide helps build the case that a reduction in the principal payoff makes the most financial sense for the lender.

Understand Your Renovation ROI

I think Lee says it best: *"The goal of your rehab is to maximize profit, not to maximize the amount of rehab you accomplish."* Working with a budget of only $52,000, Lee was able to focus those dollars on the areas that would yield the highest return. My hunch is that the highest yield came from transforming the dingy attic into a master suite. He increased not only the square footage but also the number of beds and baths.

Lee understood that this home would ultimately sell in only the mid-$100,000s. It made little sense to spend unnecessary dollars on high-end finishes, but it *did* make sense to increase the square footage. Understanding where and how to allocate those investment dollars can absolutely make or break the profitability of a renovation.

CHAPTER ELEVEN

BRETT SNODGRASS

The Substitute Teacher's Land Flip

Brett Snodgrass is the CEO of Simple Wholesaling, a company he founded eleven years ago in Indianapolis, Indiana. Until recently, he was involved in the company's day-to-day activity, but he recently moved to a smaller town so he could work remotely and focus on the company's big-picture goals as the "visionary-in-chief."

> *"I was entrenched in the routine business activity for so long that, once I extracted myself, I wasn't quite sure what to do with all the time that wasn't spent 'in the weeds.' I sought advice from some friends in leadership roles, and what really hit me was the idea that in this type of role, 20 percent of your time needs to be dedicated to just sitting and thinking. At first I thought, 'Well, that's not really doing anything,' but then I realized that, yes, it is. You can't come up with ideas and figure out your company's game-changing goals if you don't take the time to simply think."*

Meanwhile, back in Indianapolis, a seven-person team helps process acquisitions, dispositions, and closings; and nine virtual assistants help with administration. Despite the name, Simple Wholesaling's buy-and-sell process is a bit different from traditional wholesaling. It's more like "whole*tailing*," which means buying the property outright before reselling soon after.

Brett's company does about 80 percent wholetailing and 20 percent seller financing, always with the use of private lenders. Although the company began with the regular wholesaling of single-family homes—assigning contracts, double closing, and such—they found they had more options through wholetailing. For example, they can take more time with listing and accepting offers, polish the property up for a boost in asking price, or offer seller financing.

The beauty of wholesaling and wholetailing is the straightforward ability to move inventory *fast*. This point is evidenced by Brett's admission that he has honestly lost count of how many deals Simple Wholesaling has done over the years. That being said, he estimates that they have averaged 300 deals per year since 2017 and around 2,500 deals total.

The company uses some old and new techniques to bring in sellers: pay-per-click advertising and direct mail, but also television commercials and Facebook ads. Through it all, Brett keeps a strong focus on giving back to the investor community. He hosts two podcasts, *Real Estate Investing with a Purpose* and *The Indy Investor Pod*, and runs a local meetup to network and to educate investors on the process of wholetailing.

"Our company has five core values: faithful servanthood, mission-mindedness, leave a lasting impression, simple and smart systems, and enjoy the ride. We love what we do, we love people, and we want to help as many as possible. The moment we stop helping people and bringing opportunity, I don't want to do this any longer."

FINDING THE DEAL

The year Brett started in real estate was also the year of his best-ever deal, and there's a good reason for that. To be clear, it wasn't his most profitable deal, but the profit he earned impacted him in ways that would change his life forever.

In 2007 Brett was temporarily working as a substitute teacher in his small hometown of Madison, Indiana. A classic example of mid-twenties aimlessness, he was making less than $15,000 a year. The senior Mr.

Snodgrass must have known that subbing wouldn't ultimately fulfill his son, because he introduced Brett to a local land developer who also owned a timber company.

The developer's doubly profitable model was based on finding parcels of 100 to 200 acres where he could harvest and sell the timber before selling the land. He needed an extra set of eyes to help find deals, so Brett joined the team as a bird dog.

One day a giant piece of land on an auction website caught Brett's eye: 126 wooded acres close to the Ohio River. An old road cut through it, with 46 acres on one side and 80 acres on the other. The owner had died, and his six children wanted to sell it for $252,000 and split the earnings.

Insider Info There are a number of auction websites offering properties for sale all over the country. While most of them require some sort of screening process and registration up front, they offer ample opportunities for small investors to monitor auctions closely, make a lot of bids, and occasionally snag a great deal.

ASSESSMENT

The timber investor passed on the deal because there weren't enough harvestable trees, but Brett's interest was piqued. He had grown up near the area and knew there were plenty of people who would build a little cabin on land like that and use it as their personal outdoor playground. It may not have been good for timber harvesting, but it was a paradise for recreational activities like four-wheeling and hunting.

Three key components led Brett to believe the property would be a great investment:

1. It was an estate sale with six children who wanted to sell and divide the profit six ways, which he thought was a pivotal negotiation factor. Estate sales generally mean that sellers want to cash in quickly and move on. Given that, he suspected he could offer a significantly lower price overall. Plus, since the sale would be divided six ways, the difference in earnings for each individual recipient wouldn't feel as substantial as the overall reduction—for example, a $60,000 reduction in sales price would come to only $10,000 less per person.

2. He believed that dividing the property into two smaller parcels

would increase the odds of selling. Such a large property would be difficult to sell as a single parcel for recreational purposes only, but because a road ran through the land, Brett hoped to sell the two pieces separately without the hassle of having to build a fence or figure out a complicated subdivision.

3. The deed said the land had 126 acres, but it hadn't been surveyed in more than a hundred years. In the early 1900s, surveys were done much differently—this one, for example, said things like "Go to the big rock, turn left, then go to the big oak tree." Brett's hunch was that a new survey might show more acreage and yield a better return.

Brett's bird-dogging experience led him to believe he could sell the land for $1,500 to $1,800 an acre. Based on the possibility of revealing additional acreage through a new survey and his hunch that a low offer could succeed, he formed a plan.

THE BREAKDOWN

Land parcel, approximately 126 acres
Rural Southern Indiana
Asking $252,000

OFFER AND FUNDING

First, Brett needed money. He managed to convince his dad to partner with him on the deal, but that still only left them with $26,000 in cash. It's difficult enough to get a traditional bank loan on land, and their low credit scores guaranteed that wouldn't be an option. Finding more funding would be crucial.

Coincidentally, Brett had started attending a real estate meetup earlier that year because he figured it would help with his bird-dogging efforts. It was a casual gathering with seldom more than five attendees just hanging out, drinking coffee, and talking. That's where he met 72-year-old Tuffy, who turned out to be the one and only private lender he knew.

Brett had formed a solid rapport with Tuffy through their small meet-ups, so Brett told him about the deal. Like banks, private lenders tend toward reluctance on land investments, but Tuffy agreed to fund Brett's offer at a flat 12 percent monthly interest rate.

"Without Tuffy and my dad on this deal, I couldn't have done it. Tuffy because he trusted me enough to offer financing, and dad because he gave me confidence in knowing I wasn't doing it all on my own. This deal and nearly every deal since have shown me it's all about relationships. Get around people that you can build relationships and partnerships with so that when a deal comes, you're ready."

The sellers were asking $252,000 total, which worked out to $2,000 per acre, but Brett offered just $1,200. He phrased the offer carefully, offering *per acre* instead of a sum total. This was a clever move. Had he said, "I'll give you $151,200 for everything," $100,800 *less* than the asking price, the difference would have felt a lot more substantial. Instead, he softened the discrepancy with some extra layers of math.

Ken's Take Were it only one person profiting on this land, they'd prob-ably say, "A hundred thousand dollars less than asking price? No way!" But since the profit was to be divided among six people, they would really only walk away with $16,800 less per person compared to the asking price. It's not a small number, but it doesn't feel as drastic as a $100,000 reduction.

The land had been on the market for a while, and Brett sensed that the children were ready to move on, so after a few back-and-forths, they ended up accepting his offer. With his and his father's $26,000 and a $126,000 loan from Tuffy, they went into contract with a contingency on getting the land surveyed. If something funky came up with the results, they'd need to know before closing.

TURNAROUND

A month went by, and then another... The survey was taking forever. Brett hounded the surveyor, wondering why he was taking so long, and the man blamed the delay on the size of the land and the inaccuracy of the existing survey. However, during one of these calls, he leaked his suspicion that it would end up surveying for more than the initial 126 acres.

With that lead, Brett pulled the trigger. Closing without a confirmed number on the acreage was a risk worth taking, especially if there would be extra land. With the closing papers signed, he could start preparing to relist the property.

Lo and behold, the survey finally came in at 133 acres—seven bonus acres! Since they'd already closed on the deal, those were *Brett's* bonus acres, which he'd sell with all the rest. With comparable land being sold for up to $1,800 per acre, a possible $12,000 bonus took some pain out of the 12 percent interest he was paying Tuffy.

The seven extra acres fell on the larger side of the divided land, bringing it from 80 to 87 acres. Because the tracts were so large, Brett didn't have to worry about zoning—all he had to do was create a new deed for the "new" separate tracts. He listed the two properties on land sale websites, Craigslist, and the local newspaper, then waited to see who would bite.

AFTERMATH

It wasn't long before two hunters came forward with offers. Conveniently, one wanted the smaller parcel and one wanted the larger. Brett landed on a price of $1,750 per acre from both of them—bringing the total to $232,750. Minus the closing costs and two months of holding costs (including Tuffy's loan), Brett turned a net profit of more than $80,000! He had never heard the term, but he'd just started on the path to wholetailing.

> *"Some people might talk about deals with million-dollar profits, but when you're on a substitute teacher salary making $15,000 per year and bringing in about $30,000 with bird-dogging, a deal like this literally doubles your income. That's when I knew I was onto something."*

Needless to say, 2007 was Brett's last year of substitute teaching. After reinvesting the $80,000 into marketing and funding for his own projects, he began scaling his business in a way that had been impossible before. In the meantime, he continued bird-dogging for the timber land buyer and a local wholesale company.

Over the following year and a half, he found enough deals to feel certain that he could consistently earn the $30,000 to $40,000 he was making working for other investors by working only for himself. With the confidence to go into real estate full-time, he started his company, Simple Wholesaling, and never looked back.

TAKEAWAY

Find a Mentor or Work for One

Before Brett mustered up the courage to buy 133 acres to flip, he worked for somebody else who was already a successful land investor. Understanding the ins and outs of a specific niche will go a long way toward educating yourself on all the things you simply don't know. Brett says:

> *"Get mentorship. You don't have to reinvent the wheel—just do what other successful people are doing. If you want to change your life, be in the right place at the right time and around the right people."*

The only reason Brett knew how to scour the right websites and understand what the market would pay for that land was because his bird-dogging job required it. What's more effective than on-the-job training?

That said, the training doesn't necessarily have to come from a job. Another way to gain experience is by volunteering to work for a mentor on a few deals. Or maybe you find an impressive deal and invite a mentor to take part in exchange for guidance. Ultimately, gleaning as much as you can from an experienced investor will always result in better outcomes for new and aspiring investors.

Network, Network, Network

Networking is a no-brainer, yet so many investors think they can go it alone. Being around other investors and professionals is the lifeblood of a new real estate business. Take the initiative to put yourself around the right people!

Even if you feel you have nothing "professional" to bring to the table, meetups and other networking opportunities can still be about connecting on a human level. There doesn't have to be an end goal, and nobody's keeping score. It wasn't Brett's track record that influenced Tuffy to give him a loan; it was Brett's genuine personality. If he hadn't put himself out there in that tiny meetup, the land deal would never have happened.

Networking should be non-negotiable in your business. It's that simple.

Read the Seller

One reason Brett scored this deal at 60 percent of the asking price was because he understood the situation and approached the offer accordingly. Since the property was to be inherited by six children, Brett predicted a strong desire for most of the kids to cash out their share and be done.

Since he understood this dynamic, Brett could make a lowball offer in such a way that wouldn't offend the sellers. Phrasing the offer as "price per acre" made a $100,000 reduction feel a lot more reasonable. The children probably didn't know the market or what land was trading for at the time and ultimately decided that $1,200 per acre was simply the best they would get for the land.

Momentum

There's a phenomenon I've noticed with nearly everyone who enters the real estate investing business: The first deal usually takes a while to come to fruition, but once that first one is under their belt, everything changes. I always tell my students, "Once you get over the hump of that first deal, the momentum kicks in." The bottom line is that you have to persevere. Brett says it this way:

> *"All it takes is one deal, so don't quit! This just gave me so much confidence. I was really scared and nervous throughout the process—the contracts, surveying, money, and so on. In fact, I was nervous about all my early deals. Now we do twenty-five to thirty deals in a month and it's like eating breakfast—you just do it without thinking about it. It's just confidence.*
>
> *"There's an old basketball video game where if you made a few consecutive baskets, a voice would yell, 'You're on FIRE!' Listen for that voice in real estate. After getting a couple deals under your belt, you'll build momentum, you'll build confidence, and you'll be on fire."*

CHAPTER TWELVE

NANCY WALLACE-LAABS

From Small Roth IRA to Huge Payday

In 2004, Nancy Wallace-Laabs was a blood bank management consultant who knew only *one* thing about real estate: If she sold her home, she'd make an insane profit. It was the height of the housing market bubble in Phoenix, Arizona, and although she and her husband, Brian, hadn't been planning to move, the profit potential was too much to ignore.

They cashed in, leaving their jobs and taking the winnings to a new home in Dallas, Texas. But they didn't want to stop there—where else could they go with real estate? Using the remaining profit, they purchased two multifamily rentals and launched a boutique property management company dubbed KBN Homes. Game on.

It was a leap of faith, and it totally paid off. In the years since, they've owned ten rentals; worked thirty rehabs, fifteen wholesale deals, and seven owner-financed transactions; and managed 295 single-family homes. These days, they've mostly phased out property management to make room for more passive income streams like private lending and owner financing.

Investors often shy away from properties lacking a clean and clear turnaround option—hoarder situations, lien-heavy vacancies, homes in an extreme state of disrepair—but Nancy didn't build her career by being such an investor. By zeroing in on the often-leftover piece of the pie, she minimizes competition and maximizes opportunity. In fact, hunting for just such a distressed home led to her best deal ever.

FINDING THE DEAL

When Nancy isn't using her network to find deals, she's using data. In 2017, she used an online list-generating website to pull addresses from eight promising Texas zip codes with an ARV of less than $250,000.

Insider Info By filtering her search to focus on homes valued below $250,000, Nancy was boosting the odds of finding properties with minimized potential investment risk. Homes that are more broadly affordable tend to spend fewer days on the market and open the seller up to a larger pool of buyers. Plus, if she decided to hold the property and rent it, she would benefit from a strong price-to-rent ratio, which is typical in the entry-level-home price range.

Nancy then winnowed down the list to properties with out-of-state owners—she knew they'd be more motivated to offload their investments. She uploaded the resulting 6,819 addresses to an online direct mail service and sent a simple, personalized postcard that read:

Hi [Name],
My name is Nancy and I buy houses. I want to talk with you about buying your house. I'm looking to buy several houses throughout the Dallas–Fort Worth area this month.
Tired of repairs, deadbeat tenants, vacancies, or just the hassle of owning rental properties? We offer cash, pay closing costs, and never take a Realtor commission! We can even buy houses that have tenants in place.
Call today! We want to buy your house. We have solutions for everyone and every property, and we are easy to work with and close

quickly on the sale of the property.

Not ready to sell today? Keep this card with your important house papers!

P.S. We pay cash for your property, any condition... Call today for your no-obligation cash offer!

Seven days later, Nancy got a call from a man named Charles who owned a vacant home in a historic district in Fort Worth, Texas. His two-bedroom, one-bath property had been boarded up and untended for five years. Numerous investors had noticed it and made offers during this time, but Charles had rejected them all.

Timing is everything, though; Nancy's postcard arrived when he was finally ready to take action—due in no small part to the $2,000-plus he owed in code violations. If he didn't pay off the liens within the next two months, the city would condemn the property and Charles would walk away with nothing.

ASSESSMENT

Charles had grown up in the home, and Nancy sensed that an emotional connection made him reluctant to sell. Therefore, instead of discussing deal terms, she first connected with him on a personal level, asking about his family and what life was like growing up there.

Ken's Take Great deals often rely on the quality of the relationships between the people involved. It's important to build a rapport with any potential seller before beginning any sort of negotiation. As Nancy says: *"The best investors understand that people like to sell to those they know, like, and trust."*

When they moved on to discussing the property, Charles assured her that the home had good bones but one major issue: The interior foundation was separating at the joints and the front porch had already split down the middle. The house also needed new electrical, roofing, HVAC, siding, paint, and pretty much everything else. In short, it would need a complete gut.

At the time, a similar renovated home would probably have fetched around $95,000, but Charles's home couldn't be worth much more than

$10,000. She could take the easy option of wholesaling but would probably net only a $5,000 to $10,000 profit. Nancy knew she could get more.

Renovating the home for $35,000 to $40,000 would turn a higher profit, but it wouldn't come easy. Recent hurricanes in South Texas had left a dwindling supply of reliable area contractors, so Nancy preferred to avoid hunting one down—not to mention the headache of pulling permits and how she would need the local historical commission's approval for every modification. Plus, after factoring in her standard 10 percent contingency allotment for rehabs (to cushion against unexpected issues), the cost could run as high as $50,000.

Still, Nancy had spent years following the area's development of new builds, vacant lot sales, and home sale averages, and things were promising. Investors were knocking down older homes for rebuilds, and numerous homeowners were renovating. Overall, the neighborhood seemed to be changing for the better. She didn't know exactly how she'd turn the property around, but with undeniable profit waiting in the wings, Nancy called up the owner with an offer.

THE BREAKDOWN

Single-family home, 1,063 square feet
Historic Fort Worth, Texas
Asking price unknown

OFFER AND FUNDING

Although Nancy had yet to see the home in person, she wanted to strike while the iron was hot—a motivated seller can lose motivation overnight. She had $13,000 in a Roth IRA, so she made a cash offer for $10,000—enough for the owner to pay off the code violations and walk away from the closing table with a little money.

Ken's Take Using a self-directed Roth IRA (or a traditional IRA) is a great way to deploy retirement funds into real estate (as either an owner or a lender). However, unlike contributions to traditional IRAs, Roth contributions are post-tax. This means all the gains on a real estate investment are earned (and withdrawn in the future) tax-free! (Of course, consult your CPA before taking this route!)

The reality is that most people have large retirement accounts earning very little. Deploying even a portion of those dollars into creative real estate deals is a great way to crank up your overall returns.

Charles accepted the offer with little fanfare and returned a signed email contract within hours. Nancy was careful to include a thirty-day due diligence contingency, which effectively provided an out if the on-site inspection showed some surprise disaster. She wired an earnest-money deposit of $100 to the title company, and the home was officially under contract.

Insider Info Always leave yourself an out! Mistakes happen, things get overlooked, and sellers simply may not be aware of certain issues. Make sure you include long due diligence periods and other contingencies that enable you to cancel the contract and regain your earnest money should you choose to cancel a purchase.

TURNAROUND

A few days later, Nancy viewed the home in-person. It was as the owner had described it: distressed, yes, but the numbers worked. Now she just needed to prevent the city from condemning the property. A call confirming new ownership and an email with attached documentation did the trick. After extracting a promise from her to restore the home to the historic district's standards, the city reset the clock on demolition.

The only problem was that Nancy still didn't quite know what to *do* with the investment. She took a couple days to mull it over, and in the meantime, she stuck a handwritten Spanish/English *For Sale* sign in the front yard just to see what happened. Within three days, she'd received multiple calls and an offer for $50,000 and 20 percent down—but only if she'd consider owner financing.

Nancy had yet to work an owner-financing deal. Still, the strategy seemed promising: Instead of using a bank, the buyer gets funding from the *seller*. As with a traditional mortgage, there's usually a down payment.

From there, the seller holds an interest-earning mortgage note for the remaining balance, which is paid monthly the same way a traditional loan payment would be made. This type of financing—particularly due to interest—can be lucrative for sellers, and it provides homeownership options to people who can't (or prefer not to) get traditional mortgage funding.

Nancy weighed her options. A fix-and-flip would be labor-intensive and time-consuming, and wholesaling would leave too much meat on the bone. The $50,000 owner-financing offer, however, would immediately recoup the initial $10,000 investment (via the 20 percent down payment) while creating a $40,000 note at 10 percent interest over the next fifteen years. Just like that, she'd create a future income of $77,000 ($40,000 loan plus $37,000 in interest)!

Earning $77,000 on a $10,000 investment seemed too good to be true. But Nancy's favorite part of the deal was that it aligned with one of her passions—providing affordable housing.

> "For many, [renting is] not by choice. Often they simply don't have the credit history for traditional mortgages, despite an ability to pay mortgage costs. Owner financing allows me to create homeownership while supporting my own business."

After sending the buyer's information through the National Tenant Network to verify a history of reliable rental payments, Nancy drew up her first owner-financing contract. A registered mortgage loan originator (RMLO) would handle loan coordination and ensure compliance with state and federal regulations. Meanwhile, a loan servicing company would manage and report the buyer's monthly payments and deposit them into the same IRA Nancy used to fund the original purchase. Since credit-bureau-aligned loan servicing companies keep official records of monthly payments, the arrangement also creates an opportunity for tenants to show a positive payment history and raise their credit score.

For the property's physical turnaround, Nancy didn't do a thing except sweep. It's not uncommon to offload renovations to the buyer when doing an owner finance—it's *their* future home, after all. Luckily for Nancy, her buyer wasn't scared away by the foundation issue; he was equipped to fix it and simply happy to be on the path to homeownership.

AFTERMATH

Eager to move in, the new buyer corrected the foundation issues and got ready for a live-in flip. Within months, a home that had been slated for demolition was on its way to becoming a valuable asset to its community. As for the Roth IRA that Nancy nearly wiped out to purchase the home, after just two years of monthly payments from the new buyers, its value had soared to more than $34,000 (and will likely keep rising).

However, you might be wondering what would happen if the buyer stopped making payments—it happens with renters all the time, so why wouldn't that be the case with owner financing? Nancy wondered too, and here's what she realized:

> *"If I ever have to pay an attorney $2,500 to foreclose, I'll still be getting an asset worth much more than my initial $10,000 investment. I'll own it free and clear [due to the down payment], and it will be in better shape than when I purchased it."*

Since that first owner-financed deal, Nancy's done six more (and counting). She's learned that an owner-financed note has multiple exit strategies; for example, there's an active secondary market of investors looking to purchase owner-financed notes.

Insider Info It's important to know that the value of an owner-financed note varies based on the quality of the borrower/home buyer, how long the note has "seasoned," payment history, and a variety of other factors. As with any investment strategy, do your research!

TAKEAWAY
Pay It Forward

Owner financing is a win-win: Buyers get the opportunity to become homeowners, and investors typically earn more through interest than by selling at current market values. While many investors get caught in a winner-take-all mindset, Nancy's deal shows that owner financing is a great way to give back to communities while building your own business.

Don't Forget Those Retirement Dollars

Nancy didn't have much in her Roth IRA, but it was enough to buy a distressed house. Many people forget about those retirement dollars sitting in that old 401(k) or IRA that aren't really earning much. Plus, using a Roth IRA to receive income on a property means that all the incoming funds are tax-free. Find a financial custodian that handles self-directed investments and put those dollars to work!

Act Fast

Nancy ultimately made this deal because she was willing to think outside the box and act quickly. When she put the property under contract for $10,000, she knew there was some way to make money—she just hadn't mapped out a strategy yet. Sometimes you know in your gut that the price is right, so you pull the trigger. When you've worked and studied hard enough to know that your education can help you make quick decisions, which, in turn, makes you a great profit, don't hesitate.

Adapt and Grow

Careers like Nancy's are built on the bravery to strike while the iron is hot. Jumping into real estate from a completely unrelated career was a leap of faith, but she was committed to learning and growing as she went along. Nancy's journey from property management, to rentals, to fix-and-flips, and now to owner financing and passive lending proves that adaptability is one of the best tools of a savvy real estate investor.

CHAPTER THIRTEEN

ANNA KELLEY

A Big Leap from Single-Family to Multifamily

When Anna Kelley got started in real estate, she had been climbing the corporate ladder from private banking to product development at AIG, the finance and insurance giant, for ten years. However, she shared nearly $700,000 in debt with her husband for his business start-up. They'd recently moved from Houston, Texas, to Hershey, Pennsylvania, after purchasing a four-unit house hack from the sale of their home. Amid all the debt, the rental checks from the other three units flowed into their lives like clockwork.

Soon after their move, the Great Recession hit, and Anna realized that those rent checks felt like their most stable source of income. She'd dabbled in real estate since 1999 with no extraordinary success, but knowing that all her wealthiest clients had real estate investments, she decided something had to change. With four kids at home and a husband committed to his new start-up, Anna decided that real estate would be her family's path to true financial freedom.

Ten years later, Anna is now widely known as the REIMom, a fitting moniker since for her, real estate is about creating generational wealth while helping others grow through coaching and teaching. As founding partner of Zenith Capital Group, Anna manages and has ownership in a rental portfolio valued at more than $60 million and has invested in more than 2,000 multifamily units.

Anna started off with smaller flips and rental properties before scaling up to larger projects with the goal of creating enough passive income to retire early from her corporate job. She began buying larger apartment buildings with partners, focusing on buildings with thirty to a hundred units using a joint venture model with no more than four total investors.

Scaling ever upward, Anna parlayed that initial success into a syndication model using limited partners for capital while she and a small team of general partners find, finance, improve, and operate the properties. While the bulk of her deals have been sourced in central Pennsylvania, Anna has recently begun scaling nationwide:

"I moved to Hershey from Houston, Texas, where there's a ton of competition and a lot of stuff happening. Generally, real estate investors are looking for these big metropolitan areas where they can get deals, but smaller areas like Hershey are actually financially and demographically strong. We have manufacturing, industrial, trucking, medical, all sorts of things. It's a very diverse upper-scale economy, which makes for great single-family flips, rentals, larger apartments, and so on. It's a great place for people to live, and they'll pay more to live here than elsewhere."

These days, Anna is semi-retired on the passive income she's generated from her large multifamily investments. As a mom, she has created a lifestyle centered around quality time with her husband and children. As a "real estate mom," Anna also helps others get their start in the industry through coaching, speaking at events, and hosting local meetups for fellow women investors.

FINDING THE DEAL

Back when Anna was looking to score her first large multifamily deal, she was using direct mail, auction websites, and even the MLS—essentially casting lots of fishing poles to see what she could bring in. But one of the benefits of living in a smaller investment market is that people stay connected more easily. While picking up her daughter at gymnastics, Anna bumped into a friend Kay and they began catching up. When asked how her rentals were going, Anna replied that she'd recently begun looking for her first large investment.

Coincidentally, Kay's husband was planning to list their seventy-three-unit multifamily with forty-four attached storage units the very next week at $7.5 million. Anna was familiar with the property in question—it was in a Class B+ neighborhood close to shops, restaurants, highly rated schools, the Hershey medical center, and the Hershey's and Reese's candy factories. She asked if she could have the opportunity to buy it first, and Kay agreed to set up a viewing for the very next day.

Ken's Take Another benefit of smaller markets is that there are typically fewer investors competing for properties. Also, smaller markets often lend themselves to better cash-flow opportunities than large, densely populated metropolitan areas. While the MLS can be a decent acquisition strategy in a smaller market, using even basic off-market marketing can result in a number of deeply discounted buying opportunities.

ASSESSMENT

The off-market opportunity had practically walked into Anna's hands, but she still needed to know whether the deal was worth pursuing. From the looks of the three-story property built in 1985, it was still in excellent, if slightly dated, condition. The exterior was promising—the sellers had just redone the roofs, patios, siding, and parking lot, so buyers wouldn't have to do anything besides power wash.

The inside was nice and clean but, as Anna puts it, "nothing sexy." Most of the fixtures were still from the '80s, the dark wood doors were uninviting, and the monochrome antique-white paint and basic carpet felt bland. Although there wasn't anything that would wow viewers, it would take only a few bells and whistles to flip the 1,000-square-foot apartments into something more exciting.

With units renting for around $750 per month, Anna immediately knew the rate was well below market value. With or without renovations, she was certain there was room to raise the rent by at least $200 monthly.

She explains:

> *"There was a ton of upside on the rent. The seller hadn't raised rents much since building the units in 1985. They had paid off the mortgage and had the attitude of 'the devil you know is better than the devil you don't—keep your tenants there, keep them happy.'"*

Anna's vision was to do a minor flip and repositioning effort, investing $3,000 to $4,000 into sprucing up each unit depending on whether it was a one- or two-bedroom. Meanwhile, she'd aim to cut overall expenses with energy savings and raise the rents as tenants moved out, increasing the total value while generating more net income.

After a few years of this, Anna hoped to turn around and sell the property for a couple million dollars on top of the almost-guaranteed cash flow she'd earn throughout the repositioning effort. As a plan B, she could also do a cash-out refinance, then continue to hold at the new valuation.

Insider Info Anna was already considering the age-old question in multifamily: Sell or hold? Once a property has been successfully repositioned—meaning renovations completed, rents increased, and occupancy where it needs to be—there's typically newly created equity that can be utilized. If an investor decides to sell, they immediately cash out the equity and likely use a 1031 exchange to move their earnings into the next project. However, some investors prefer to refinance the property using the new, higher appraised value in an effort to pull out all the original invested equity. For the long-term investor who prefers cashing out their limited partners and enjoying ongoing cash flow (and appreciation) for themselves, this can be a great option.

Anna's confidence centered on knowing the amount of room there was for rent bumps based on relatively minimal renovation expenses. As long as she could translate that rental upside into an increased valuation, the deal seemed no-fail. There was one hitch, however: She didn't have funding.

THE BREAKDOWN

Multifamily, 73 units, 44 storage units
Hershey, Pennsylvania
Asking $7.5 million

OFFER AND FUNDING

Anna met with the owner at his kitchen table on the very same day she viewed the property. She'd run the numbers and decided to offer $5.5 million based on its existing rental rates. The seller countered using a prior appraisal and the broker's pre-marketing package. A week later, they met again and settled on a purchase price of $6.5 million.

Anna needed at least $2.2 million for the down payment, closing costs, operation, and renovation expenses, and with no funding to speak of, she had to act fast. Having worked with private placement securities in her corporate background, she understood syndication but wasn't sure she could sponsor that large a deal without having a significant amount of capital herself. Rather than go it alone, she aimed to create a joint venture that would bring in funding from other general partners.

Racking her brain, Anna recalled meeting up with a fellow investor just weeks earlier specifically to discuss tackling larger projects together. When she told him about the deal, he wanted in. Although he couldn't front all the money, a friend of his came aboard to cover the difference. With their combined resources, they could take down the deal as three general partners without the need for limited partners.

However, with three partners came three opinions on how to divide profit. Anna's nonnegotiable was a six-figure acquisition fee: It would be a ticket out of debt and a running start toward early retirement. To get the fee she wanted, she negotiated a higher ownership and cash-flow percentage for her partners.

"Structuring joint venture deals like this really boils down to figuring out what is a win-win for everybody. When I came into the deal, I thought, 'I found this, I negotiated it, and I want X percent,' but when

I brought partners on, they of course had their own opinions and desires. They pushed back with what was important to them, and it wasn't necessarily aligned with what I wanted. But I understood the power of not having to go out and syndicate and of being able to create a great relationship with people I could potentially continue doing deals with. I had to swallow my pride and negotiate to find what was a win for the money partners and what was a win for me. Depending on how long we hold it, it's a high $700,000s to $1.4 million deal for me, so it was a home run no matter how I looked at it."

With two partners willing to invest the $2.2 million in up-front equity, there wasn't much reason to go outside the box for obtaining a loan. The three of them simply opted for a traditional thirty-year multifamily loan at 5 percent interest and 25 percent down. Anna explains:

"I'm a firm believer in not using bridge loans unless it's absolutely necessary for just a couple of months. The great thing about these large apartment buildings is that you can get agency financing like Fannie Mae and Freddie Mac at thirty-year, fixed-interest financing."

TURNAROUND

With the exterior in near-mint condition and nothing crying out for immediate change inside, Anna was already on the way to cash flow by simply raising rents. With the building almost 100 percent occupied, they didn't want to scare everyone off and lose out with turnover costs. That said, the units were renting for at least $200 below market value, so tenants would be hard-pressed to find comparable accommodations in the area even after a rent hike.

"We thought if we put in $3,000 to $4,000 per unit, we could eventually raise the rent $200 a month. But first, we wanted to try keeping the tenants we already had. We opted to see if they'd take a $75 increase, and we knew most would because they wouldn't even be able to downsize into a similar neighboring apartment complex for the same price. They knew they wouldn't be able to find as nice a

place for anything less than $100 to $125 more per month. By rais-
ing the rent by just $75 and assuring them of all the improvements
we would make, we kept 95 percent of the tenants in place without
spending a dime."

Simply raising the rents by $75 enabled Anna's team to meet third-year projections by the end of year one! When tenants did move out, the units received interior upgrades: bedrooms got new carpet, luxury vinyl plank flooring went into living spaces, and bathrooms got rolled vinyl floors. They painted the interiors in greige with bright white trim; redid bathroom vanities, mirrors, and lighting; painted the dark brown doors bright white; and replaced mismatched appliances and brass doorknobs with brushed nickel.

When finished, not only could they justify a $200 monthly rental increase, they could even push to the top of the market. For example, a two-bedroom apartment that had been renting for $750 jumped to $995 as one of the best options on the market. On top of that, they cut thousands in monthly expenses by installing LED lights and water-saving devices in the bathrooms of all the units.

Behind the Scenes:
"One of the reasons the seller chose me as a buyer was because we agreed to work with his property manager, who was a relative. We hesitated to do this but thought it was worth a try. He was an old-school manager who loved the property and the tenants, but he didn't know technology or advertising and was slow to turn the units. We thought he might not make it with our company, but he pleasantly surprised us. He created a seamless transition with the existing tenants, learned the technology, learned to market and use the internet, and learned to do unit turns at our speed. He has been an incredible asset to the property, and we wish we could clone him!"

AFTERMATH

As Anna and her team continue pushing the value of their complex, they'll eventually decide whether to sell or refinance. If they sell in five years, they'll gross at least $3.5 million (including the cash flow that will have come in over the years). However, they could also put a sizable chunk of change in their pockets through a cash-out refinance and continue collecting cash flow well into the future. Either way, they hit a home run on this deal.

Five months after closing, Anna was able to retire from her twenty-year career at AIG. With just three owners raking in all that amazing cash flow, it's an easy bet that Anna will continue to cruise through retirement with passive income paying for the lifestyle she worked so hard to create. She and the other general partners have since purchased and syndicated two additional multifamilies and today own hundreds of doors together. Anna explains their ongoing strategy:

"All our owners enjoy the tax benefits, appreciation, and cash flow generated by these rental properties, but my investors don't have to worry about day-to-day management. What is so powerful about this model is that we essentially flip apartment buildings. We go through all the updates on the interior and exterior, just like you would a smaller single-family flip. It's just that these are valued more on operations and net operating income than on a comp basis and generate significantly higher returns than doing it on many homes over and over again."

TAKEAWAY

Leverage Partners to Scale Up

Using partners and carving up ownership to make *more* money may seem counterintuitive, but for Anna, taking that step toward scaling got her out of debt and into early retirement. For years, she'd been going it alone as a smaller-scale BRRRR investor, finding moderate success, but once she decided to snag a multi-million-dollar property, she was forced to bring in partners. She puts it this way:

"For a long time, I was kind of a lone ranger flipping a lot of small rentals on my own. Eventually, you start to get tapped out. I was doing it on a transactional basis to fund the next deal to the next by doing everything all on my own. You can borrow hard money like most of us do, but if you're able to partner with other people who can

*each bring something different to the table, it becomes less stressful
and needs a lot less of your own time and money for significantly
larger returns.*

*"I learned to give up a little control and to give a little bit on my
idea of the percentage I 'needed' in order to create a win-win for
everybody. It has propelled me to continue that model, be flexible
in the type of joint venture partnerships I create, and really have
confidence that I can take down much larger deals even if I don't
have the capital to do so."*

Repositioning Doesn't Have to Involve Reno

Anna saw an opportunity to reposition a property that didn't at first seem
like a value-add opportunity. Honestly, a $7.5 million apartment complex
with seventy-three units earning $750 monthly might not sound all that
enticing to most investors. The property was already in decent condition,
and most investors would just assume there wasn't much upside.

However, Anna realized the real opportunity was the potential to
raise rent with little to no renovation. In the end, her insight was 100
percent correct—they quickly bumped up rents by $75 monthly without
anybody batting an eye. That move alone represented more than $67,000
in additional revenue for the first year. Combine that with the fact that
she negotiated a million dollars off the purchase price and *voilà!* you have
the makings of an incredible deal.

Overcome the Next Level of Fear

Anna's story is a great example of overcoming fear and doubt. She had
been in the business for twenty years before working up the courage to
take on a property of this magnitude. All too often, investors prevent
themselves from scaling into bigger opportunities because of self-lim-
iting beliefs. In running and managing a business, mindset is everything. Yes, hard work and persistence are still important, but the belief
in yourself and your ability to achieve your goals are ultimately what
fuel success. Anna says:

*"This deal gave me another level of fear to overcome. Even invest-
ing for twenty years and knowing real estate, you're always a little
afraid when it comes time to do the next bigger thing. When I found
this deal, I was like, 'Can I really pull this off?' In a small town where*

everybody knows everybody, you don't want to get something under contract and not be able to close. I just said: 'I'm going to do it. I'm going to figure this out, get creative, and find a way to make the deal work.' Now that I've done it, I have no more fears there and I'm doing bigger and bigger deals not only here, but throughout the country."

CHAPTER FOURTEEN

GLENN AND AMBER SCHWORM

Massive Profits in an REO Mistake

Glenn and Amber Schworm got their start as entrepreneurs and just never stopped. The thing is, they weren't always successful. After Glenn founded a profitable security and alarms company at age 19 and sold it fourteen years later, his and Amber's next foray ended up leaving them broke. With two children at home, $80,000 in debt, and the 2008 housing market crash just around the corner, they decided to jump into real estate.

No doubt it was a particularly terrible time to get started in real estate, but Glenn and Amber fought through and managed to find one single-family deal by the end of that year. They renovated and sold it themselves—adding even more to their debt through the process—but netted a profit on the sale. The following year, they found three deals, seven the next, and twenty by the fourth.

To date, Glenn and Amber have bought, sold, or wholesaled more than 600 houses and counting. Now debt-free (to say the least!) and based in upstate New York, they focus on turning eighty to ninety deals per year with a team of ten employees who help find deals and manage administrative tasks. The bulk of the deals are wholesales, but they cherry-pick ten to fifteen renovations yearly while maintaining a rental portfolio of around twelve long- and short-term rentals.

FINDING THE DEAL

Like many investors, Glenn and Amber use direct mail and referrals to find deals, but they set themselves apart with formidable branding efforts. Instead of being another faceless investor team, they use social media and local television ads to promote themselves. Their acquisitions team always asks how callers found them; the catchy jingle used in their TV commercial is often the culprit!

Ken's Take TV ads are definitely not for the faint of heart, but I have a number of friends around the country who swear by them for generating motivated sellers. It's tough to measure results over a short period of time, but those who do it well have committed to the long game and claim that TV ads earn a solid return on investment. Glenn says, *"Television makes the phone ring the most and provides credibility and legitimacy to what we do. Plus, we get recognized on a daily basis."*

Inventive marketing not only helps them find new clients, but it also keeps them top of mind among their existing network of sellers and agents. And they don't stop there: They also offer payouts on *both* sides of any deal an agent brings them. Most investors only disburse on the front end, but because Glenn and Amber share the wealth throughout, they often get that first call.

Case in point: When an agent got the job for a real estate owned (REO) property in upstate New York that nobody else knew about, they immediately called Glenn and Amber to dish the inside scoop.

The bank that owned the single-family home opposed listing it on the local MLS due to "internal politics" between themselves and the agency. That meant the agent could only list on an MLS that was thirty miles away, where the property wouldn't be on most buyers' radar. Sensing that most investors would jump on this deal under normal circumstances, Glenn and Amber hopped in the car to check it out. About their deal-finding strategy, they say:

"We feel it is much better to leverage your time by letting people know to call you when they see a deal that meets your criteria. No one else really saw this deal except for this agent, who knew we would pounce. It would have been a multiple-bid circumstance under normal conditions."

ASSESSMENT

The quiet, upscale town of Guilderland, New York, has great schools, rolling country landscapes, and homes that routinely sell for more than $500,000. As Glenn and Amber drove up the private, secluded road leading to the property, they knew they were seeing huge potential. Amid a picturesque two and a half acres stood the three-story, 3,000-square-foot brick Cape Cod home. It had four bedrooms, three and a half baths, a basement, a sunroom, a detached four-car garage, and an in-ground pool.

At first glance, the $125,000 asking price seemed too good to be true. But on getting out of the car, they glimpsed an old landfill peeking through trees on a nearby property. Though it was mostly covered with grass, the agent informed them that its built-in methane vents often spread the smell of sulfur during hot summer days. It wasn't exactly a backyard amenity.

As for what was *supposed* to be an amenity—the pool—it was nowhere to be found. When they approached a fenced-in area filled with weeds and overgrowth, Glenn began stepping carefully through the greenery. One of his footfalls eventually landed on what felt like a waterbed, followed by a huge section of overgrowth swooshing down into a long, pool-shaped wave. He'd found the pool, but an entire ecosystem had grown on top of the cover—another strike for backyard amenities.

Continuing along the property's perimeter, they also noticed a few huge dog pens dotting the yard. Upon entering the home, an overwhelming smell told them why: Dogs had *definitely* been living there. In fact, there'd been twelve great Danes living in the house. At the very least, the home would need new floors, walls, and doors to get rid of the scratch marks and odor.

The dog cleanup wasn't too much of a setback, though, because the outdated interior would need a cosmetic overhaul anyway. The walls were covered in garish flowery wallpaper, the ceiling lights were large and overbearing, and the kitchen and bathrooms were straight out of the '70s.

Glenn and Amber envisioned a full renovation that would include a new kitchen, new bathrooms, and a basement build-out. They would also add a fifth bedroom by converting the unused upstairs loft space into a luxurious master suite. There weren't any huge structural issues to fix, and the exterior would just need a little touch-up.

If things went according to plan, they would put around $100,000 into the home and exit with at least a $90,000 profit. When finished, it would offer a stately, rural retreat in one of upstate New York's most esteemed suburban towns. Insofar as the adjacent problem, they explain:

"The neighboring landfill was definitely a concern that we knew might stifle some interest. At the same time, we predicted that some buyer would come along who would love the home so much it wouldn't matter. We knew there was at least $90,000 in the deal if we did it right, and even if we screwed up or missed something, we still would clear $50,000."

 THE BREAKDOWN

Single-family home, 3,000 square feet
Guilderland, New York
Asking $125,000

$ OFFER AND FUNDING

The agent hadn't received any calls on the property from the distant MLS listing and had only reached out to Glenn and Amber. Knowing they had no offers to compete against, they landed on a $122,000 cash offer. The bank was eager to offload the property and accepted without a hitch.

> *"The asking price was already a steal, but we still offered less than asking to see if we could create more profit. The highest per-hour pay you will ever earn is from negotiating—one fifteen-minute call can earn you $10,000 or more. If you did that every fifteen minutes, that equals $40,000 per hour. Where else can you make that but in real estate?"*

Glenn and Amber had built an amazing reputation among their lender base, so they were able to get 100 percent private funding for the purchase and renovation. The loan was structured at 10 percent interest with no payments due until the home sold.

As the Schworms' lawyer got the closing papers in order, she called Glenn to confirm a few details. When she casually mentioned the property's seven acres, Glenn interrupted to say that the property had only two and a half. The lawyer sent over the land survey to prove her point—and she was right! The survey confirmed seven acres divided into three lots. One was a separate three-acre lot just across the home's driveway, and the other was an isolated half acre toward the edge of the property. The bank had overlooked the extra acreage, but it was nearly triple the land at the same $122,000 price.

TURNAROUND

With closing papers signed, Glenn and Amber got started with the renovation. They hired a contractor to carry out what they expected to be a straightforward job, but they soon learned they had hired a crook. He took the money for the job and permits, but he never actually applied for the necessary legal paperwork. When Glenn and Amber found out, they fired him, only to have him retaliate by turning them in for the construction *he* did without permits. About that misstep, they explain:

> *"We went against our own cardinal rule: Always do a background check! We just assumed that this seasoned contractor, who was in his seventies, was here to help us manage the project. As it turned out, a simple internet search would have prevented huge losses. He was a convicted felon who had just been released from prison after his last con, with which he'd landed his own daughter in jail.*
>
> *"He was a bad dude, and we brought it on ourselves. Always vet everyone and do background checks to save yourself a major headache."*

As the owners of the property, Glenn and Amber were technically the "responsible" party, so the city showed up asking for proof that everything had been built correctly. They had to rip out an entire new wall and the kitchen's new granite countertops to prove that, despite lacking paperwork, everything had been built according to code. Then, of course, they had to redo all the work. The shady contractor had set them back a month and added $5,000 to their renovation cost.

Lesson learned, Glenn and Amber selected a new project manager and cautiously moved forward with the rest of the renovation. They tore off the flower wallpaper and gave the home a fresh coat of paint, renewed the hardwood floors, restored three once-beautiful fireplaces, completely replaced the kitchen and bathrooms, and brought the swampy swimming pool back to life.

Finally, building out the loft space added valuable square footage with a fifth bedroom. The work took about four months and came in at $110,000. Having invested a total of $232,000, they were a painful $20,000 over budget, but the home was a jaw-dropper and would hopefully pay off. Glenn says:

> *"Amber makes sure all our homes pop above the competition and sell the fastest. She has the designer's touch when it comes to staging. The outside is the first impression that always wows viewers, but the inside is what makes them fall in love."*

As for the extra acreage, Glenn and Amber knew that a house on seven acres could actually turn off potential buyers due to all the upkeep. On top of that, they believed they'd profit best by subdividing the land. They paid $4,000 for new surveys and some red tape at the county office, and with the parcels officially recorded, they were finally ready to list.

Ken's Take Buying houses with sub-dividable land is one of my favorite strategies. Extra acreage associated with a house is rarely as valuable as a smaller, stand-alone parcel. As a builder, I find that subdividing into smaller parcels is a great way to source less-expensive lot inventory.

AFTERMATH

Within days, a local builder jumped at the half-acre lot for $43,000. Another buyer soon followed, purchasing the fully renovated home for $387,000. With the $122,000 purchase, $110,000 renovation, $4,000 subdivision, and $33,000 for closing, commissions, and holding costs, these two sales already cleared a $161,000 profit.

The three-acre lot across from the home had yet to sell, and Glenn and Amber wanted it gone so they could move on to the next deal. Since the acreage sat within view of the single-family house, they figured it was in the home buyer's interest to buy the land to prevent someone from coming along and building on it. The buyer was hesitant, though, so with a stroke of artful insight, Glenn hired someone to go survey the land.

Once the new homeowner saw the surveying equipment sizing up the acreage for a possible build, he thought better of his reluctance and purchased the three acres at a rock-bottom price of $60,000. With profit from the house and two additional parcels, Glenn and Amber walked away with $221,000, saying a quiet thank-you to the bank for overlooking the acreage that made up more than $100,000 of the profit.

TAKEAWAY

Examine All Angles

Most properties have multiple ways to maximize return on investment. Some are better suited for rentals, some for flips, some for rezoning, some for teardowns—you get the gist. Always analyze properties with extra land with the possibility of subdividing into smaller parcels.

As investors, don't pigeonhole yourself into one way of thinking. Every deal should be analyzed closely to determine how to best maximize your return. In Glenn and Amber's case, it just so happened to come in the form of easily dividable land dropping into their lap. As they say:

"Look for every opportunity to maximize a deal. This deal had a lot of moving parts, but we learned to always be on the lookout for ways to make as much money as you can on your flip."

Unicorns Do Exist

If you've learned anything from this book so far, it's that amazing deals happen to real estate investors all the time. Sometimes it's their first deal, but typically the really special deals come from consistent grinding. The more deals you do, the higher the likelihood that you're going to land a unicorn. The Schworms put it this way:

"Sometimes we make the mistake of thinking we got lucky with this, but we're not lucky—we're out there doing our deals. We're grinding and working. Deals like that don't happen every day, but like every baseball player, if you swing the bat enough, you're going to connect. And sometimes you'll connect with a big one. We find deals because we're in the game. You win the game on singles, but every now and again, you hit a home run."

The bottom line is this: If you're not out there doing it, you won't find the unicorns.

Vet Your Contractor Thoroughly

Glenn and Amber turned a handsome profit on this deal, but the fact that they got burned by their first contractor is one of the most valuable lessons here. My guess is that they were using a new contractor on this home since it was outside of their typical investment area. When taking on a large renovation like this one, vetting a contractor properly is of the utmost importance. Here are five basic rules investors should adhere to when hiring a contractor for a specific job:

1. Collect bids from at least three different contractors to make sure pricing is competitive and in line with the job.
2. Make sure the bid details every possible line item in the renovation. A vague bid is a recipe for disaster.

3. Make sure the contractor is properly licensed, insured, and in good standing. Do your own research to verify.
4. Call at least three recent references to discuss their experiences with this particular contractor.
5. Make sure you have a clearly defined draw schedule, and don't be manipulated into deviating from this schedule during the project.

CHAPTER FIFTEEN

NICK AALERUD

Cutting Through Red Tape Pays Off

Like many Bostonians, Nick Aalerud keeps busy. His real estate business encompasses wholesales, fix-and-flips, sales and brokerage, property management, and even debt settlement. With a goal of providing five-star client service no matter the type of deal, Nick explains, "We try to help more than a hundred sellers a year."

When Nick jumped into real estate back in 2005, he was pivoting from his first career as an investment banker. Through managing mutual funds, stocks, and bonds, he came to understand the irresistible allure of real estate investing. From there, he founded his real estate acquisition firm, AA Real Estate Group, and renovated five great buy and holds within the first three years.

Then the 2008 downturn hit, and due to poor due diligence and a bad partnership, he lost every single one of them to short sales or foreclosure. On the loss of his properties, Nick says:

"It was a very tough time in my life. I blamed everything on the partner who had lied to me, when in fact, I needed to look in the mirror and revamp my strategies. 'Failure is not an option' is the worst quote I've ever read—failure is not only an option, but it is

necessary to move forward. This was the first of many 'reset buttons,' as I now call them."

It was a tough pill to swallow, but Nick would never again make the mistake of ignoring real estate market cycles. He started over with new rules and systems and has been cranking ever since.

By now, his company has completed more than $70 million in closed real estate transactions and manages more than fifty rental units across New England, Pennsylvania, and Florida. Over time, he has developed a strong network of private lenders and investors to help fund a career built mainly on fix-and-flips. Lately, however, his company trends more toward wholesales and limits renovations to the lowest-risk and highest-upside properties. As he learned back in 2008, flexibility is the key to success from year to year.

Ken's Take Wholesaling homes isn't just a great strategy for beginners. There are plenty of veteran investors who manage risk by wholesaling the majority of their off-market acquisitions. This is especially true when investors sense market volatility.

FINDING THE DEAL

Most of Nick's deals come from marketing through direct mail, texts, and voicemails, but when you spend nearly fifteen years in a city doing great work, you get access to one of the best marketing techniques around: referrals. They come in at zero cost per lead!

Linda, a friend of one of Nick's private lenders, needed help selling her mother's property, so she got in touch with Nick. Eight months earlier, her mother—who'd lived alone in her home for decades—abruptly moved into a nursing home, and Linda inherited somewhat of a mess. Nobody had dealt with the property (or even entered it) since.

As the home sat untended, neighbors began complaining about mold, disrepair, and a dangerous uncovered pool. Code violations were issued and lost amid the stress and paperwork of her mother's move. By the time Linda caught up with the backlogged mail, the city was all over her with liens and threats to condemn the building.

On top of that, Medicaid wanted a piece of the home's value. In the absence of other known funding options, Medicaid was actually covering the nursing home costs. When they discovered the home's existence—and how it was a potential source of funding—they slapped a lien on it for an as-yet-unknown amount. A cryptic letter arrived that simply said "Before you sell this property, give us a call."

In short, Linda wanted to sell fast and pay off her mother's debts before things could get worse. Almost certainly there was more *owed* on the home than she could get by selling it, but if she could walk away without debt or legal action, she'd count that as a win.

Insider Info Most people don't realize that the federal government (including Medicaid) can put a tax lien on a home. It's important to do a title search as soon as possible when attempting to purchase an off-market property. Oftentimes, you'll find that even the sellers are unaware of outstanding issues clouding the title.

ASSESSMENT

Just behind the front yard's overgrown vegetation, you could make out a once-beautiful two-story Cape Cod home. Built in the 1940s, it had three bedrooms, two bathrooms, and a basement. A large in-ground pool sat in the backyard, but because it lacked an adequate liner and pumps, it was more of a swampy maintenance nightmare than an amenity.

On the upside, it was in suburban north Boston, and the Class B+ neighborhood had excellent school systems and a high average income. Deals were few and far between, and Nick knew that pretty much any project he could get his hands on would sell—it just had to be worth the effort.

A *lot* of seasonal change can occur over eight months in Boston, and this home sat vacant during a particularly rough winter. Most New Englanders fear the worst of winter home disasters: frozen pipes. Left unmanaged, the water eventually thaws, and expanding heat causes pipes to burst. Since Boston is an old city with lots of old, uninsulated plumbing, it's a frustratingly common issue.

Lo and behold, a water line had burst over the winter, and the resulting leak had gone unnoticed for months. Cold water had filled up the entire basement and even seeped onto the first floor. As warm spring weather approached, it created a contemptible recipe for mold.

"Lots and lots of really cool colors of mold grew throughout the entire property. Hot yellows, bright oranges, things I'd never seen before!"

Adding insult to injury, the leaked water had frozen, thawed, and re-frozen so many times that recurring heat expansion created cracks throughout the entire foundation. The moisture impacted everything—ceiling tiles were falling apart, plaster was bubbling, floors were rotting, and anything that could peel was done for.

The home would need serious work. By Nick's calculation, the cost of repairs would exceed the value of the house itself. Plus, the neighborhood's other sizable homes demanded a bigger and nicer product for a renovation effort to be worthwhile. For the numbers to make sense, he would have to demolish the house and start over from the ground up.

Nick's idea was to build a custom colonial-style home with four bedrooms, two and a half bathrooms, and a two-car garage in keeping with the feel of the neighborhood. Knowing that most buyers would value additional living space more than pool maintenance, he'd get rid of the pool, instead adding 1,450 square feet to the home's footprint, boosting it to a spacious 3,200 square feet.

Ken's Take The decision to keep an existing pool really depends on numerous factors. In some warm-climate markets, pools are a must-have and almost always worth restoring. However, in cooler areas, a pool might not actually add much (if any) value to a home. In Nick's situation, adding square footage to the house would absolutely be a better use of space than a pool.

Nick estimated that a new build would cost $360,000, with demolition at $10,000 and construction costing around $110 per square foot at the time. The amount owed to the city in liens was nearly $2,000, and some sleuthing showed that Medicaid would probably ask for up to $210,000. Nonetheless, with a resale value estimated at $725,000, he decided the deal was worth pursuing.

THE BREAKDOWN

Single-family home, 1,750 square feet
North Boston suburbs, Massachusetts
Likely owed more than $210,000 in liens and fines

OFFER AND FUNDING

With the numbers being what they were, Linda didn't stand to profit, but Nick found a way to sweeten the deal for her regardless. His offer was to take the property off her hands as-is and deal with the city and Medicaid himself. Essentially, his "purchase price" would be the time, money, and effort it took to pay off the liens. In exchange, Linda could simply walk away from the stress, angry phone calls, and mounting bills. Linda was beyond relieved to accept his offer, and they drew up a contract with the sole contingency relating to resolution of the outstanding liens.

Nick lined up a private lender, but working through the pile of regulatory issues would probably take months. In the meantime, he paid the lender a couple thousand dollars to keep the funds available until needed.

Ken's Take Private lenders typically get paid only when their money is deployed. However, sometimes a purchase transaction can be difficult to time perfectly and may hinge on title or some other unresolved variable. In those cases, I find it's worth paying your private lender some amount of interest while their money sits in an escrow account to fund your project at a moment's notice.

TURNAROUND

The first order of business was to get the Medicaid situation resolved. Nick had never dealt with them before as lienholders, but he knew that, just as with any other claimant, the two parties would have to reach consensus on the home's value. Medicaid had used recent comparable sales to come up with their valuation of more than $200,000, but given the city's liens and the home's deplorable state, Nick knew they were gravely overvaluing it. To defend his stance, he made repeated requests for Medicaid to send out a representative to see for themselves, but they were resolute on using computer-generated comps instead.

With fingers crossed that he'd eventually be able to talk them down, Nick meanwhile began dealing with the city. He paid off the overdue liens, then remedied the code violations by filling in and securing the pool, blocking off doors and windows with nailed plywood (to keep the home secure from squatters), and shutting off the utilities. That was a lot of time and money to put into a home he still didn't own, but he did so in the expectation that by dealing with those issues now, he'd be ready to start construction once he finally settled things with Medicaid.

"Normally, you should never put money into a property that you don't own yet, as there's a risk you'll never get that money back. We knew the risks, however—and we knew by doing this, we would help Linda by getting the building inspectors off her back. She would be grateful, and we would be a hero to the neighborhood!"

With the city liens paid off, Nick went to apply for a construction zoning variance. It didn't take him long to realize that the zoning office regarded him as an evil new developer. They made it *very* clear that things would be strictly regulated for any new construction—at least, as long as Nick was the one doing it.

Adding insult to injury, the local historical commission caught wind of his plans and decreed that the home was on the register of historic homes. Nick pointed out the unlikelihood of a 1940s home being "historic" (especially since most of the area's historic homes were built in the 1800s), but because the commission defined it as postwar Cape Cod style, they would have their say.

Two months of meetings with the historical commission were fruitless. The obstinate president had his heart set on his own *personal* desire: plans for either a 1960s-style Cape Cod or a ranch home. But the plans Nick had presented weren't for an outlandish modern new build—the colonial build made financial sense and fit in well with the other houses. Nick recalls:

"One moment stands out in my mind that I've still never seen in my fifteen years in the business. The chair of the historical commission threw some pictures of 1960s ranches at me. He pounded the table in front of the commission and all those in attendance, and he boomed, 'Don't you know the Golden Rule? The Parthenon was built by the Golden Rule. Look it up. And I must say—if it's good enough for the Parthenon, it's good enough for [Johns Ave.]!'

As an outsider to the area, Nick suspected the commissioners were just making a power play. Nevertheless, he'd need their approval for the zoning variance. With things dragging into the third month of negotiations, Nick finally came up with a checkmate. At the final meeting, he presented evidence of the commission's several recent approvals for colonial-style builds and rehabs that varied little from his own proposal. Egg on their faces, the commissioners signed off on the plans.

He was slowly reaching the finish line, but the Medicaid lien amount remained unresolved. They'd refused to send anyone out to value the property, so it was on Nick to keep fighting for a fair valuation. Finally, he had a lightbulb moment. He would reach out to the building department and ask them to do what they had been threatening to do all along: condemn the house! The very next day, the building department was at the house, posting *Condemned* signs all around the property.

With photos of *Condemned* signs on the boarded-up home, Nick was finally able to prove to Medicaid that their "asset" wasn't worth nearly what they'd desired. Realizing that the longer they waited, the lower the home's value would drop, Medicaid was right where Nick wanted them. He offered $115,000, and after a little negotiation, they settled on $145,000 to release the lien.

The property was a five-month headache, but Nick had accomplished nearly all the necessary legwork to get it ready for new construction. While waiting on final approval for the zoning variance, he put a *For Sale* sign in the front yard. Even though he was happy to proceed with the rebuild himself, he suspected he could profit almost as much by offloading the project to another investor.

One month later, the final permits were granted. Just as Nick was getting ready to pay for them, a local builder called to declare that he would buy the property at any price. He was well established and well connected in the area, and he wasn't afraid of jumping through any regulatory hoops for building; Nick had cleared most of them out, anyway. The builder offered $325,000, *double* what Nick would soon be paying to Medicaid. Nick thought about it:

> *"So, we don't have to drive forty minutes to get to the site every day, we don't have to fight with the town councils, and we don't have to be the evil developer? This guy will just take all that from us and we'll literally double our money? I'm sorry—are you kidding me?"*

The opportunity was too good to resist. Nick drew up a contract, and at closing, he took the builder's $325,000 and paid off the negotiated Medicaid lien of $145,000. After paying $28,000 in attorney, engineer, permitting, and minor construction fees, this meant a $152,000 profit—an amazing payoff for some phone calls, paperwork, and council meetings!

AFTERMATH

Getting this property ready for new construction took nearly six months of greasing wheels and cutting through red tape—which is no easy task when you're operating without a guarantee of ownership. Not only was it time-consuming, it also ended up costing Nick nearly $30,000.

Nevertheless, it was that very work that got the home to a point where a different builder could come in and start construction immediately. Nick had dived in with the faith that he'd somehow turn a profit, and it paid off. He walked away with $152,000, one of the highest spreads he'd ever made on a house he'd never even owned!

> *"While the spread was excellent, most aren't like that. We position ourselves in our community as helpers and problem solvers, and the community knows that. We are there to make a new relationship and solve problems—and sometimes that ends up as a deal. Be in the position to truly help and impact others, and with preparation, the profit will follow."*

TAKEAWAY

Position Yourself as the Problem Solver

It may seem odd that Linda was willing to essentially give the house away. However, put yourself in her shoes: dealing with the countless phone calls from code enforcement, mounting fines, and the nagging thought of incurring more liability than the house was even worth. This was no longer the home that held sweet memories of her mother—it had become the house from hell.

Nick realized that solving this headache was the most important thing—even more important than trying to squeeze out some equity. Linda's best-case scenario was Nick's offer to take on the burden so that she could walk away without fines or expenses. In this case, he was no longer simply a home buyer but the guy who could make it all just go away.

Red Tape Can Equal Profit

Many investors would analyze the facts surrounding this property and assume there was no money to be made. Between code enforcement fines, liens from the city, and a whopping Medicaid lien, they'd figure there wasn't much meat left on the bone. However, those investors didn't see that putting in the time and effort to negotiate with lienholders might pay off to the tune of more than $100,000.

Additionally, some investors are intimidated at the thought of working through rezoning boards, historical commissions, city council meetings, and so on. However, learning to navigate this kind of red tape can absolutely mean the difference between a no-profit deal and a home run.

A Bird in the Hand

Whenever my coaching clients ask me whether or not they should wholesale a particular deal or buy/fix/flip, I ask them if they've truly thought through the risks and rewards of both scenarios. While large renovation projects often look good on paper, it's been my experience that investors rarely estimate costs accurately. Among holding costs, unforeseen repairs, inaccurate ARVs, market fluctuations, and more, large projects simply carry an inherent amount of risk that rarely gets factored in appropriately during the decision-making process.

The longer I've been in this business, the more I lean toward the old adage "A bird in the hand is worth two in the bush." If I can take a *defi-*

nite $20,000 today versus a *maybe* $50,000 in six months, I'm taking the $20,000 without a doubt. I've seen too many *maybe* deals go sideways and not work out as planned.

I suspect Nick felt the same way. Taking $152,000 to walk away versus the huge amount of time and exposure required to build an expensive house—all while dealing with a difficult municipality—was a no-brainer.

CHAPTER SIXTEEN

JOE LIEBER

No Money, No Financing, No Problem

One lazy Saturday, a 17-year-old boy named Joe sat watching TV when an infomercial caught his eye. A dignified man stood amid swaying palm trees dangling the promise of oceanside living and telling viewers about the endless wealth they could create through real estate. Carleton H. Sheets was his name, and he vowed that you too could have beach-life riches by simply following his program. Young Joe Lieber was fresh out of high school, and he was hooked.

When an infomercial inspires you to invest in real estate, how can you go wrong? Yet in the nearly twenty years since that fateful viewing, Joe has completed more than 1,000 single-family transactions and a solid handful of multifamily deals. After renouncing his pursuit of some big one-off score, Joe now turns so many deals that his whole portfolio is one big score.

Joe got his start in Cleveland, Ohio, in the early 2000s, when he could find downtown properties for between $5,000 and $20,000—they were practically free! With investments that cheap, it was easy to take the rental income (which tends to remain consistent no matter how the sales market is performing) and funnel the earnings into purchasing more homes. Joe says:

"I was financing with private notes from private lenders for these properties on five-year fully amortized loans. Even paying 15 percent to lenders, I was still breaking even or cash-flowing! That's how I got my whole portfolio paid off so quickly. The rental income I was earning during the downturn years hasn't changed much, even though the sale price has fluctuated greatly. Even then, I could get $800 in monthly rent on a $10,000 house after putting in just $10,000 for the rehab."

Through cashing in on the cheap housing extravaganza, Joe built a single-family rental portfolio of more than 200 doors within just a few years. However, hitting such a high number eventually left him with the choice of either downsizing or hiring more staff to go bigger. Rather than scaling up, he opted to maintain his sanity by keeping around 100 to 150 properties at a time.

Given his investment model, which is built on accumulating numerous smaller sources of income, managing his own properties is key to Joe's success. When a home is only going to make between $5,000 and $8,000 net per year, that profit can easily disappear when paying someone else to fix issues and manage renters. From clean-outs to turnover to evictions, property managers can bleed profits and make something profitable only break-even.

Ken's Take Having been in a mastermind with Joe since 2012, I've always admired his willingness to get in the trenches. Even with a property manager, you as the owner are usually still the quarterback. You're the one calling the plays and making the key decisions: what to fix, how to handle a tenant situation, and so on. Since Joe believes property managers make most of their money on repairs, he saves tons of money by finding labor or fixing things himself. Instead of paying $200 to install a kitchen faucet, he pays $75. Those little gains add up!

All those years spent developing his reputation in the Cleveland market means that Joe has built a reliable pool of lenders and investors. While he's been involved with all sorts of projects over the years—brokerage, management, rehabs, landlording, wholesaling, and multifamiles—his bread and butter comes from focusing on the local MLS and REO listings for low-cost properties to either add to his rental portfolio or sell as turnkey, owner finance, or retail.

FINDING THE DEAL

Long before Joe accumulated the balance sheet he has today, he was on the search for another buy and hold to add to his burgeoning portfolio. Most of his funds were tied up in other rentals, and because he lacked low-interest options for a purchase, he'd have to get creative to find and fund another deal. He began scanning the MLS for properties that had been sitting for a while. If something hadn't sold, somebody needed a better solution, and Joe planned to offer just that.

Sometimes great deals are hiding in plain sight—Joe found a property that had been sitting on the MLS for 150 days. The seller was asking $100,000, and Joe's familiarity with the neighborhood immediately told him it was priced too high. He called up the Realtor, who was so "over it" that she was actually in the process of releasing the listing. Joe was happy to deal directly with the seller, so he called her up and introduced himself.

ASSESSMENT

The property was a 1919 duplex called a "double," meaning the two units sat atop each other rather than side by side. Each unit was a spacious 1,050 square feet with a street-facing porch, two bedrooms, a living room, and a dining room. They shared a grassy private backyard and a basement for storage.

The seller, Jeanie, had always lived in the double's lower unit, and as Joe says, "*We all know the difference between a tenant-occupied home and an owner-occupied home.*" She'd kept the property in good shape overall. The charm wasn't overpowering, but it was there. Considering her upkeep over the years, Joe suspected that, if nothing else, the rent-ready property wouldn't require any rehab investment.

Although the neighborhood was spotted with both run-down and renovated homes, Jeanie's double stood on a nice, tree-lined brick cobblestone street. With downtown Cleveland, Lake Erie, and the airport all within a fifteen-minute drive, the area would likely continue developing with investment potential.

Jeanie was ten years in on her thirty-year mortgage, but she still owed $88,000 on the property and was struggling to make payments. Unfortunately, a friend who had been renting the upstairs had taken advantage of her kindness by rarely paying rent before disappearing. At this point, selling seemed like the only way she could avoid an eventual foreclosure.

The existing mortgage was $550 per month, and with taxes and insurance, the total payment bumped up to about $700. Even though amortization was beginning to chip away at her principal balance, the prospect of ever paying off the property seemed like a hopeless uphill battle. Ready to wash her hands of the whole situation, Jeanie hoped to somehow sell for $100,000—just enough to pay off the mortgage and cover closing costs.

Joe couldn't imagine the unrenovated double being worth more than $70,000, which was likely why it had sat on the MLS for so long. However, although there was no deal in her asking price, he predicted the value would increase over the next few years. Experience told him he could expect at least $550 in monthly rental income from each unit.

The numbers weren't adding up to ideal cash flow at a $100,000 purchase, but Joe had an idea: If he could keep Jeanie's mortgage in place and simply take over the payments, she could walk away from her debt and Joe would be on the path to owning another buy and hold.

Enter the subject-to agreement.

Insider Info Subject-to is a type of purchase where the buyer takes title to the property, but the existing mortgage stays in the name of the seller. In other words, the sale is "subject to" the existing financing (i.e., the mortgage Jeanie secured when she purchased the home). Joe proposed that Jeanie simply walk away from the loan and let him assume the mortgage obligation.

However, in many subject-to deals, the seller will actually sell at a price above their mortgage balance. In these cases, the buyer can pay the difference in cash, or the seller can even carry back a second loan that the buyer pays in addition to the underlying mortgage.

If Jeanie signed on to the plan, she would deed Joe the property title and he would take over the payments. True, she wouldn't make any money outright, but she could stop throwing more money into a home that was likely slated for foreclosure. Meanwhile, Joe planned to easily offset the $700 monthly payment by renting out both units. With effectively no money down, Joe would take ownership, generate cash flow, and eventually sell the home for pure profit!

THE BREAKDOWN

Double (stacked duplex), 2,100 square feet
Cleveland, Ohio
Asking $100,000

OFFER AND FUNDING

With unattractive interest rates and his cash tied up in other projects, it was better for Joe to keep Jeanie's mortgage in place rather than attempt to get a new one in his name. Her interest rate was simply better than anything he'd be able to get as a non-owner-occupied borrower, and certainly better than a hard-money loan. However, allowing Joe to take over her financing would require a huge degree of trust from Jeanie. If he defaulted on the payments, it was *her* credit on the line.

What did Joe do to make her comfortable with the situation? I'll let him explain:

"In this case, I was the one who was there making this a personable transaction. If you're sending an acquisitions manager out for your 'big company,' it's just not the same—it's too impersonal. I wasn't hiding behind some company name; I'm just a guy trying to buy some houses, trying to make my mark, and I'm going to do the right thing.

"When I meet a seller, I bring a little box of cookies. We talk about family and friends; we build rapport. I spoke from the heart. I didn't just act genuine, I was genuine. There weren't any crazy sales tactics—I was just looking her in the eye and saying, 'Jeanie, I know you want out of here, and I'm going to do what I say. If I don't, what's the alternative? It'll probably just go into foreclosure and nobody wins.'"

In short, Joe's sales tactic was being genuine and offering a solution that Jeanie hadn't even known existed. He also promised that when the market turned, he would refinance the property in his name so she could wipe it off the books completely. If Joe didn't make the payments as outlined with their subject-to agreement, the property would foreclose,

Jeanie would have her credit ruined, and Joe would lose the deed to a home into which he had invested time, effort, and money.

Ken's Take As is the case with most investors, Joe's goal is to acquire properties where low risk and minimal out-of-pocket cash meet high potential upside. Could he have gone to a bank and put a conventional loan on this property? Probably. But then he would be putting 25 percent down on a $100,000 purchase with a likely higher interest rate. On top of that, he'd have to personally guarantee a loan that would occupy valuable space on his credit report. All of a sudden, it's no longer a deal. As was the case with Joe's transaction, the subject-to model often works for investors when a traditional purchase won't.

The stakes were high, and although trusting someone you had barely known for a month to pay your mortgage was risky, Jeanie wanted out. She signed a quitclaim deed granting Joe title to the property and trusted him to keep his word on the payments. Though Joe knew he'd never break his side of the deal, he also knew a cardinal rule of negotiation:

> *"He who cares least wins. You have to find people who have a 'situation' in a real estate deal. There's massive opportunity there—those are the ones who are most motivated."*

TURNAROUND

With no money out of pocket and nothing needed for rehab, Joe now had title and a $700 monthly payment. Despite its rent-ready state, he anticipated the old home needing maintenance more often than not. Instead of dealing with all that work himself, he decided to market the double as a master lease, where along with the house hacking opportunity, the lessee would take on the responsibility of property maintenance.

The master lease option meant the tenant could live in one and rent the other, or they could rent out both in an effort to create cash flow. Joe sweetened the pot with what's called a *lease option*, which gives the tenant first dibs if they want to purchase the property at some point in the future.

His offer included a monthly rent credit toward a locked-in purchase price of $110,000 if executed within four years of signing the lease. The property wasn't worth that much at the time, but establishing the number was a great way to incentivize the tenant to move toward a purchase. That being said, it could also backfire if market values eventually surpassed the $110,000 price.

Insider Info With lease options, it's typical for the lessor to offer a monthly rent credit toward a future purchase option. This is typically the allure for the lessee, who will feel that their monthly rental payment isn't going to waste but is actually adding to a future "down payment." It's worth noting that such agreements should be structured *meticulously*—certain court rulings over the years have left investors with messy surprises.

Within weeks, Joe found a lessee willing to lease the whole place for $1,100 monthly. They seemed eager to work toward exercising the option while living in the bottom unit and renting out the top. They signed the lease, and Joe crossed his fingers that the deal would remain effortless.

AFTERMATH

For three and a half years, Joe didn't hear a peep from the property besides the sound when he opened an envelope with the monthly rent check. He was netting a cool $400 per month—it was like creating equity and cash flow out of thin air.

Lo and behold, at the close of three years, the lessee decided it was time to exercise the lease option. It was Joe's dream come true: She had already been preapproved for a loan and was ready to close on financing. Jeanie's mortgage was thirteen years in with a balance just less than $80,000, so a $110,000 sale would net nearly $30,000 in profit on top of all the cash flow he'd already made. Joe says:

> "At closing, I gave a seller concession of $4,000, but I didn't care—at $110,000, if I pay $4,000 in closing costs, I'm still getting $106,000 on top of all the cash flow I made. When you're talking big numbers like that, I'm not penny-pinching, I'm just grateful. I had been making $400 monthly and was about to get a huge check, so yeah, I'm giving them a seller concession."

Looking back, it's interesting that nobody else had come up with the subject-to option during the 150 days Jeanie's home sat on the MLS. While everybody else saw an overpriced double, Joe sniffed out an opportunity. He hadn't just bought and held a house, he had used a subject-to and a lease option to create mailbox money for three years, plus a $30,000 payday at the end. With his confidence (and bank account) bolstered, he set out to find more creative investments to continue feeding his real estate empire.

 # TAKEAWAY

Adapt to the Market

Joe wasn't keen on getting a traditional bank loan (and the interest rates that come with it) when he found this deal, so it took a high degree of creativity to create profit. Knowing there had to be sellers with "problem" properties, Joe scoured the MLS for someone in need of a creative solution. This pursuit led him to the subject-to model, something that worked for both him *and* the troubled sellers. As he puts it:

> *"Real estate markets are ever changing. A strategy that works today won't necessarily work three years or even three months later. You have to be on the cutting edge of what's going on. People need to sublease houses, sometimes even when they have mortgages. Subject-to deals are still out there every day."*

The Power of Lease Options

Having spent time with Joe in Cleveland and even purchased properties from him, I'm not surprised that one of his best deals involves a lease option. He's literally done hundreds of these over the years.

Joe's model of buying older housing stock (typically in less-than-fair condition) tends to come with a set of never-ending maintenance issues that are costly and time-consuming. Offering a lease option that delegates the property's upkeep to the tenant removes Joe from the maintenance equation. It's a win-win for both parties.

Scaling Isn't Always Better

In a strong seller's market, finding houses at all tends to be an investor's biggest challenge. But throughout the Great Recession, Joe was able to find and buy houses for next to nothing. It took him only a few years to build a portfolio of more than 200 homes!

Back then, it was keeping up with all the houses that was the real challenge. Finding deals was easy, but not every cheap house was worth owning. Although Joe could have hired additional staff to help him run things, he ultimately decided to scale down to a size he could easily manage himself. He says:

> "There was a period when I was just buying to buy. If someone offered me something and it was cheap, I would take it. Eventually, I realized that was a mistake. These were heavy cap-ex homes that needed work and weren't in the best neighborhoods. I just figured that instead of trying to scale up and create more chaos in my life, I would scale down."

I can personally attest to the allure of scaling even when doing so doesn't make the best sense. Sometimes scaling just amounts to more headaches, more overhead, and ultimately less profit. As investors, it's important to truly analyze and understand the risks, headaches, and potential upside of scaling a business before blindly assuming that is the best course of action.

CHAPTER SEVETEEN

ZEONA MCINTYRE

From Rental Nightmare to Short-Term Rental Dream

A lot of people fall into Airbnb investing by accident: A property performs poorly, the owner decides to try out short-term rentals, and suddenly it outperforms anything they've ever dreamed of. Zeona McIntyre isn't one of those investors. She "fell" into short-term rentals intentionally—and ahead of the curve—all the way back in 2012.

After learning that a friend had made $50,000 from his first year on Airbnb in New York, she saw an opportunity for the ultimate side hustle. At the time, she was attending college for massage therapy in Boulder, Colorado, and she started using the Airbnb platform to rent the second bedroom of her condo when her roommate moved out (note: Zeona used Airbnb but the same idea applies across any vacation rental platform like VRBO or any others). If it didn't go well, she figured she'd just find another roommate.

It worked out. Now Zeona owns seven short-term rentals and manages a total of twenty-five from Seattle to Spain. A property management software program schedules cleaners, lists her properties on multiple websites, syncs scheduling, and provides 24/7 receptionists for nearly all guest communication. Meanwhile, an operations manager handles accounting and atypical guest issues. With these systems in place, Zeona can focus on balancing her business pursuits with pleasures like travel and adventure. She explains:

> *"If you're interested in rentals, just start getting the experience. List what you have, go away for a weekend, and see if you like it—it's the easiest way to get into rentals, and you don't have to invest anything! Everybody lives somewhere—you could be living in a van and rent it out in someone's driveway. Some people even rent out their backyard and put tents in it. People want a unique space—treehouses are some of the most popular listings overall!"*

Zeona's business model is notable for its relatively hands-off approach. First, using property management software minimizes firsthand interaction—it's an investment with an amazing ROI for both money *and* time. Second, her acquisition strategy keeps physical labor at bay; instead of dealing with remodeling and managing crews, Zeona buys homes that are rent-ready. After listing a property online, once the inspection clears, she arrives the day of closing to furnish the place, and she usually has it booked the day she departs.

FINDING THE DEAL

These days, Zeona keeps things simple: Since Airbnbs and other vacation rental sites fill such a unique niche, she finds plenty of profit by simply buying homes off the MLS. However, back in 2015, she still hadn't purchased a home and was earning rental income by "rent and re-rent" (also called master leasing). She was essentially Airbnbing rooms in the property she rented as a co-venture with the property owner. Under this model, she earned 25 percent of the rental income, essentially skimming off the top, on rooms she didn't own, didn't furnish, and didn't even invest in.

Insider Info

Finding a master lease option is easier than people think. Zeona says, *"It's really just coming up with a couple of really good terms that would be hard to say no to, then shooting out a cover letter to fifty places on rental sites. I tell people we'll do a long lease—two or three years—and we'll guarantee rent increases. For lessors, this means no vacancy, guaranteed rent (with increases), and professional maintenance. The main idea is to ensure owners that you'll go above and beyond to take care of the place. You might be surprised how many are eager to say yes!"*

Around this time, she attended a friend's wedding in St. Louis , Missouri. Amid small talk, she discovered that the average three-bedroom house with a garage and backyard generally had a monthly mortgage of only $300. Once she returned home, she dived into research on the St. Louis single-family market, also contacting local Airbnb hosts to understand their numbers, visitor seasonality, and area features. Two weeks later, Zeona was back in St. Louis furnishing her first out-of-state home.

That investment quickly began crushing the 1 percent price-to-rent ratio (known as the 1 percent rule, which I'll explain in more detail later) through Airbnb rentals, and Zeona wanted more. Assuming she could find yet another successful investment in the same area, she hit the MLS and found a similar home just six doors down. The owners had purchased it for $96,000 ten years earlier (before the downturn) and had been losing money on it ever since. They listed it at $63,000, not knowing that someone like Zeona could come along and spin it into her best deal ever.

ASSESSMENT

The 1906 property was a charming two-bedroom one-bath home in good condition. It had been renovated twelve years earlier, and Zeona judged that it wouldn't need any major work before she could list it on Airbnb. The original hardwood floors and nine-foot ceilings kept the 930-square-foot home feeling spacious, and a large fenced-in backyard provided a beautiful, private respite.

The Class B neighborhood of University City consisted mostly of blue-collar residents and student renters from nearby Washington University. The location seemed ideal for short-term rentals: It was only fifteen minutes from the airport and twenty minutes from the convention center and downtown. The home was also close to Restaurant Row, a walkable area with shops, theaters, a concert hall, and trendy dining.

Although the property was in a lower-income area, Zeona knew that by going the Airbnb route, she wouldn't have to deal with many issues common with low-income, long-term renters. Even if Airbnb didn't work out, a long-term rental would bring in an easy $850 to $900 monthly (Airbnb estimates were well over $1,000 per month). Either way, if she purchased the home for $63,000 and it needed only furnishing to be rent-ready, this property would crush the 1 percent rule!

Insider Info Most investors consider the 1 percent price-to-rent ratio, known as the 1 percent rule, a good basic indicator of the efficacy of a potential rental investment. The 1 percent rule refers to the gross monthly rent compared with the total investment cost (acquisition plus repairs). If Zeona could purchase the property in rent-ready condition for $63,000, she would need only $630 per month in rent to meet the 1 percent rule. In her case, a standard long-term rental would conservatively bring in $850 monthly, which is actually 1.34 percent of the acquisition price. Even as a backup plan, a long-term rental made investment sense.

THE BREAKDOWN

Single-family home, 930 square feet
St. Louis, Missouri
Asking $63,000

OFFER AND FUNDING

Zeona decided to offer $52,000 cash from her personal savings with the option to close in only two weeks. The property had been listed for more than four months, and the distressed California-based owners were eager to accept, close fast, and get it off their hands.

Ken's Take Always be creative—take a step back to consider other ways to spin investments. The sellers didn't realize that their house was a wonderful investment opportunity. As they say, one man's trash is another man's treasure! This is especially true for out-of-state owners, who often have trouble managing a property long-distance. Some of my best investments have been made by purchasing from out-of-state investors who have gone sour on their once-promising investment.

TURNAROUND

As soon as the property passed inspection, Zeona took the risk of listing it on Airbnb with photos from the owners' MLS listing. Although the photos showed unfurnished empty rooms, she knew that by listing with low, competitive rates she was still likely to get bookings. By assuring viewers that the home would be fully furnished by their rental date, she started getting bookings before she even owned it!

Insider Info Use that lead time. The first month of operating a new Airbnb rental tends to be spotty, so listing it early puts it on the map and allows you to get bookings that you might miss by waiting for a finished product. Also, listing at below-market rates helps to get those initial bookings and—perhaps more important—early positive reviews.

While Zeona was preparing to fly out to sign the closing papers, the title company discovered an issue caused by an outstanding lien. They were confident they'd be able to work things out with the owners to get the lien paid off, but it would be another month or two before they could finalize things. With closing delayed, Zeona saw an opportunity: What if she could get the current owners to rent out the property to her in the meantime? Then she could rent and re-rent, just like the old days! They agreed to Zeona's proposal, and she signed on as a lessee for her future home at just $420 per month.

After quickly finding some furnishings for around $4,000, she began to Airbnb the property. The first month she earned $1,600 in rent, and the second came in at $1,800. Minus her $840 for two months' rent, that meant a $2,560 profit—positive cash flow before she even owned the house.

Ken's Take What an amazing example of finding a distressed seller and negotiating terms to create a win-win. Because of the title issues, Zeona couldn't buy the home as quickly as she wanted, but she enabled the owners (and herself) to start making money by offering to pay rent until it closed. In and of itself, this is a great investing strategy, and one that scores of investors have used to build successful Airbnb businesses. Who says you need to *own* real estate to build a profitable rental portfolio?

AFTERMATH

Zeona was already in the groove of things by the time she closed on the home, and to keep vacancies low, she used pricing software that maintained competitive listing prices relative to the time of year and other local rentals. She enlisted boots-on-the-ground cleaners for the turnovers, and from there it was mostly hands-off.

These days, the home generates $1,500 to $3,000 per month in Airbnb rental income. After expenses, that's a cash flow of more than $10,000 per year, and because Zeona paid cash for the property, that $10,000 in yearly net profit amounts to a 20 percent ROI. However, if Zeona decides one day to put financing on the property, this return becomes infinitely higher. She could easily BRRRR, get a loan for around 5 percent, and put her original $50,000 investment to work on another property. But at the end of the day, Zeona prefers to leave her $50,000 investment alone instead of putting debt on it, which is completely understandable at 20 percent ROI. Describing her zen-like approach, Zeona says:

> *"I'm less traditional—I don't feel the need to leverage everything. I'm just aiming for early retirement and enough properties to maintain my lifestyle."*

TAKEAWAY

Look at Other Markets

Perhaps you've heard the adage "Live where you want; invest where it makes sense." In Zeona's case, she found that owning and managing Airbnbs all over the country makes sense when you put the right systems in place to manage them. Because of this, she's able to keep her passion for travel and adventure at the forefront of her lifestyle.

The reality is that there are markets all over the country that may be less "popular" but have much higher long- and short-term rental returns than markets with higher entry points. Savvy investors take the time to research these areas and build teams and systems to support investments there, building profitable rental portfolios as a result. Don't get stuck in the mindset that you can only invest in your own backyard!

Understand What Makes a Good Airbnb

Having managed a handful of Airbnbs already, Zeona could recognize the potential in this St. Louis property. While the long-term rental rates were not exceptional, the Airbnb rates were disproportionately higher—but why?

Simply put, short-term renters typically want to stay in locations that are convenient to specific amenities. Urban locations like this one are usually successful when within walking distance of restaurants, bars, coffee shops, shopping districts, airports, and so on. In this particular case, the nearby college and proximity to downtown played a crucial role in the location's popularity.

However, don't assume that an area is going to yield a great Airbnb investment if it meets the above criteria. I've seen some of my own Airbnbs diminish in performance as specific submarkets become saturated with other Airbnb offerings. Talk to other hosts and explore numerous online analytical tools to help make informed Airbnb investment decisions.

Rent Arbitrage

Master leasing is one of the oldest strategies in the book, and it's become especially popular when combined with Airbnb. Aspiring real estate entrepreneurs can reach out to landlords with long-term rentals and employ the same method as Zeona: propose long leases, better upkeep than normal renting, and guarantee that they'll see rent increases.

For someone who is just starting out or isn't ready to take on the risk of buying a property, this strategy earns you experience *and* profit, and you don't even need to own real estate. Essentially, it's just an arbitrage game of what you (the lessee) negotiate with the owner (the lessor) and how much rent you can achieve through Airbnb. Even if you average just a few hundred dollars a month per property, with so little skin in the game, it's an easy win.

CHAPTER EIGHTEEN

LIZ FAIRCLOTH

The 2 Percent Duplex Using Other People's Money

Liz Faircloth caught the real estate bug back in 2005 after she and her husband, Matt, acquired their first single-family flip. Eager for more deals, they founded a real estate company—the DeRosa Group—in their home base of Trenton, New Jersey, and got started on their mission to "transform lives through real estate."

At the time, Liz was a successful business management consultant, so Matt managed the real estate hustle full-time while she balanced her day job with their new venture. Like most small-team investors, they began with single-family flips and rentals. By 2013, after enough real estate success, Liz was able to leave her day job and work full-time with the DeRosa Group.

Over years of building up their portfolio, they have scaled their business focus from single-family properties to large multifamilies with anywhere from fifty to 200 units. Their focus on Class B neighborhoods allows them to specialize in the value-add sector, where they take advantage of market disparities by adding value to or repositioning properties.

Rather than carry a heavy payroll, Matt and Liz have built a team of independent professionals who each get a piece of the action for finding deals, evaluating opportunities, coordinating transactions, and managing properties. By leveraging their experience and strong network, Matt and Liz have come to control nearly 700 units of residential and commercial assets throughout the East Coast.

In line with that initial goal of transforming lives through real estate, Liz launched *The Real Estate InvestHER Show* with co-host Andresa Guidelli in early 2018 to provide "straight talk and inspiration for existing and aspiring women investors." The hosts have also created online and in-person communities that offer support and encouragement to women who are interested in real estate investing.

FINDING THE DEAL

For Liz, finding properties is all about her network. Most of the time, local commercial brokers and wholesalers are the ones laying deals at her feet, which is precisely what happened when a wholesaler friend called her up about a brick side-by-side row house duplex for $50,000. Liz and Matt had been looking to add a multifamily rental to their portfolio, so she set up an appointment to find out more.

"You build real estate relationships just like you build any important relationship—it begins with finding the right people. First, you need to find the movers and shakers that specialize in your target asset class and target geographical market. Then you need to reach out to them, connect with them, and cultivate a relationship with them.

"Remember, as soon as you reach out, they will be evaluating you and asking questions, such as: Can I take this person seriously? Are they qualified to even be evaluating deals of this size/type? What is their track record? Are they well funded? Lasting relationships, whether business or personal, take constant cultivation and attention."

Ken's Take Building relationships with local wholesalers can turn into a wealth of inventory for your flipping and rental business. Wholesalers typically email deals to a large database of prospective buyers.

However, if you can build trust and credibility with even one or two high-producing wholesalers who will let you see their deals before anyone else, the sky's the limit.

✅ ASSESSMENT

The Trenton neighborhood was a typical urban Class C with a mixture of both renovated and dilapidated row homes, but the area was developing and increasingly popular with renters. The early-1900s duplex was in comparatively fair condition, and each unit came in at 1,100 square feet with two bedrooms, one bathroom, and an unfinished basement.

On the bright side, there were formal dining rooms, private fenced-in backyards, relatively large rooms, and gas heating. Less promising were the lack of parking, backyard access through the house only (inconvenient for an owner or landlord if there are tenants), and poorly insulated crawl spaces that foreshadowed frozen pipes during the cold Jersey winters.

None of the issues seemed insurmountable, though, and Liz predicted that an additional $50,000 for a cosmetic rehab would raise the resale value to well over $100,000. Hoping for a buy and hold, she figured it could bring in nearly $2,000 in monthly rent. If correct, she could then refinance to pay back the total investment and be on her way to a cash-flowing multifamily rental.

Insider Info Many investors aim to buy and hold rentals using the 1 percent rule: If the monthly rental income equals 1 percent or more of the all-in investment (acquisition and renovation), the investment is probably worthwhile. If Liz was all-in at $100,000 ($50,000 purchase plus $50,000 rehab) and earned $2,000 per month in rental income, the price-to-rent ratio would hit a whopping 2 percent!

🏠 THE BREAKDOWN

Duplex: two attached row houses, 1,100 square feet each
Trenton, New Jersey
Asking $50,000

OFFER AND FUNDING

There was one major hitch: After six years of relying on friends, family, and their own savings or credit lines to finance deals, Liz and Matt had reached a point where all their funding options were tied up in other holdings. It was a good problem to have, but they'd need new investors if they wanted to keep scaling.

It was 2011 and Liz was still working as a consultant, so she began pondering how to leverage an upcoming consulting job in New York City—a city *full* of possible investors. Combining business with pleasure, she arranged a coffee date with an old Wharton grad school friend named Jason who had become a successful financial planner in the years since they'd graduated.

By then, Liz and Matt were managing forty successful rental units and had a solid track record of deals. When she mentioned this to Jason, he exclaimed, "I love real estate! I want to invest, but I just don't have the time." Liz responded that she did have the time and skills for investing, just not the financial resources.

They immediately saw the possibility for symbiosis: Jason could finally get his start in real estate by lending to a team he could trust, and Liz and Matt could continue their upward growth. The next weekend, Jason flew down to Trenton to learn more about their operation and, as it happened, the duplex deal. Just like that, Liz and Matt had their first equity partner.

Liz, Matt, and Jason formed an LLC partnership separate from the DeRosa Group under which they would purchase, renovate, and rent out the duplex. Within the partnership, Jason would be "the money" as an equity partner, fronting $50,000 cash for the purchase with faith that the refinance would pay him back in no time.

Meanwhile, Liz and Matt would be the boots on the ground and de facto mentors for Jason as he learned about the process. When the property eventually sold, they would split the profit 50/50. If everything went according to Liz's plan, Jason would not only see how easy and lucrative real estate investing could be, but he would also be eager to keep doing deals with them.

Insider Info There are infinite ways to structure a partnership—it really depends on what each party brings to the table and how each is willing to value their contribution. For example, some partners bring cash to the equation, others bring experience and management, and some simply help raise capital. At the end of the day, each partner contributes in some form or fashion, and their ownership percentage is typically reflective of the value they bring.

Once all parties are in agreement, it's imperative that expectations, ownership percentages, and other partnership factors are clearly defined and documented in writing. For an LLC, this is typically mapped out in the operating agreement.

As for the $50,000 they would need for the renovation, another investor was waiting in the wings. Matt had met a private investor named Anika through a business networking group, and she was looking to use her self-directed IRA for a real estate investment. Anika was familiar with Trenton real estate and had several properties herself, so when Matt called her up, she immediately recognized the good opportunity. Together, they agreed on a loan amount of $50,000 at 12 percent annual interest, plus one point at closing.

Ken's Take One point and 12 percent annual interest may seem high, but it's actually average for most private-money loans. They're still typically cheaper than hard-money loans, which can run as high as two to four points and 15 percent interest. As you gain a solid track record and build lending relationships, it's easier to find less-expensive lenders and negotiate better terms, such as zero points, a lower interest rate, or a balloon note. At the end of the day, investors need to become experts at using other people's money (OPM) to scale their business.

TURNAROUND

Liz hired a contractor for the units' facelifts, which she and Matt oversaw. They updated kitchens with new appliances, countertops, and cabinets; installed new bathroom vanities; and refinished the first-level hardwood floors and upstairs carpet. Finally, they threw on a top-to-bottom fresh coat of paint.

As for the crawl space, they added insulation to keep utility bills low and protect the pipes from freezing. As predicted, it all came in at a smooth $50,000—minus one small bump in the road. Liz explains:

"Our contractor was removing a small shed in the backyard of one of the homes. In the dirt below the shed, they found several large bones. At first, we thought it was from a large animal. But upon further inspection, the bones appeared to be from a human. We immediately called the police and they confirmed that those bones were indeed human (from many years ago). They shut our job site down for two days while they performed an investigation and removed the remains. They never found out who the bones belonged to!"

With Anika's private loan accruing interest daily, they were motivated to get the duplex leased as quickly as possible. Showing strong rental income was also likely to boost the bank's refinance assessment, so Liz hired an aggressive local real estate agent to list and show the units. Within two weeks, she had secured two leases for $950 a month. As planned, Liz soared past the 1 percent rule and nearly hit an amazing 2 percent!

The next step was approaching a local community bank for the refinance. If the numbers came through as hoped, she would be able to pay back both the private loan and Jason's investment. The bank appraised the duplex for $150,000 with a cash-out option of $100,000 at 4.5 percent interest locked in for five years. The appraisal was far beyond the $50,000 purchase price and $50,000 rehab, confirming that they'd achieved an additional $50,000 in equity.

Insider Info Including Jason as a partner also benefited the LLC because his strong personal financial position helped secure the refinancing loan. He not only fronted the original $50,000 to acquire the property, but he also became an additional guarantor on the long-term loan.

Using the cash-out refinance to pay back Jason and Anika, Liz and Matt were then ready to start reaping that cash flow. Though Liz hadn't heard of the BRRRR (buy, rehab, rent, refinance, repeat) strategy yet, it described exactly what she'd done.

AFTERMATH

Liz created a solid, clean deal to give her business the boost it needed. To avoid a personal capital investment, she created both a partner and a private lender who were able to regain their original investments within six months. Beyond that, both units spun off tremendous cash flow until Liz, Matt, and Jason eventually decided to sell.

After seven years, they sold the duplex for $160,000—a profit of $60,000—and split it 50/50 with Jason as promised. It's been eight years since that sale, and wouldn't you know it—they've worked six more deals with Jason and five more with Anika since that time. It goes to show how making that first foray into working with other investors can propel your business onward and upward.

TAKEAWAY

Start Small and Build a Track Record

This deal was a quintessential base hit—the type of deal that leads to winning the game. You don't need to buy a huge multifamily to get started with private money lenders or partners. Quite honestly, it often makes sense to start with a single-family home—something real, tangible, and relatively easy to deal with. New investors don't necessarily want to start off lending tons of money, and they have good reason to be cautious. Start small, let people see that you're going to do what you say you'll do, and scale up from there.

> Liz says, "No matter what level, somebody needs something. Start getting experience, or if you already have experience but need a bigger cash pool, focus on creating a track record. Don't say, 'I'm just starting out' and dismiss what you've done—a track record is a track record. Show that this is where we are, this is what we've done, and this is where we want to go. Don't undersell yourself, but don't oversell yourself. Share your work with confidence. Lenders have money, you have time."

Don't Ask for Money—Offer an Opportunity

Offering to pay a private lender 12 percent interest on a loan should be perceived as an opportunity by both you *and* the potential lender. As a new investor, it's important to present your financing objective not as a need but as an opportunity your lender shouldn't miss out on.

Liz says, "Be willing to pivot your mindset. When people talk about private money, you're not asking for money, you're giving an opportunity. We gave our lenders an opportunity to make money while protecting their money."

Leverage Other People's Money (OPM)

Liz and Matt found both investors simply by leveraging their network. Liz says it best:

"Talk to everyone you know—not just real estate investing groups but business networking groups, fundraisers, accountants, attorneys, engineers, and so on. Lots of people want to invest but just don't have the time, so put yourself in situations where you'll connect. Be a resource for them, and let them be a resource for you."

Remember that giving up some equity is often a better option than putting your own money at risk. Liz and Matt gave up 50 percent of this deal's profit, but it ultimately spurred them forward when they were otherwise tapped out. Not only that, as they built trust with Jason, he became a partner for even more deals. Sure, they didn't walk away with 100 percent of the profit from the duplex's sale, but they more than made up for it with the numerous deals that followed.

CHAPTER NINETEEN

SHAWN WOLFSWINKEL

The Same-Day Purchase

Shawn Wolfswinkel was just a freshman in college when a late-night infomercial popped up on the television. It advertised a speaker who would soon be coming to town teaching how to build wealth through real estate with no formal training, no money, and no credit. Shawn didn't have any of those things, but he did have big ambition and the entrepreneurial itch.

He showed up for the event and the speaker ended up selling him on a wholesaling course and mentorship package. Lo and behold, it worked. While going to school, Shawn started wholesaling properties on his own and partnering with his mentor on several fix and flips.

> *"My parents had given me a small amount of money to attend college, and I ended up spending it all in the back of that room signing up for courses and mentorship. They were extremely angry with me when they found out—they had no idea where this would end up leading me. But as I saw it, I was an 'adult' and had to figure it out on my own. I was going to school in the morning and buying and selling houses in the afternoons and evenings. I did end up finishing to get*

*a degree in entrepreneurial studies. After graduation, I continued
to grow my real estate business and never looked back."*

Shawn's story is proof that you can start very young and with little
to no money. Out of the 1,650 deals he's turned in his career, he and his
wife, Joni, still manage 1,350 properties through their company, Texas
Turnkey Properties. They and their skilled team of thirty-four employees
find up to a hundred deals per year, specializing in buying, selling, and
managing properties for investment partners in Houston, Texas, and
Albuquerque, New Mexico.

Interestingly enough, Shawn entered the turnkey space specifically to
build a property management business. Many turnkey providers do it the
other way around, feeling forced into property management to help sell
their buy and holds. However, when Shawn saw how the value of a flipping
business mainly boils down to the current inventory's profit potential, he
opted instead for the reliable yearly residuals of property management.

Targeting single-family homes and duplexes, Shawn's company either
renovates or builds new construction to sell as turnkey, thereby creating
new property management clients. Occasionally, they flip or wholesale,
and no matter the method, the business focuses on providing exceptional
service to everyone involved.

Ken's Take I love the build-to-rent model, but it only makes sense when
you can find lots that are cheap enough. Shawn has created
huge demand for his new builds through the ability to sell for less than $100
per square foot—which is nearly impossible to find anywhere else. His company's secret is concentrating on infill lots, tear-downs, and dilapidated homes to
keep construction costs low. For marketing, they then put up their own bandit
signs on the land saying *We Buy Lots!* instead of *We Buy Houses!* After finding
these lots of one to seven acres, they build duplexes at 1,600 square feet, three
bedrooms, and two and a half baths per side. They sell for $285,000, rent for
$1,300 per door, and there are no HOAs.

You can understand why investors gobble these up! Shawn explains:

*"We've figured out how to cut costs by building quantity and fol-
lowing the same model over and over again. Plus, we get great deals
on the lots, so we manage to pass that on to the clients. As usual, I*

jumped right in when moving from rehabs to new construction. I made mistakes—overpaying for lots, buying where there was no sewer or water available, and so on. You live and learn. Now that we have things dialed down to the penny, the only real surprise issue has been thieves who target new construction."

FINDING THE DEAL

The thing about managing 1,300-plus properties is that it tends to keep you in touch with lots of construction professionals. When one of Shawn's Houston-based contractors was working for a woman named Nicole, his ears perked up when she mentioned a home in Round Rock, Texas, she wished to sell. Nicole's son was a "big-time" Houston developer who'd purchased the home for her decades earlier. She hadn't lived there in more than two years and was by now comfortably established in Houston.

The home had foundation issues, and rather than fix them, Nicole's son suggested it would be more profitable to knock everything down and build a new home to sell. His advice was to either get maximum value out of a new build or else sell for the land's value. Since neither Nicole nor her son wanted to undertake a construction project, she preferred to get it off the books as easily as possible.

Luckily for Shawn, his contractor immediately recognized an off-market seller who preferred a fast buyer over the hassles of time and paperwork. Since getting Shawn on board would mean a job either remodeling or building a new home, he picked up the phone.

ASSESSMENT

Round Rock was about three and a half hours from Shawn's Houston offices, but he knew it to be a popular upscale area near booming Austin, Texas. Public tax documents showed the assessed land value of the 1,707-square-foot, three-bedroom, two-bath property at $20,000, and Shawn knew it must be a mess of a house if Nicole wanted nothing beyond that. However, an online search showed the ranch-style home, built in 1978, to be in decent shape.

Shawn convinced a friend in Austin to drive by the property and set the story straight. By the friend's account, it not only looked perfectly livable but also stood in a lovely suburban residential neighborhood. It had been vacant for two years and needed a bit of work, but that didn't seem to extend past cosmetic touch-ups.

Figuring Nicole's asking price had to be a gimmick, Shawn called her up. When they discovered that she lived close to Shawn's Houston office, she invited him over to chat in person. She explained that she'd lived in the home for thirty years before moving to Houston, and although it was paid off, she never felt like making the long drive to deal with it. Ultimately, the whole situation just felt like a hassle.

Not knowing the extent of the foundation issue—and frankly, not caring—Nicole was adamant: She just wanted the land value. Shawn offered to cut Nicole a check right there, but she didn't feel comfortable taking his money before he saw the property for himself. Not wanting the deal to slip away, he borrowed the keys and promised to drive down that day. The thing was, the roads were smattered with black ice—a rarity in Texas—and the three-and-a-half-hour drive was now looking like a dangerous four-plus-hour slog.

"Houston is known for being hot and humid, right? But it freezes about five times a year, and for whatever reason, that day it had frozen and nearly everything was shut down. Roads were covered in black ice, and Texas vehicles just aren't equipped to handle that—everybody freaks out and stays home. I had a four-wheel drive truck, and I figured, 'Let's just go, and I'll figure it out.' If you hustle, you can make it in this business."

Ken's Take Many of you might be thinking that Nicole's son gave her bad advice. Was it Shawn's job to tell her she should reconsider? Ultimately, I don't believe it's up to the investor to decide what's the best use of someone else's time and money. Don't get me wrong: I don't think an investor should take advantage of ignorance—that crosses a moral line. However, this seemed like a clear case of *nonchalance*, not ignorance. Nicole likely could have found a buyer for more than $20,000 (even without fixing the foundation), but she preferred passing those savings along to someone else *as long as* it made her life easier. While most investors would agree that the son gave her "bad" advice, we simply don't know all the factors in play. My hunch is that, as far as he was concerned, his mom was already "set," and hassling with the home just wasn't worth their time.

Setting aside excuses, Shawn hit the road and found the home as expected. Yes, it needed updating—new paint, flooring, fixtures, and other hardware—but apart from that, the foundation was the only serious issue. Since nearly half the homes he'd ever dealt with had foundation problems (due to the shifting of Texas's clay-filled ground), he would just fix it—probably for less than $15,000. From there, he'd get a lifetime warranty on it and be good to go.

Insider Info A handful of intimidating home issues scare away most buyers, but they often spell opportunity. Mold, termites, fire damage, and foundation problems are the most common culprits, but knowing how to deal with them gives the savvy investor an edge. Having done more than 1,000 deals, Shawn wasn't put off by a trifling foundation problem.

Whatever he did with it, the bread-and-butter home would appeal to that area's largest buyer *and* tenant pools. Even as-is, Shawn guessed it could be worth an easy $135,000. At such a low purchase price, he figured a quick renovation for about $25,000 would make flipping the home the most lucrative turnaround option. Hopping back in the truck for the long trek home, Shawn put his cellphone to work. If he didn't strike while the iron was hot, another buyer might snag Nicole's amazing offer.

THE BREAKDOWN

Single-family home, 1,707 square feet
Round Rock, Texas
Asking $20,000

OFFER AND FUNDING

The wheels were in motion, but Shawn still wondered if he was somehow being conned. Suspecting that there must be an issue with the title or liens, he called up his title company. They quickly got to work, but at a cursory glance, everything was clean and taxes were current.

Ken's Take At the time, Shawn was doing lots of pre-foreclosure invest-ing, so he was accustomed to doing quick title pulls. While this deal's preliminary title search was not as thorough or extensive as it could have been with more time, he had enough information to merit taking the risk on this $20,000 deal. Even if issues did arise, they likely wouldn't cost more than what he could eventually get with a sale—even without lifting a finger on the home! It was a calculated risk, but one that would probably pay off.

The too-good-to-be-true deal was only hours away from becoming a reality, so Shawn arranged for a notary to meet him at Nicole's Houston home along with a prepared warranty deed. If he could swing it, he'd try to close that very night.

Arriving back at Nicole's house, Shawn cut her a check at the kitchen table and she signed the warranty deed over to him. Although he typically uses private lending, he decided to self-fund the predicted total cost of only $45,000 to keep up with the opportunity's whirlwind pace. He still lacked title insurance to protect that $20,000, but he'd hopefully wrangle that the next morning.

TURNAROUND

The contractor who found the deal was ready to get to work, so he simply moved into the home to carry out the flip and manage subcon-tractors. In the meantime, Shawn locked in a title policy on the house and found insurance, breathing a sigh of relief at getting all his bases covered.

As one team tackled the foundation issue, another got to work gussy-ing up curb appeal and rebuilding the backyard deck. From there, they modernized the kitchen and bathrooms and updated the home with recessed lighting, wood flooring, and granite countertops. With a fresh coat of paint inside and out, they wrapped up the job within a month.

AFTERMATH

The foundation work came with a $12,000 price tag, but the cosmetic turnaround only cost $13,000. Adding that to the purchase price, Shawn was all-in at just $45,000. Although he considered selling the property as a turnkey, he felt he'd be able to sell the house quicker and for more money on the retail market. He found a local Realtor, who quickly sold it on the local MLS for $165,000.

A mere fifty-five days had passed from getting the lead to closing with a new buyer—which is incredibly fast for a flip. Closing, commission, and other minor expenses came out to $18,000, netting Shawn a profit just shy of $100,000. It's definitely rare to clear six figures on a house that sells for only $165,000, but you hustle in this business long enough and eventually a deal like this will fall in your lap.

TAKEAWAY

Speed Is Everything

I've been in this business long enough to know that the early bird really does get the worm in real estate. There have been times when I pushed my team to immediately lock down a deal that ultimately paid big dividends. Other times, we dragged our feet and missed out on thousands in profit.

For Shawn, this meant driving to meet with Nicole in Houston, then driving more than seven hours in a day to visit her property, come back, and close before the end of the day. That's hustle, and it's why he pulled down almost $100,000. He puts it this way:

> *"The most important thing is that you're willing and prepared to act quickly. It's all about the hustle. My staff and I are currently reading a book called* Relentless: From Good to Great to Unstoppable, *by Tim Grover. He talks about the mindset of the cleaner [on a basketball team], summarizing it as 'Don't think, just act.' They are ready to step up when called.*
>
> *"We could have come up with a ton of excuses for why to wait on this deal—even to just push it back one day because of the ice on the road. But between now and then—especially in today's market—another investor can swoop in and snatch the deal away. If you don't act quickly, you don't get the deal."*

Taking Calculated Risks

Investing in real estate is 100 percent about risk and reward. What's the possible payoff for investing the time and money into finding, funding, and fixing a property? Even wholesalers, who don't necessarily take on the risk of ownership, must weigh the risks of putting up earnest money and investing time and reputation to get houses under contract.

Shawn had to carefully weigh the risk of buying a house with a foundation issue without knowing for sure that the title was 100 percent clean. However, with an opportunity to buy at well below the likely market value, the possible upside was ultimately worth a $20,000 risk.

Every investor has their own risk tolerance. Some are overly conservative—they tend to operate in the buy-and-hold space, use less leverage, and buy in "safe" neighborhoods that achieve moderate yields. At the other end of the spectrum are the gunslingers who never met a deal they didn't like and who never met a loan they weren't willing to guarantee. These are the investors who land a few whoppers over their careers but also rack up losses, often finding themselves over-leveraged and ultimately broke.

I would venture to say that most successful real estate investors land somewhere in the middle. They don't have an aversion to risk, but they only take risks that make financial sense. They study the numbers carefully—the comps, renovation, upside potential, and worst-case scenarios—before committing to a project. Over time, these wins (and occasional losses) stack on each other and build a balance sheet well beyond those of peers stuck in the 9-to-5 grind.

Use Your Personal Network to Source Deals

One of the coolest houses we renovated in season two of *Flip or Flop Atlanta* was a mansion on seven acres in Conyers, Georgia. In fact, it had such a striking facade that the house made the show opener for the entire second season. Interestingly, this house was brought to us by our HVAC contractor, with whom we'd done tons of business. When one of his employees was trying to help their family navigate a probate situation, our HVAC guy put us in touch.

Shawn's contractor thought of him as someone who could help Nicole, and the contractor also saw an opportunity to snag himself another gig. Plus, he got the benefit of saving on rent by living in the house at the same time—a win for both him and Shawn!

It's amazing how many deals will end up coming through your network. At any point in time, there's nearly always someone you know connected to a motivated seller. Whether it's a contractor, another real estate professional, or even an acquaintance, if people know what you do for a living, they *will* refer real estate opportunities to you. Sometimes it boils down to the fact that people just feel good about making connections.

The best way to capitalize on this is by making sure everybody knows what you do. This is where networking and social media really pay off. If you're constantly flipping houses but nobody in your circle knows what you're up to, you're missing out on the low-hanging fruit. Spend time letting friends know what you're looking for, bolster your social media with regular content about your work, and network with other industry professionals. Over time, this effort will absolutely reward you with new opportunities.

CHAPTER TWENTY

FELIPE MEJIA

Pioneering the Single-Family Room Rental

When Felipe's mother gave him the unconventional high school graduation gift of a mobile home, he house hacked it throughout college with a renter in the second bedroom. After college, he started a moving company in Tennessee and sold his mobile home, putting the profit toward a down payment on a three-bedroom single-family. He placed a long-term renter in one room and Airbnb guests in the others, so the mortgage was covered from the start.

By not spending a dime on living expenses since leaving home at 18, Felipe was tightening his grip on the power of passive income. Still, he kept growing his moving company while real estate remained a side hustle. After getting married and moving in with his wife, Cristina, he started renting out the third room in the home he'd left behind. When Cristina caught on to his rental numbers, she agreed to rent out the two spare bedrooms of their home. Felipe explains:

> *"The rooms were rarely empty, and the income was paying our mortgage. At this point, things really clicked. Someone, somewhere would always need a place to stay, and I could give them rooms. When the return on my time was greater with real estate, I left the moving business and became a full-time investor."*

Today Felipe owns eight (and counting) single-family homes, operating each bedroom within as a single-unit rental. Few of today's investors have even considered the rent-by-the-room model, but it's likely to become more and more prevalent in coming years. Felipe may be young, but he's an investing pioneer.

Though he inadvertently began building his real estate model in college, the wheels had actually begun turning in the aftermath of his mom and dad's divorce when he was only 11 years old. Felipe explains it best:

"When my dad left, so did the money. With the last of her savings, my mom added a bedroom in the home's downstairs to rent it out and supplement the income. She took her third-grade education and now runs two separate, successful businesses.

"Once I began investing myself, I asked her, 'Mom, what did you do in 2008?' With a straight face, she turned to me and asked, 'What happened in '08?' Which is to say, the crash didn't affect her at all. If anything, she had more tenants than she knew what to do with. My mom told me something important: 'If you want to get wealthy, get wealthy on Walmart money. Whether it's a downturn or an upturn, Walmart never closes its doors.'"

Felipe's target properties nearly always have an additional living space in the form of a simple basement and adjacent two-car garage. After purchasing, the formula is simple: Convert the basement into a large master suite with an adjacent kitchen, put two bedrooms and a bathroom in the garage, then provide separate entrances to both "units." It's a clear-cut business model targeting specific houses, specific renters, and a specific area that requires an approximate investment of $20,000 in each project.

Insider Info While renting individual rooms to different tenants is a great way to maximize rental income in a single-family home, it's important to check whether your municipality has an unrelated-persons ordinance before going down this road. Some cities and counties actually prohibit more than two or three unrelated people from living under the same roof.

FINDING THE DEAL

Felipe beats out investor competition by using specific, unique criteria to find homes. While most single-family investors seek low-cost, dilapidated options, Felipe targets homes built in 1960 to 1975 with three bedrooms and one bath, 1,400 to 1,800 square feet, and a value around $200,000.

Insider Info These smaller three-bedroom homes often lack a true master bedroom. This means that, on top of other investors passing over these properties, regular home buyers also tend to stay away in favor of homes with an existing master suite.

The MLS is all Felipe needs to find the single-family homes that meet his criteria, which keeps acquisition costs to a minimum. Whenever his Realtor finds something, they schedule the soonest available viewing, and the home is usually there for the taking.

"Nobody's looking for these properties. If I go online right now, I'll find three or four that I can make bids on. Since nobody else is buying them, I can underbid by 20 percent and still get them much of the time. Who's looking for a three-bedroom, one-bath home with no true master, a two-car garage, and a fifteen-by-twenty basement space? It sounds like a big waste of space, but I see gold."

Knowing your market is key, and Felipe can typically gauge a home's potential just by knowing the street it's on. So when his Realtor called him up a couple years ago about a $220,000 home that seemed to check all the boxes, he was so confident in the details that he asked his plumber, electrician, and framer to join him for the viewing so they could immediately form a plan of action.

ASSESSMENT

The solid brick home was well built, with no structural issues or need for exterior touch-ups. With three bedrooms and one bath, the home was practically rent-ready as it stood. It was located in a quaint

Class B residential neighborhood with nearby access to the interstate.

A stairway led down to an unfinished basement with one large "room" and a door leading to the garage. Wasting no time, Felipe had his plumber and framer draw up plans, discussing options with the electrician so they would all be ready come game time. They estimated between $15,000 and $18,000 to build out the lower level and garage, which gave Felipe confidence that the home would fit his model perfectly.

"In real estate, it's all about time, efficiency, and staying in front of the curve. My rule is that we need to be able to renovate the property within thirty days in order to move on to the next project. In the assessment, my plumber ensures the ease of adding an extra bathroom, and my electrician makes sure the electrical box has space to add the extra kitchen and bedrooms. If we need extra space or permitting on these two big issues, I don't buy the property."

Ken's Take Felipe goes far to make sure he's not walking into something that will hurt him later. Most investors pay for a typical inspection before buying a house, but Felipe takes it a step further by paying to have his skilled laborers on-site. Not only do they inspect for issues Felipe might not catch, they also map out a game plan and a specific bid to transition the property into Felipe's rental model.

THE BREAKDOWN

Single-family home, 1,400 square feet
Nashville, Tennessee
Asking $220,000

OFFER AND FUNDING

Felipe came in with an offer of $180,000, knowing full well that he would go up to $200,000 if he had to. With a bit of haggling, they landed at $190,000. A local bank loaned him 20 percent down at 5 percent interest, and he planned to use his own money for the renovation. After letting the loan season for about a year, Felipe would pull his cash back out of the home using a line of credit (that his local bank would provide against the same house), then recycle the funds into yet another project.

Insider Info A commercial equity line of credit is a simple way to tap into a home's equity without the hassle of refinancing. Granted, the maximum loan-to-value (LTV) ratio that most banks will lend on a non-owner-occupied property isn't nearly as aggressive as on an owner-occupied home, but for investors with strong equity—either through original cash invested or through appreciation—a line of credit can still be a great tool to access that equity quickly.

TURNAROUND

With the renovation plans already mapped out during the pre-purchase inspection, all Felipe's team had to do was follow the formula. Just like the three homes they had already flipped, this one would get a master suite with a private entrance in the large, lower-level den; two 10' × 10' bedrooms, a 5' × 8' bathroom, and a private entrance in the garage; and a small kitchen accessible to both units.

The crew broke ground by removing the garage door and closing off the space to match the exterior as closely as possible to the home's existing aesthetic. Then they framed everything out and put the pieces in place. After they knocked out electrical, plumbing, drywall, and paint, what was once a basement and garage became two mini-apartments almost overnight.

Ken's Take An interesting feature of Felipe's renovation process is that many of his renters are also traveling professional laborers. With their six- to twelve-month job contracts, they often find it easier and more cost-effective to rent a room than an apartment. By providing their housing, Felipe also has a direct line to professionals who are often interested in taking up an extra side hustle. Leveraging this renter base creates a cash flow win-win: Felipe gets a deal on labor, and the laborer gets a deal on rent. This symbiosis means most of his renovation expenses go to material costs.

At just three and a half weeks in, Felipe was ready to rent out all the units. There will always be people needing a place to live for less than $600 a month, and by being one of the few landlords providing this option to transient renters—cooks, nurses, construction workers, and so on—Felipe was thriving on word of mouth alone. Although he'd used online listings to advertise rooms in the earlier homes he'd rented, by the time this deal was finished, his reputation had created a waiting list of potential tenants. He explains:

"I get renters the same way the restaurant in your hometown is always in business and the same way that barber shop in your town always seems to be full: consistency with my product."

AFTERMATH

With a $190,000 purchase, $20,000 in renovations, and $10,000 in purchase and finance expenses, Felipe was all-in at $220,000 with $1,100 in monthly PITI (principal, interest, taxes, and insurance). The three upstairs rooms ended up garnering a hefty $1,500 per month at $500 each. Plus, by creating and renting the lower-level master and two-room space for $700 each, Felipe scored an extra $1,400 in pure cash flow. He left the 1 percent rule in the dust!

"Most investors might stop at a three-bedroom house, renting out the rooms at $500 each and thinking, 'Fine, it's close to the 1 percent rule.' But that's a model that may or may not work. If my mortgage is $1,200, I wouldn't get out of bed for just an extra $300 a month. When I was getting into real estate and really thinking about what I wanted to do, I wondered: 'How do people live off this 1 percent rule? I don't want one hundred houses in order to retire—I want ten.'"

Ken's Take One of the great things about Felipe's business model is that he rarely has to worry about negative cash flow. Unlike a traditional single-family rental, where a vacant house means zero revenue, Felipe's multi-unit approach spreads the risk across multiple renters. At any given time, he could have one or even two units vacant and he's still cash-flow positive. It's similar to a multifamily property in this regard. Felipe says, *"I have to lose 40 percent of my tenants to get down to a point where I'm just breaking even."*

By now, Felipe has developed eight homes just like this one, and by following the same formula every time, he's achieving at least $1,400 in monthly cash flow on each property. What started as a convenient college house hack has grown into a scalable model that will continue fueling his success as a multi-tenant landlord and investor.

TAKEAWAY

Know When to Go

When I went into real estate full-time, I literally walked into my boss's office one day and quit. My Fortune 500 corporate job promised a great career path, but I knew it wasn't for me, and I couldn't fake it any longer. Luckily, even in my blind naivete, I was able to grind it out that first year as an investor and more than replace my corporate income. However, after being in this business for fifteen years, I'm not so sure that strategy makes the most sense for everyone.

Felipe took a calculated approach toward leaving his moving business. Once he had purchased enough houses and figured out a replicable model, the return on his time became higher with his real estate business than with his moving business. At that point, the decision was easy: He let the moving business go and spent his time building real estate investments.

Unless you've saved up a decent amount of runway to go full-time as an investor, a gradual transition might make more sense. Many of our coaching students have taken this approach and successfully left the workplace when the timing felt right. While the thought of working a full-time job and a real estate side hustle may seem overwhelming, it's often the smarter way to transition into full-time real estate.

See Space Differently

Real estate investing comes with the ever-present need for creative and analytical thinking. Finding ways to increase value and rents with existing space is one of the greatest real estate art forms. Whether it's finishing out an attic or a basement or just finding room to squeeze in another bathroom, these types of creative decisions can have a huge impact on sale and rental pricing.

Any given property has innumerable strategies for capitalizing on potential upside: Is it better to flip or buy and hold? To tear down and build new or renovate? A modest $30,000 renovation or a high-end $90,000 renovation? Finish out the basement for extra square footage or leave it be? These questions bounce around my office daily.

Felipe saw an asset that nobody else considered an attractive investment and *made* it profitable by reconfiguring the space for the highest possible ROI. While a downstairs living area might be nice for a traditional tenant, it doesn't necessarily bump up the rent. The same goes for a two-car garage—it's nice, but plenty of tenants live in homes without garages. By taking these two spaces and creating *three* new rentable rooms, Felipe produced an extra $1,400 per month.

Know Your Niche

Felipe grew up with room rentals, house hacked through college, and rented out Airbnb rooms. His community's need for room rentals was as obvious to him as its need for single-family homes or apartment complexes. When the lightbulb went off that he could make providing them his *living*, Felipe was off to the races.

Countless investors avoid focusing on niches where they've seen measurable success in favor of continuing to experiment—like the guy who decides to open up a "new market" in another state when he's barely scraped the surface in his own backyard. Or the agent who shuttles buyers around in her car on the weekend, works on a flip an hour away, and is also trying to manage a couple of rentals for a friend. By spreading themselves thin, they often lose the ability to really capture economies of scale. (I know because I've been guilty of it over the years!)

There isn't anything inherently wrong with trying to expand, but it's often a misguided way to grow and scale. People like Felipe, Zeona McIntyre (Chapter 17) and Jack Bosch (coming up in Chapter 25) find their niche early and stick with it. It may not be sexy, but it builds serious cash flow. If there's one thing I've learned through interviewing hundreds of real estate investors over the years, it's that focusing on a specific niche is often the fastest way to scale a successful business.

CHAPTER TWENTY-ONE

ANDRESA GUIDELLI

Candy Shop Triplex

Brazilian-born Andresa Guidelli landed stateside in 2008 to earn a master's in business communication from La Salle University in Philadelphia. However, after reading *Rich Dad Poor Dad* during her last semester, she pivoted away from the world of business suits and conference rooms and toward the world of real estate.

Inspired by the book, she dived into educating herself on real estate and purchased her first live-in flip within six months. Although she "definitely overpaid for construction," she got that first investment out of the way and was ready for more. (For the record, she still maintains this property as a cash-flowing rental, and its value has more than doubled!) Andresa recalls:

> "*My husband at that time spent a lot of time analyzing the market and understanding each block of the neighborhood we were considering buying into. This property came on the market during Memorial Day weekend, and I remember vividly that I called our Realtor and said, 'Jack, we need to see this house ASAP.' He said it was a holiday weekend, so he was unavailable.*
>
> "*Then, my Italian heritage kicked in and I said, 'Jack, I love*

working with you and I would like to continue. I am telling you I am going to see this property tomorrow morning with or without you.' The next day, we were the first ones inside that house—and we immediately made a full-price offer and closed 45 days later!"

Andresa bootstrapped her way through a few more residential flips, advancing the learning curve one deal after another. Scaling quickly, she was a full-time real estate investor within only five years—overseeing up to fifteen flips at a time and even incorporating new construction into her portfolio.

These days, while managing her own renovation and construction projects, Andresa is also the director of real estate development for a Philadelphia firm that focuses on medium to large commercial developments. In her "spare" time, she co-hosts *The Real Estate InvestHER Show*, a podcast she co-created with Liz Faircloth (who you met in Chapter 18) to highlight and inspire female real estate investors. In addition to wearing all those hats, Andresa also manages a personal portfolio of rental properties.

Although Andresa is undeniably a skilled multitasker, she relies on a special sauce of automated systems and foolproof processes created to ensure efficiency and quality every step of the way. One of her favorite investing strategies is using multifamily properties for long- and short-term rentals, and you'll soon learn why.

FINDING THE DEAL

Andresa was on-site rehabbing a small home in the South Philly neighborhood of East Passyunk when she noticed garbage bags and furniture being jettisoned to the curb from a neighboring building. Like any good investor, she had an inkling that the property was being prepared for new ownership. If it was about to hit the market, she wanted to be the first investor to know.

After unsuccessful attempts to reach out to the owners using the contact information listed on the local tax assessor's website, Andresa discovered through a neighbor that they had passed away. Assuming the home had likely gone into probate, Andresa checked a local public notices website, confirmed her suspicion, and located the phone number for the estate's executor. The executor was happy to hear from Andresa—she'd been overwhelmed with paperwork, so selling directly (rather than using public auction) would ultimately make her life easier.

Ken's Take While probate situations are certainly not the happiest of buying scenarios, they do tend to be great acquisition opportunities. Some investors go online or to the local courthouse to look up public probate records, but you can usually find someone selling a list of these properties—at a premium price. We have students who have even built relationships with probate attorneys and sourced consistent seller leads through these relationships.

ASSESSMENT

The property was a three-story 4,500-square-foot traditional brick and wood-frame home with each level (including a basement) connected by interior stairs. Though the house was originally built to be a triplex, one family had been living in both the second and third stories for decades, taking it upon themselves to convert the two levels into a "single-family" with six bedrooms and only one kitchen. Meanwhile, they'd been operating the first floor as a (recently shuttered) candy store since 1950.

Just two miles south of the city center, East Passyunk was a stable residential neighborhood with charming parks and traditional historic brick buildings. It was a highly walkable foodie hot spot that was growing increasingly popular among young families who worked in the city but didn't want to pay city prices. Plus, it was near a large hospital, making it ideal for traveling nurses whose rental costs were covered by stipends.

The executor informed Andresa that the first floor was zoned with a residential option that no longer existed in Philadelphia. However, given the candy store, the zoning regulation had been ignored anyway. This meant that the first-floor zoning existed in a type of no-man's land, and if Andresa wanted to do any construction on the property, she would need to apply for new zoning permits.

Insider Info It is of the utmost importance to understand current and desired zoning during the due diligence phase of a purchase. Don't assume that your code violation or noncompliance will be "grandfathered" in. This is especially true for properties that aren't in compliance and require some amount of work. The simple act of obtaining a permit can trigger a municipality to require that your property be brought into compliance with current zoning regulations. Be sure to understand all these implications *before* you purchase a property.

The second and third stories were properly zoned as separate residential units, so Andresa wouldn't have to deal with zoning permits on that front. But the family's unpermitted reconstruction had created a layout that simply wouldn't work—one of the units wouldn't even have a kitchen!

Unless Andresa opted to sell as-is or wholesale the home, a profitable flip would require a full gut and reconstruction. It wouldn't come easy, either—not only was the renovation projected to cost $150,000, but the building was utterly full of stuff the family had left behind: furniture, clothes, store supplies, and endless odds and ends that would need to be cleared out.

If Andresa could find a purchase price that worked, she envisioned restoring the property to a true triplex and renting out each level for a total of $4,500 monthly. As it stood, she predicted the building's value hovered around $250,000. With a solid renovation to bring in competitive rental income, Andresa foresaw getting the appraisal number up to $600,000. If she was right, she'd refinance (the BRRRR method at its finest) for a cash-out loan to cover the purchase and renovation costs, hopefully with cash left over for future investments.

While nearly all renovation projects come with unpredictable setbacks, Andresa's plan already had one glaring hitch: The zoning board could ultimately reject her application to zone the first level as residential. Since it had operated for decades as a candy store, they might decide to apply commercial zoning instead. Though a mixed-use property wasn't ideal, Andresa was confident that it would still be profitable.

In any case, Andresa's total investment needed to work under the best- and worst-case scenarios. It was too early to know what the board would say, but if she didn't make an offer soon, the executor would auction the property at an upcoming estate sale.

THE BREAKDOWN

Triplex, 4,500 square feet
East Passyunk, Philadelphia, Pennsylvania
Pending auction

OFFER AND FUNDING

Regular single-family homes in the neighborhood were selling for $180,000 to $200,000, but knowing the construction expense would be massive, Andresa offered $210,000 for the property as-is—meaning the executor could offload it without having to deal with clearing out the property's leftover items. They went back and forth on the number a couple times, but thanks to having developed a rapport at a few in-person meetings, they eventually agreed on a sale price of $230,000, which Andresa would pay under a traditional bank loan.

Having just purchased a much smaller *single*-family property down the street for $200,000 (which also needed a complete gut), Andresa knew she'd scored a great price. The property was still in probate, though, so paperwork and litigation would prevent them from closing for another three months.

Although a three-month waiting period is typically not ideal, Andresa had a plan to make it work in her favor. The executor, as the property's interim caretaker, was the only person allowed to apply for rezoning. But if Andresa could get the executor to confer these rights to her, she could go ahead and apply for the permits before closing. If the zoning board approved everything, not only could she get started on the renovation but the property would likely get a higher appraisal, and therefore a more favorable loan, for the purchase. Securing the zoning as soon as possible also meant that Andresa would skip the holding costs of applying for permits *after* the purchase—a process that often takes up to three months (or more!).

> *"My construction numbers and ARV were all based on a triplex, so I really needed to get the property zoned as such. Otherwise, my*

lender would not be able to lend 75 percent LTV and 100 percent on the renovation if the zoning was not corrected prior to closing."

Nevertheless, it was a risky gambit: After investing time and money into zoning applications, Andresa still faced the chance that the sale could fall through. She worked with a real estate attorney to carefully vet the title and probate situation, and they concluded that since the sale was likely to proceed without a hitch, it was a worthwhile gamble. Luckily, the executor formally agreed to allow Andresa to begin rezoning the property, and Andresa was off to the races.

Ken's Take Starting the rezoning and permitting process before owning the property is only advisable if you're comfortable taking a gamble that the deal may or may not close. Putting time and money into permits only to end up with a canceled deal can be a big blow! Similarly, purchasing a property with the hopes of obtaining a particular zoning can be risky as well. The zoning board may simply have a different idea for the property. Ultimately, a move like this is only advisable if the numbers make sense in any zoning scenario.

To boost the odds of approval for the zoning variance, Andresa first aimed to garner support from the community. She knew that proof of community interaction can go a long way toward securing support from the local government, so she arranged to speak at a community meeting to educate the neighbors on the proposed project.

The proposal fit well with the area, but the neighbors inexplicably wanted nothing to do with the triplex plans—but they didn't want a commercial store, either. It seemed like the only thing they *knew* they wanted was to say no to any proposal. Andresa was at a loss.

"In the midst of all the disapproval, there was a very funny moment. One of the neighbors stood up and asked me if I was planning on keeping the chicken coop on the roof. I was extremely confused, and a board member clarified by saying, 'Sir, that's not a chicken coop, it's called a pilothouse. That's how people access the roof deck.'"

Without community support, the odds of getting a zoning variance granted were diminished, but Andresa remained hopeful that the city would come around to her vision. She then set up a meeting to make her case to the zoning board. After she highlighted how the property was initially built as a triplex and would fit in perfectly with the numerous surrounding multifamily properties, they approved her plans without a hitch. It's a beautiful thing when governments are easy to work with!

Three months in, Andresa was permitted, the probate process was finished, and both parties were ready to close. A local bank gave her an interest-only loan for $323,000 at 10 percent interest, which required an out-of-pocket equity contribution of about $50,000 but also included $150,000 for the renovation. Content with these terms, Andresa closed on the project and got to work.

TURNAROUND

The first step was working with a construction team to clean out the property and strip it down to the studs for the remodel. Working from the bottom up, Andresa began dividing the basement into extra living space for the first-floor unit and separate storage spaces for the other two units. They'd barely begun when they discovered that the support beams between the basement and the first floor were almost entirely rotted. It was an ominous start. Tapped out on the bank loan, Andresa had to dip into personal savings for the extra $50,000 it took to refortify the foundation.

Insider Info Andresa was fortunate to have the personal savings to deal with the foundation, but not everybody has $50,000 lying around. As you saw in Liz Faircloth's deal, this type of situation can also be remedied with a private lender or equity partner. While you'll likely have to give up more of a stake to bring additional capital into the project, doing so can be a deal-saving maneuver.

Luckily, the rest of the renovation went according to plan: new framing, drywall, paint, doors, windows, HVAC, electric, plumbing, and finishes. In an effort to create efficiencies with the new layout and utility installations, they stacked all three kitchens and bathrooms directly on top of each other. They also separated out the utilities on every floor to ensure that each unit was metered independently.

Ken's Take When renting out small multifamily units or even separate spaces within a single unit, it's *much* easier to make tenants responsible for their own utilities. When utility usage isn't separated across multiple tenants, it often falls upon the owner to cover the utility bill, then attempt to collect these expenses from the tenants. This just creates more work for everybody. The other option is to attempt to include utility costs in the rental price. As a landlord, I can tell you this is never an ideal scenario; utility costs often exceed what you've budgeted for (there's always that person who takes thirty-minute showers), but you've formally agreed to be the one to pay them.

As things shaped up over the ensuing six months of renovation, Andresa predicted that the first floor—with a basement and backyard—would rent for around $1,700 a month. The middle unit—the smallest one and without an outside area—could operate as an Airbnb and earn $1,300 to $1,800 per month. The third floor—smaller, but with a roof deck—would hopefully fetch $1,625.

AFTERMATH

With $50,000 added on top of the estimated rehab of $150,000, Andresa was all-in at about $430,000. She paid a local property manager the equivalent of one month's rent to show the property and qualify tenants, and as predicted, between the two long-term rental units and the middle Airbnb unit, total rent came in at nearly $4,600 from the start. With an outgoing interest payment of about $3,000 per month on her bank loan, that meant immediate cash flow of more than $1,000 per month!

With renters in place, it was time to refinance. Small multifamily properties are typically valued based on two approaches: the *comparable sales approach* and the *income approach*. Since there weren't many comparable sales in the area, Andresa knew that rental income would have to play a strong part in proving the property's new, higher value.

Insider Info As a property owner, it's important to identify strong comps and highlight income compared with other similar properties in an effort to help maximize the property's appraised value. Appraisers aim to be objective, but none are immune to overly conservative valuations.

Andresa estimated that a new appraisal should come in at $600,000 minimum. When the appraisal came back at $560,000—a whopping $130,000 above her all-in cost—she was still somewhat disappointed. Philadelphia is dense, so she figured the appraiser's familiarity with the neighborhood wasn't as granular as her own. Confident that there had been a mistake, she decided to challenge his number.

Challenging a lender's appraisal requires a thorough defense, so Andresa began poring through the report. She quickly noticed a few key flaws:

1. The triplex's sale value had been compared with properties that were zoned as *single*-family residences. Of course, it should have been compared with other multifamilies.
2. The zip codes used for comparison were too far away. In downtown Philadelphia, property values vary greatly from street to street, let alone zip to zip.
3. Some of the rental comps were for multifamilies that weren't actually being rented; the appraiser was using their *estimated* rental income value.

With the report's inconsistencies outlined, Andresa created her own opinion of value for the lender's review. The bank informed her that they would need the original appraiser's approval before reviewing her proposal, so Andresa prepared herself for a mildly awkward phone call to the appraiser. Politely informing him of her real estate experience and familiarity with the area, she requested consent for the bank to review her appeal. The appraiser agreed—perhaps Andresa's business communications degree came in handy here—and she quickly sent off the confirmation.

Ken's Take If you spend any amount of time in real estate, it won't take long to learn that disappointing appraisals are not uncommon. Rather than react emotionally (which is an understandable response), it's important to remember that there are rational steps you can take to solve the problem. Andresa knew that she had plenty of ammunition to discredit the original valuation approach—all she had to do was keep cool while making her case. While some appraisers won't budge on their "expertise," many will be reasonable enough to consider additional data.

After a week of bated-breath waiting, the new appraisal came back at $675,000—$115,000 higher than the initial number and $245,000 higher than Andresa's all-in cost. Under a new refinance, she was able to cash out up to 75 percent of the appraised value. With this, she reimbursed herself for the original equity investment and out-of-pocket repairs *and* created an additional $76,000 of equity.

Insider Info If you've created enough equity—either through a below-market purchase or renovation or through an appreciating market—consider the potential of either (a) an equity line against the property, or (b) refinancing your primary loan in order to access new increased equity.

Remember, pulling equity out of a property is not considered taxable income. In Andresa's case, she was able to deposit $76,000 of tax-free money into her bank account to put toward other investments.

TAKEAWAY

Communicate with the Community

Andresa left Brazil for the cold Philadelphia winters to get a master's degree in business communication. Many people wonder why she traded in her degree for a real estate career, but to Andresa:

> *"Real estate is all about communication—it comes down to how well you communicate, how well you engage with the seller and the buyer, and deal negotiation."*

Andresa didn't just create equity through a solid renovation, she created equity through research and communication. Her ability to sniff out a potential deal and work with the seller to navigate the probate process enabled her to capitalize on this opportunity. Throughout the process, Andresa also communicated with neighbors and local zoning boards to source and structure a project that ended up being a highly profitable venture.

Pursue the Highest and Best Use

Andresa likely could have purchased the property and renovated it as a single-family residence. Perhaps she could have sold it to an owner-occupant and turned a modest profit. However, she quickly identified that the highest profit potential for this property was as a triplex. This particular neighborhood commanded high rents, and by splitting the building into three rentable units, she achieved a total rental income that was out of the park.

As investors, it's important to analyze the highest profit potential for any given project. If it's feasible to rezone a particular property and the time and cost aren't prohibitive, why *not* take that approach? If a few thousand dollars in legal expenses could net an additional $50,000 to $100,000 in profit, I would argue that rezoning is worth pursuing.

Don't Settle for Less

It's easy to assume that banks, brokers, and appraisers are part of a secret club that doesn't care about what any of us outsiders bring to the table. But the people behind the titles are just people, and many of them are more reasonable than you might think. Instead of being angry or giving up, Andresa kept her cool, put in hours of work to research a new appraisal value, and ultimately scored a valuation $115,000 higher than the initial appraiser's number. That's an amazing rate of return for the work she invested!

In fact, Andresa had done this before. On her very first home purchase, the bank initially quoted a home equity line of credit (HELOC) of $25,000. Andresa didn't realize it was uncommon to go against the appraiser report, so she put together her own report, got in touch with the appraiser, and ended up raising the HELOC to $68,000.

CHAPTER TWENTY-TWO

CORY BOATRIGHT

Short Sale to Tall Profit

One of my favorite things about Cory Boatright is that he's an investor who will admit he can't *stand* doing rehabs. After cutting his teeth more than twenty years ago as a bird dog for Oklahoma City wholesalers, he realized his time would be better spent finding deals for himself. In light of the heavy competition among wholesalers and his aversion to rehabs, he would need to find a unique niche for himself.

When Cory stumbled across the concept of short sales, a lightbulb went off. Nobody else seemed to be doing them, even though Oklahoma's laws were extremely favorable toward the practice. He began learning everything he could and, as they say, the rest is history. Cory's companies now manage more than 430 doors through apartment syndications, wholesale more than one hundred single-family houses a year, and own more than $20 million in real estate holdings.

Cory credits his success to reliable systems and processes carried out by an even more reliable team. Still based in Oklahoma, his ten-person team handles acquisitions, dispositions, transactions, underwriting, and project management. Over the years, his aim has shifted to scoring wholesale deals while cherry-picking off-market multifamilies (particularly affordable housing) for syndications or an occasional short sale.

FINDING THE DEAL

Even in his bird dog days, Cory knew that the best thing to score was an off-market deal. Having worked in Oklahoma for more than twenty years, he could count on his network as the best source for such deals. However, direct-to-seller marketing techniques like mailers, texts, cold calls, and pay-per-click advertising also help him zero in on properties whose owners are motivated to sell.

To this end, Cory was compiling a pre-foreclosure list for Oklahoma City in 2008 when he noticed an address in the renowned historic neighborhood of Heritage Hills. Knowing that renovated homes in that area sold quickly for prices anywhere between $500,000 and $2 million, Cory called the owner to get the scoop.

The owner was grateful to hear from someone who might be able to help, but the outlook was grim: The home had zero equity *and* three mortgages owing more than $530,000. The owner had no way to even come close to paying off the mortgages, and only sixty days remained before he would lose the title to foreclosure.

Cory knew that if he could convince the lenders to take a discount on the home's debt, he might have a deal on his hands. Enter the "short sale," in which a property sells for a lower ("shorter") price than its principal balance.

Insider Info Remember, it was 2008 and the recession was in its heyday. Home values had plummeted and myriad lenders were left stranded with upside-down mortgage notes. In an effort to get these underwater assets off their balance sheets, banks were motivated to discount mortgage notes and allow properties to sell for far short of their principal balances—hence the name "short sale."

ASSESSMENT

Meander down the streets of Heritage Hills, and you'll see château-like mansions, statuesque elms, and exquisitely manicured lawns—but the house Cory went to see was an absolute eyesore. Standing three stories tall with seven bedrooms, three and a half baths, and 4,670 square feet of living space, it had once been a majestic Victorian home.

Now the paint was peeling, there were holes in many of the walls, the roof leaked, and cockroaches scurried around as if they owned the place. A musty smell emanated from the basement, and Cory descended to find standing water and splotches of mold along the walls. The smell was overpowering, but Cory still smelled money—he knew that mold discourages most investors while encouraging discounted prices.

Amid the disrepair, Cory could see strong structural bones and huge potential. Much of the property—including the staircase, doorknobs, hardwood flooring, and crown molding—was original. On the plus side, neighborhood residents would certainly support a full rehab, but on the downside, the rehab would be tedious, pricey, and historically exacting.

Nonetheless, Cory had been in the market long enough to know that certain niche buyers would lose their minds for the opportunity to restore a home like this. If he could snag it before they did, he could turn around and sell it for a cool profit. Time, however, was running out—he would have to act fast and negotiate smart.

Ken's Take Renovating homes in a historic district can be a double-edged sword. These areas are often in high demand, so homes can fetch top-end pricing. However, local historical commissions are usually involved, and they can slow down projects and impose unreasonable requirements in an effort to maintain "historical integrity." Sometimes, the work and tedium involved make the profit not worthwhile. As with all things real estate, know the forces you're up against and approach on a case-by-case basis.

As for the mortgages, the first loan was for $400,000, the second for $100,000, and the third for $30,000. This insane debt had turned away most traditional off-market investors because they simply weren't considering the possibility of negotiating these loans down. However, Cory suspected higher odds of a successful short sale since the home had more than one mortgage. Essentially, banks would look at all those loans and realize how hopeless it was to expect to get their money back. As Cory describes it:

> *"Debtors can either take what's offered from a purchaser or risk the very likely chance of the house going into foreclosure. If that happens, they won't get anything out of the deal. In situations like these,*

it's not uncommon for a debtor asking $100,000 to take $5,000 to $10,000 and simply exit the deal. The fact is, there isn't a better alternative—they're going to take what they can instead of foreclosing."

THE BREAKDOWN

Single-family home, 4,670 square feet
Heritage Hills Historic District,
Oklahoma City, Oklahoma
$530,000 owed to three mortgage lenders;
asking unknown

OFFER AND FUNDING

With Cory as his only hope, the homeowner signed a letter of authorization to give him negotiation rights with the lenders. Cory explained on the phone with the first lender that the only way to prevent foreclosure would be with substantial debt forgiveness. In response, they sent a real estate broker out to assess the property and submit a broker price opinion (BPO) of its value. The broker would then submit the BPO to the lender, and from there, they'd land on a new "asking" price to pay off the mortgage.

Cory predicted that the property would appraise for around $550,000—but he didn't tell the broker this. If they appraised it for *lower*, then all the better. When the broker clutched his stomach and dry heaved from the overpoweringly musty basement, the appraisal came in at $350,000!

The foreclosure clock was ticking down. Knowing that the first-position lender was motivated to unload this property rather than proceed with foreclosure paperwork, Cory decided to take an aggressive approach and offer a mere $220,000 for the property. While the lender wasn't quite willing to swallow that big of a loss, they did agree to accept $250,000.

TURNAROUND

With a settled price for the first-position loan, Cory still needed to negotiate a payoff for the second- and third-position lenders. Since the first-position lender would have to approve any money put toward the junior loans, Cory got them all on a conference call to duke it out. As he describes it:

> *"The junior lenders realized they were in second and third positions. They knew they wouldn't get anything if the property went to auction. It was fun getting them on a three-way call and listening to them argue back and forth on who should get what."*

After this multilevel negotiation, Cory agreed to a total offer of $261,000—$250,000 for the first lender, $10,000 for the second, and only $1,000 for the third. The homeowner, having been so trapped by the debt and impending credit destruction, felt lucky just to be walking away without a foreclosure on his credit history.

Insider Info To put it bluntly, the first-position loan/lender holds all the cards in the lender hierarchy. When there's more than one loan on the house, they have priority position on any collateral in the case of a foreclosure liquidation event. Such an event likely wouldn't get them their entire loan back, but they would at least get proceeds from the sale of the property.

If the first-position lender opts for foreclose, that completely wipes out any junior loans. As such, when negotiating short sales with multiple lenders, the "junior" lenders are lucky to recoup much—if any—of their principal balance.

With the house on its way to Cory's inventory, he needed to decide how to pay for it and what to do about the rehab. As you're probably learning, it pays to be connected: A contractor friend who specialized in historic repairs called Cory about a possible buyer. The man in question coveted historic homes, and the contractor predicted he'd buy it at any price. If this turned out to be true, Cory could utilize what's known as a "double close," essentially buying and reselling the home in a single stroke.

Cory reached out to the historic home connoisseur, and the contractor was right—the man had been eyeing the home for years. They landed on a sale price of $430,000 cash, covering Cory's $261,000 purchase price and leaving a $169,000 profit. And just a reminder: Cory hadn't lifted a finger on the property.

AFTERMATH

Cory essentially bought and sold the house at the same time, describing it as "using the B-to-C to pay the A-to-B." Using funds from the second buyer to make the initial purchase means he never had to secure funding for the deal, let alone pay any interest.

Insider Info While Cory's score was common among short sales back in 2008, many banks have since caught on and begun imposing deed restrictions. These rules set a limit on the percentage increase at which an investor can resell the property during a specific time frame following the initial purchase.

Although Cory's buyer originally planned to do a fix-and-flip, he loved the property so much that he ended up living there. Plus, by working with the historical society, he earned credits toward fixing up the house in accordance with historical standards. For every dollar he spent, he earned 25 cents as a tax credit—a hefty sum when you put thousands into a rehab! In short: Cory breezed through a purchase and sale, the homeowner got a fresh start, and the second buyer was elated. It was a true win-win-win for all three—just maybe not for the banks.

TAKEAWAY

Don't Let Lack of Equity Scare You Away

Most people assume that a house with a mortgage (or multiple mortgages) above or near the home's value are a lost cause for investing. Cory's story clearly illustrates that this doesn't always have to be the case.

As usual, it's important to get *all* the facts before deciding whether or not to pursue an opportunity. For pre-foreclosure properties, the devil is definitely in the details. Just as in Cory's deal, multiple loans may lead to a negotiation resulting in better terms and numbers than if there were only a single loan. When you are solutions-oriented, who knows what you might come up with to save the day? Particularly when banks are involved, try to empathize with them, even if that's a scary idea. Ultimately, a foreclosure doesn't work in their favor.

Profit Potential: Change Your Mindset

This particular deal changed a lot of things for Cory, including his bank balance. But the most important change was in his thinking. Up to that point, he had been making between $5,000 and $10,000 on wholesale deals. He knew there was more to be made out there, though, so he searched for new investment techniques and educated himself on the short sale niche.

When he found the home in Heritage Hills, he didn't look at it with a wholesaler's perspective—a wholesaler would have simply walked away. Instead, he was thinking like a short-sale investor. Not only was the $169,000 profit a home run—it was a complete game changer.

Sometimes investors just have to experience a deep purchase to realize that this type of deal is more attainable than they might think. Once they've tasted success, investors gain the confidence to negotiate harder, buy deeper, and ask for more when selling. Intangible beliefs can absolutely lead to tangible profit.

Pick a Strategy That Fits Your Market

Understanding what market you're in and what strategies to employ is critical to any investor's success. The reality is that Cory's deal probably wouldn't have happened in a strong real estate market. In a good market, lenders are likely to recoup most, if not all, of their principal loan balance, so they're less motivated to sell at a deep discount.

This doesn't mean there aren't numerous other great strategies for a strong real estate market—you're seeing a lot of them played out in this book. Most important, Cory's deal reminds us that it simply pays to be prepared. Markets change, so there will probably be another day to employ short sales. Those who are educated will be ready.

CHAPTER TWENTY-THREE

STERLING WHITE

Owner-Financed Multifamily

Unlike 95 percent of the investors I know, Sterling White started off with nearly all the odds stacked against him. Raised by his single mother with "Section 8 housing, food stamps, and any type of government aid you could think of," Sterling and his twin brother often had to fend for themselves in a downtrodden neighborhood of Indianapolis. The only investor "role models" Sterling had were local street dealers, and he still recalls a stray bullet flying through their kitchen window when he was just 6 years old.

Sterling knew he didn't want the lifestyle he saw on the street, so he forged his own path with what he could find. As an elementary school entrepreneur, that came in the form of Kool-Aid. Mixing the powder with sugar in plastic bags, he'd sell the mix to friends throughout the day. From Kool-Aid, he moved on to selling Pokémon cards; from Pokémon cards, to honing his skill (and scaling his earnings) with actual playing cards.

The entrepreneurial bug bit him early and never went away. After finishing high school, Sterling supplemented his income with a construction job mixing mortar for bricklaying. He fell in love with the process, but it wasn't the manual labor he liked—it was seeing the transformation of a property. Once he realized that he'd rather be managing from the outside than working in the trenches, he hatched a plan.

The following years were based on a strict schedule of studying self-development and the patterns of the ultra-wealthy. Noting the book *Think and Grow Rich* and speaker Earl Nightingale as key early influences, Sterling found that the more he learned, the more obvious it became that all his biggest influences had real estate in their investment portfolios.

Just four years into his self-taught studies, Sterling bought his first single-family flip with no credit and negative funds in his bank account. Just three years later, he had scaled up to a portfolio of 150 single-family rentals. In 2017, only eight years after that fateful summer construction job, he was able to shift his focus entirely to multifamily investing.

Today Sterling is the founder of Sonder Investment Group, which manages and operates about 400 doors through multifamily syndications in markets across the Midwest. A core team helps with administration and construction so Sterling can focus on idea generation and building relationships with investors, brokers, and property owners.

Sterling has capitalized on creating a reputation for himself locally and nationally. His investor base comes from leveraging multiple channels—often through digital marketing—to generate interest in his projects, then funneling investors through a process that sells them on the value of working with his team over others. Thanks to a prolific flow of online content, marketing, and interaction building his personal brand, it's often out-of-state (or out-of-country) investors who reach out to *him*. Sterling says:

> "I'm able to filter potential investors through my personal brand because I've built up a presence in the real estate world that's focused on value. Gary Vaynerchuk's book Jab, Jab, Jab, Right Hook—which talks about providing value to potential clients [the 'jabs'] before asking for anything [the 'hook']—was a huge influence for me in this area. By being myself and offering free content, I become trustworthy. I don't need to ask anything of anybody—instead, they ask to work with me."

Although his multifamily foundation was built on snagging Class C assets that needed heavy lifting, Sterling now focuses on Class B apartment buildings of 75 to 200 units for buy and holds. Acquisitions typically come through cold-calling buildings that meet three criteria: They haven't sold within the past five years, rent is between $750 and $1,000 per month, and they were built between 1980 and 2000. Nearly all his deals are sourced off-market using what Sterling calls "ninja techniques" based on follow-up, commitment, and creativity. He explains it best:

"Everyone needs to understand that creativity follows commitment. When I send an offer to property owners and don't hear anything back, I follow up with a small Rubik's Cube that says, 'Hey, let's figure this out.' Thinking outside the box with little things like that ensures that I stay top of mind versus other investors who just keep following up with, 'Now are you interested in selling?... Now are you interested in selling?'"

FINDING THE DEAL

After building a strong portfolio, Sterling knew that next-level investing meant scoring a multifamily property. He had built an amazing pool of investors through single-family investments and planned to take them along as he scaled up. He knew that true focus on that goal meant dropping the 150-home distraction, so he sold the rental portfolio to go all-in on the multifamily pursuit.

But first, he needed to find a deal. Having grown up in Indianapolis, Sterling knew the neighborhoods to scout for signs of development. While driving around a working-class area of south Indianapolis, he noticed something about two run-down apartment buildings he'd been watching over the years: One had just sold and was slated for renovation, and the other seemed emptier and more dilapidated than ever. Noting the address of the latter, he started researching as soon as he arrived home.

Although he'd spent months cultivating relationships with local brokers, they had yet to bring him any results. So instead of going back to what seemed like an empty trough, Sterling went to the county and researched the property himself. It was owned by an LLC, and after some more digging, Sterling found the owner's name, skip traced his phone number, and called him up.

Insider Info Sterling used an approach he learned during his single-family acquisition days: research and skip trace. One of the most effective ways to find an off-market deal is by doing your own research through tax records, the secretary of state's website, social media, and so on. Then, take it a step further with a thorough skip trace that can include the person's current address, multiple phone numbers or emails, and even possible relatives. It's the investors who go the extra mile to hunt down a potential seller who end up scoring the deals nobody else knew existed.

> *"Before this, I'd been going the route of trying to nurture relationships with area brokers and it just wasn't working well. Instead of taking the mindset of 'Maybe it's just not a good time to shift to multifamily. I'll just wait for a correction to happen… if it ever happens,' I decided to take destiny into my own hands and say, 'How can I go directly to the owner and beat the broker to the punch?'"*

The good news was that the owner, Frank, was already motivated to sell. The apartment had been listed at $1.4 million on the local MLS for several months, but Frank had recently taken it down because of low interest. Interestingly enough, he was shifting careers into being a debt collector for people who had fallen behind on rent, which was perhaps useful intel on what Sterling could expect if he took on the property. With no alternative plan to get the property off his books, Frank hoped that the solution had fallen into his lap.

Ken's Take New real estate agents are typically taught to call through expired listings to find potential clients, so it's amazing how few investors use this approach to find deals. It's a numbers game, but there's definitely gold in expired listings if you make enough phone calls and talk to enough sellers.

ASSESSMENT

According to Frank, a California investor had purchased the ninety-nine-unit apartment building across the street from his own, and it was slated for an upscale rehab. This would almost certainly raise the entire street's value, and if Sterling could get a good deal on Frank's place, he would take part in the upside.

However, Frank didn't have to tell Sterling that his property was in rough shape—that much was obvious just from driving by. From the "alligator back" parking lot, which Sterling described as *rough and cracking all over the place*," to the crumbling brick siding, and stained, time-worn signage, the place didn't exactly invite prospective tenants inside.

Even so, the two-story garden-style complex showed potential. Built in 1952, its forty-six units were split between two adjacent buildings, each with its own grassy, tree-lined common area. All the units were about 750 square feet with two bedrooms and one bath, and many had covered balconies.

Unsurprisingly, the interior hadn't seen updates in years. The dark wood fixtures were sourced from the '80s, the paint scheme was blindingly whitewashed, and the depressing commercial carpeting felt more appropriate to offices than living rooms. On the plus side, the bland appearance was at least broken up by original hardwood flooring in the bedrooms, which Sterling knew would be a selling point after a refinish.

There was also this: A month earlier, one of the two buildings had been partially burned down after a cooking accident. Add to that the hail damage the roof had suffered months earlier, and you get the lovely fire-water formula that had reduced occupancy to a mere 70 percent. Although the fire and roof damage accounted for most of the vacancies, several of the units were empty simply because the owner had become a lazy marketer.

Sterling and his partner, Jacob Blackett, ran the numbers and landed on needing at least $400,000 to bring the complex up to market. They would aim for a repositioning effort that gave the building a complete overhaul: new landscaping, signage, parking lots, common areas, and siding and updated interiors. They'd also start charging residents for water usage, a huge expense in temperature-volatile Indianapolis that the owner had been eating.

Each unit's rental income averaged about $485 per month, and although they hoped to raise rents by at least $100, they also knew predicting finances for Class C units warranted extra prudence. If everything went according to plan, though, all their moves would raise the overall value and put it at the top of its class.

However, the progress wouldn't come easy. Frank wanted $1.4 million for the property, but Sterling was singing more to the tune of $700,000. He wanted to keep his all-in number close to $1 million, so they hit the negotiating table.

THE BREAKDOWN

Apartment building, forty-six units at 750 square feet each
Indianapolis, Indiana
Asking $1.4 million

OFFER AND FUNDING

With renovation expenses predicted as they were, Sterling couldn't meet any sales price over $1 million. After haggling, they finally found a solution in a $900,000 purchase through seller financing. They would put $200,000 down on a twenty-five-year amortized loan with a stair-step interest rate that started at 3 percent for the first year and 5 percent the second, then stayed at 7 percent after hitting the third year. Sterling explains:

> *"We were stuck on the financing question, but my partner, Jacob, had the idea to have the owner carry back a portion of the loan while we raised the down payment from investors. Jacob came through like that throughout the whole deal, from coming up with the underwriting model and financing solutions to getting the transaction to closing. Having solid partners has always turned out to be the key to making deals like this a success."*

Insider Info Sweetening Frank's side of the deal by agreeing to a stair-step interest rate was brilliant. Since Frank wanted the property completely off his books, increasing interest would incentivize Sterling to refinance (or sell) before reaching the three-year mark or else face rising rates.

The threat of increasing interest loomed over the already intense effort this complex would require, but Sterling did what he had to do to get the deal. As a concession, the owner agreed to replace both roofs before closing, but he'd leave the fire damage to Sterling's team.

Using virtually the same investors he'd worked with while building his single-family portfolio, Sterling syndicated a $685,000 second-position loan at 8 percent fixed interest and 50 percent profit split upon exit. With $200,000 as a down payment, $438,000 allocated for repairs, and $47,000 for closing and fees, they planned to be all-in at $1.37 million.

Ken's Take Structuring second-position lenders (versus equity investors) on big deals like this means adding the obligation of debt service atop an already risky and capital-intensive deal. Since Sterling had been a single-family investor using lenders before this deal, he went back to the same pool to fund the multifamily. These investors were accustomed to fixed interest rates and debt financing, so that's what he went with (albeit second-position debt rather than first).

It would turn out to be the first and *last* time he used second-position debt on a multifamily project, because lenders expect their interest payments no matter what. Equity partners, on the other hand, agree and understand that they'll participate in the investment's upside *and* downside.

TURNAROUND

The renovation would have to move quickly to get occupancy and rental income paying out interest and recouping costs as soon as possible. However, the city was in the throes of an incredibly aggressive winter when Sterling finally got the keys. When he'd found the property four months earlier, he'd predicted the worst of the cold would be over by closing, but it was approaching March and winter carried on.

Weather setbacks created two months of construction delays, which led to a cascade of other setbacks. Even though they'd expected repositioning to take up to a year and a half, the delay in getting the vacant units filled meant an early shortfall in predicted rental income. The issue was soon compounded by a surprise $20,000 expense to replace the complex's boiler unit.

Sterling's team was operating within a tight margin, but they stayed afloat until April, when they finally could get down to business. In the meantime, he renamed and registered the complex as Garfield Place, associating it with Indianapolis's oldest park, which reigned beautifully just a block away. Then the team updated the signage, painted the building's trim, redid the parking lot, painted the deck rails a flashy blue, and spruced up the landscape so the whole exterior popped.

Once they could begin renovating the vacant units, they retouched the hardwood floors, recoated the walls with two-tone paint, resurfaced the cabinets, replaced the countertops with renter-friendly Formica, and tore out the commercial carpeting. As leases renewed for existing tenants, they were offered a renovated unit for a small price hike. Many were eager to take the option, which helped Sterling avoid turnover costs amid getting units renovated as quickly as possible.

While Sterling was scaling up his new multifamily portfolio, he was also developing a property management business. With this project as its first run, the business became responsible for scheduling maintenance and managing renters and payments, slowly raising the rents by $50 to $100 per month.

AFTERMATH

After a year and a half, Sterling had deployed the full $438,000 toward renovation and brought occupancy up to 95 percent. Despite the impressive boost to occupancy, the ability to raise all rents by $100 hit a ceiling—and making matters worse, the complex was turning out to be more operationally expensive than expected.

Ken's Take One important factor to remember when investing in Class C properties (especially ones that rent for only $485 a month) is the potential of dealing with flaky tenants, *especially* when you're inheriting them rather than screening them yourself. I advise students to use a very conservative delinquency component when building a proforma for a property like this. Of course, there are plenty of quality tenants that live in Class C (and lower) properties—it's just important to be extra prudent during the screening process to give yourself the best chance for success.

As he approached the two-year mark, Sterling noticed that, despite the huge boost to occupancy, dealing with renter issues was creeping into his ability to cover the investors' 8 percent monthly interest. For whatever reason, he couldn't seem to find the higher-caliber tenants he was looking for.

Given this, Sterling began wondering whether the repositioning efforts might have already paid off through the property's increased value. If he could hit the investment's projected numbers with an exit, it would save the hassle of fighting against the rent threshold they were hitting. He got an estimate on the building, and although he'd predicted its value to reach $1.5 million by the fifth year, it had appreciated much more in only *two* years—to $1.9 million! Sterling says:

> *"There had been back-and-forth between investors and me because we were barely hitting their returns. For some, it was also their first multifamily deal, and it made many of them nervous. But they were willing to stick with it because, ultimately, they felt we were getting them where they wanted to go. And they were right—at the end of the day, we got them caught up on the interest and then some."*

As they say, all's well that ends well. Sterling's team listed the property with a traditional broker at $1.85 million, and that's exactly what they got after multiple bidders. After getting their investors caught up on interest payments, they split 50 percent of the remaining $310,000 net profit with them. Each investor walked away with a 16.3 percent internal rate of return (IRR), and those numbers easily meant they would be happy to keep scaling with Sterling on his journey to multifamily success.

TAKEAWAY

Expect the Unexpected

Sterling learned lots of amazing lessons by nailing down his first multifamily. After snagging a large deal like this, it's easy for initial excitement to cause investors (myself included) to put on rose-colored glasses. Sterling didn't foresee the full extent of the rental ceiling possibility, but he was conservative where it mattered, and it paid off.

This multifamily venture is a great reminder that rents won't always rise to the values we project—we just can't control every aspect of a large property's performance. That being said, Sterling analyzed the market and made predictions as well as he could, accepting risk as the price for getting a multifamily under his belt. He says:

> *"Even though we knew it would be difficult, we wanted this apartment complex. Repositioning and selling forty-six units—even when they're difficult—enables you to reach economies of scale much more quickly than single-family."*

Ultimately, he overcame the setback because it was a savvy purchase and a strong renovation. In this business, you can expect to miss the mark on occasion, and no doubt that will be some of your best training. If you've made a smart purchase, though, it will hit the mark in other ways. By taking a conservative, thoughtful approach when vetting and managing projects, you'll find that expecting the unexpected might be one of the most important steps toward ensuring success.

All Relationships Require Healthy Communication

Telling private lenders that they might not get a month's interest payment is difficult no matter how you look at it. What pushed Sterling and his investors through was mindset—*Sterling's* mindset. He knew that at the end of the day, this property would still be a winner. Because he knows how to work with people, he could assure investors that an interest payment was a small piece of the overall profit pie. All it took was helping them adjust their mindset to see the endgame and the huge potential this project was moving toward fulfilling.

Other investors in this situation might not have fared so well. Something in human nature causes people to avoid conflict and duck responsibility. I've known plenty of industry "professionals" who simply disappear when there's bad news to report. The thing is, bad news never gets better with age. It's always better to face it head-on, overcommunicate, and work together to reach a solution.

Sterling earned his investors' faith that the project was moving in the right direction. Eventually, the lenders came to realize how two years of consistent effort had put them right where they needed to be. The sale earned them everything they'd signed up for and more.

Mindset Is Everything

Sterling is one of the most positive, inspirational people I've ever met. While I don't know what it's like to grow up as a low-income member of a minority with a single parent in the inner city, I do know that a person with such a background doesn't see many others who share their experience in the investor space.

That's not how it should be, but success in real estate gets a lot harder when you have few, if any, real-life role models encouraging you to believe in yourself. Sterling shows us that this industry (or any industry, for that matter) shouldn't be about where you came from but about where you want to go.

Sterling didn't get to where he is today by accident or through favors—he did it through *intention*. Once you've decided to break down barriers and challenge the status quo, knowledge and skill drive the engine, but mindset is the fuel. Sterling says:

"For the longest time, I thought investing in real estate was only for the ultra-wealthy with a lot of cash. I didn't have that, but I was still able to get my foot in the door and not let any obstacle be a barrier instead of a problem to solve. Whatever happens, I'm going to partner, learn, make money, and break down all the barriers that keep me from the success I desire."

CHAPTER TWENTY-FOUR

MELISA CLEMENT

Great Reputation Equals Built-In Buyers

Melisa Clement barely spent two years in the real estate game before she was flipping half-million-dollar homes like a seasoned pro. Did it come easily? Actually, kind of. Did it come without skill? Not at all.

Unlike most of this book's investors, Melisa can credit much of her success to her skill as an artist first, with her skill as a businesswoman a close second. Prior to being one of Austin, Texas' most sought-after house flippers, Melisa was a stay-at-home mom for nearly two decades. It wasn't until all five of her children were in high school and college that she tapped into her background as an art major, drawing on her education and creativity to remodel her and her husband's home.

When a real estate agent friend named Siobhan visited the remodeled digs, she asked if Melisa would stage a couple of the homes she was selling. Melisa had a go at it, using furniture and decorations she already owned, and received rave reviews for her work. When a local flipper happened to view one of Siobhan's homes, he persuaded Melisa to stage some of his projects too.

It wasn't long before this flipper was asking for Melisa's opinion on tile, paint, and overall layout. As she gained an understanding of house flipping from the inside out, she realized she could probably do it herself. She shared this idea with her husband, Dallas, who agreed it was worth a shot.

Just like that, Melisa and Dallas sold their home, downsized, and used the profit to purchase their first single-family flip for $285,000. After hiring a crew and overseeing the home's meticulous renovation, Melisa resold it for $450,000. With a first-time net profit of nearly $100,000, she realized she was definitely onto something.

"My husband believed in me so much that as we became successful, he suggested we roll over all of his IRA into a self-directed IRA, and that's actually how we've funded all thirty-five of our flips. Which is to say, after all those years as a stay-at-home mom, I'm now in charge of all our retirement money!"

In the nine years since, Melisa has orchestrated three to four flips a year, and with each one, the line of people waiting for her work grows longer. Austin has a booming home market, and since Melisa is design-intensive, she's been able to concentrate on higher-end properties. As she puts it, she's *"super picky and detail oriented,"* which has turned out to be an excellent way to differentiate herself from the competition.

Melisa's buying formula is simple: Find the worst house in the best neighborhood with the best school district. She focuses only on properties near her own home in Northwest Austin, where there's lots of business and residential growth (including a new billion-dollar Apple campus).

Ken's Take Melisa's location choosiness is worth highlighting. A lot of investors, especially when they're just getting started, feel they have to go after anything and everything, no matter the commute time. It's not just about finding the right market, but about finding the right market that works for *you*. Maintaining balance between hours spent in a car and hours spent enjoying your life has a value too.

By focusing on specific neighborhoods, Melisa has single-handedly raised values for the entire area through the thirty-five (and counting) projects she's overseen. These days, she aims for homes around $500,000 to renovate using her small crew of seven, plus a few specific subcontractors. After creating the design and orchestrating the magic touches, she relists in the high $800,000s and low $900,000s. Melisa explains:

> "I try to find homes that are more than 2,500 square feet, and I won't buy a house if I can't get four bedrooms out of it somehow. Four bedrooms, three-plus bathrooms, and an office is ideal. Sometimes that means adding a second floor to the house, adding a bathroom, or modifying the layout. I have often added a second story to a small 1970s house in order to double the original square footage. If I'm buying it for $195 per square foot and selling it for $250 per square foot, and it costs me around $150 per square foot to do an addition, then it makes sense if I have the funds available and the patience to wait for permits to be pulled."

Melisa's model, based on developing a specific reputation in a specific part of town, is so successful that when someone is planning to move into that area, they often want anything she's put her stamp on. It's almost like being a sought-after custom home builder, except Melisa gets to keep her hands clean as the visionary behind design-centric flips.

Melisa's business model also relies on the social media presence she's built, particularly on Instagram. Her Austin follower base is so numerous that many are on a waiting list and plan on moving to Northwest Austin simply to be in one of her homes.

Ken's Take Melisa's success highlights the fact that quality can absolutely trump quantity. With a small renovation team and a modest goal of four homes per year, she's built a lucrative business without the complexity and overhead of a high-volume flipping organization. *More* does not always equal *better*.

FINDING THE DEAL

If it's not clear by now, let me say it again: Sometimes a great reputation is all you need to find deals. When people are bringing you properties and *asking* you to buy, how's that for cost per lead? Such was the case when a local wholesaler approached Melisa about a home he'd got under contract in "her" zip code.

One man had lived in the 1970s house for more than forty years, raising his children there and remaining in the home as they all eventually moved out of state. When a health issue required that he suddenly move into an assisted living facility, he wasn't able to clean out the home before leaving. The asking price of $507,000 seemed fair, so Melisa went to have a look. She says:

> "My favorite houses to look for are those built in the '70s. For the most part, they are well built and lacking some of the challenges I've found in older homes. Sometimes there's aluminum wiring and the team has to change it to copper, but overall, these homes feel like a safe bet and are often overlooked by buyers until they can see them brought back into this century."

✅ ASSESSMENT

The stone home stood two stories tall on a spacious one-third acre in one of Austin's most prestigious neighborhoods. At 3,638 square feet, it had four bedrooms, with three full and two half baths, a pool, and a huge detached garage workshop. However, with its popcorn ceilings, old wallpaper, and dark wood paneling, it wasn't hiding its age so well.

> "The stone was ugly—a big rust-colored rock mix—and the pool was filled with algae and cracks. The house and garage were filled top to bottom with decades of family life, tools, collections, and mementos. While the owner's children were trying their best to sort through it all and pack it up, it was clear that this was going to be an 'as-is' purchase."

Despite the mess, Melisa could envision a beautiful remodeled home with spacious rooms, a refinished pool, and a complete makeover to the tiny, cramped kitchen. Since the house was in good shape and needed no major repairs, she was confident that most of the budget could be spent on the pool, kitchen, and bathroom remodeling. Her plan would be to follow the tried-and-true formula of getting it renovated for around $150,000, then selling in the high $800,000s.

THE BREAKDOWN

Single-family home, 3,638 square feet
Austin, Texas
Asking $507,000

OFFER AND FUNDING

With her intimate knowledge of the neighborhood, Melisa was fine with the asking price and paid it outright with her self-directed IRA. There was one catch: As part of the wholesaler's agreement with the children, they would get some time to pack up their dad's stuff. Happy to comply, Melisa offered a fifteen-day lease-back option for a $5,000 deposit, which she would return once the house was cleared.

Insider Info It's not uncommon for a seller to ask for additional time to move out of a property even after it's sold. Often, they need the cash from the sale in order to pay for moving expenses or a deposit on their next residence. The key to negotiating this scenario is making sure you have a short-term rental agreement secured in case they decide not to move out and you're forced to evict. Melisa took it a step further and held $5,000 from the proceeds of their sale as a deposit to ensure they would move out in the agreed-upon time frame.

TURNAROUND

As it turned out, the kids weren't exactly prepared for the forty years' worth of stuff their dad had accumulated. With the lease-back terms approaching the closing date and the kids losing interest by the day, Melisa realized there was no way they'd get everything out of the home in time. She ended up keeping the deposit and invested the $5,000 in a cleaning crew to clear out the home.

"It took us two weeks to get everything either resold, trashed, or donated. The three-bay garage was also overflowing with tools and other stuff. If I had been smarter, I would've held an estate sale and just opened up the house and sold everything out of it. I did get some very cool original artwork out of the house, though!"

Ken's Take I've purchased many properties over the years that needed major clean-outs. Some just required dumpsters, but others contained enough interesting items to justify an estate sale. If you don't want to deal with that yourself, you can hire someone to oversee it in exchange for a percentage of the sales, or just find a professional company to run it for you. While the resulting income likely won't make you rich, it can potentially offset the cost of trash removal and demo.

Melisa's crew spent the next six months pulling permits, gutting the home, and implementing her renowned design style. First, they scraped the popcorn ceilings, floated the walls to get rid of their uneven texture, removed the old wallpaper, rearranged the kitchen, and opened things up for better flow. As the crew removed the kitchen's original ceiling, they quickly realized that one of the walls they were going to take down was load bearing, which was a dangerous problem in a two-story home.

Though Melisa had wanted to remove the wall to create flow into the dining room, building structural support in that space would be too costly. Instead, she kept the wall and created a sense of flow by installing uniform flooring throughout the rooms and opening the kitchen to the family room instead.

"I didn't like that the stairs were right by the front door, but I felt that if I could take down the wall there and install a modern railing, that would help. The formal living and dining rooms were dark and closed off with no overhead lighting to speak of, but just by opening up the doorway between the two spaces, adding a cool wood-paneled accent wall, and adding some recessed lights and new fixtures, the whole space felt rejuvenated."

From there, they updated all the bathrooms, revived the pool and patio area, and solved the exterior stone color problem by painting the entire house in a creamy white and adding gorgeous ipe hardwood accents. At six months and the predicted $150,000 renovation budget, Melisa was finally ready to relist.

Insider Info It's important to note that there are strict rules around using self-funded retirement accounts for investing. They boil down to the IRS's need to ensure that funds are used solely to build the *retirement* account, not present-day personal accounts. All expenses related to the property must be paid out of the account or a business representing the retirement account (in Melisa's case, an LLC for the IRA). Melisa's role is then limited to being manager for the LLC—or think of it as being a fund manager. She can oversee the purchase, project manage, designate materials, create the design, and manage the funds, but she cannot lift a finger on the property itself (meaning no physical work, permit applications, materials delivery, and so on).

The look-but-don't-touch approach can be a pain, but a profitable one. Understanding the guidelines and nuances surrounding IRA real estate investing is crucial before utilizing your retirement account as a funding source for your next project.

AFTERMATH

Melisa listed the home for $899,000, and within twenty-four hours she had multiple offers that led to a winning bid of $925,000. She and her husband had spent $150,000 on the renovation and about $47,000 on taxes and transaction fees, so that left a whopping $220,000 profit. Even better, it all went right back into their IRA as tax-deferred income! Melisa explains:

> *"For that neighborhood, we always sell at the top of the market and push the comps. If the buyer needs to have an appraisal done, then I provide my own comps for my own houses. Appraisers don't always do a good job giving you credit for really nice finishes. They're looking at square footage and bedrooms and baths—it's just not apples to apples. They're not always looking at the quality and effort that went into the build."*

TAKEAWAY

Build a Solid Reputation

I've known of house flippers who create a following among agents, but it's very rare to find someone like Melisa who has reached beyond agents to the buyers themselves. When someone is trying to renovate or move into a property within Melisa's "domain," it's almost guaranteed they know about her. That's the power of building a specific reputation. She says it best:

"I believe in doing the very best quality you can. In fact, I would always spend extra to do it right rather than cut corners. I've seen flippers literally paint over rotted wood (among other things), then sell the house for a great price. But you don't build a reputation by doing things like that. You don't get multiple offers on the twenty-fifth house you've done in the same neighborhood by cutting corners. I'd rather make less money on the first five, then build up my name and reputation to the point where people are lining up to buy my houses."

Abundance Mentality

Melisa spent years working with the same Realtor friend who first hired her as a home stager. Selling such high-dollar homes means that the 1 to 3 percent agent fee is quite a hefty sum. Even though Melisa could have become a licensed Realtor herself long ago, she believed that keeping her agent on board and sharing the wealth was more valuable than the extra profit.

"At a certain point, since so many people were coming to us, I knew that I didn't necessarily need my friend to sell homes, but we kept working together because of our friendship. It's the 'cast your bread upon the waters' idea. We worked out a deal where Siobhan would get 3 percent for the initial purchase and 1 percent for the resale. Meanwhile, the buyer's agent got the typical 3 percent. It was a lot, but it felt good to pay it forward.

"Honestly, I feel like the times when I've been stingy in business— whether it's with my crew or otherwise—have been when I don't do as well on the sale. I've learned that lesson. As I open my heart and am generous, I am generously rewarded."

Self-Directed IRAs

When Melisa was getting started, she had the money to invest, but it was locked away in retirement accounts managed by institutions. By moving those dollars into self-directed accounts, she freed up the money for their real estate projects. In fact, she and her husband now manage two self-directed IRA LLCs.

Melisa's business framework has created a tremendous amount of wealth without creating a huge tax burden. The profits from each flip are simply returned to the IRA, further building the capital for their next project as well as a handsome nest egg. In thinking through the benefits of this strategy, Melisa says:

> *"Back in 2019, when the stock market was doing really well, I was curious and nervous about whether our decision to liquidate my husband's IRA (which would have been following the stock market) had panned out as well as if we had left the money alone. When I did the math, it turned out that we'd done better than the stock market, by far! It was great confirmation for his trusting me with all the money he'd worked so hard to earn over the years."*

Many new or would-be investors keep themselves from flipping properties due to lack of available cash. By now, hopefully this book has opened your eyes to the numerous ways investors can profit through various creative techniques and strategies that use none of their own cash. Bear in mind, investors are restricted from doing any of the work *themselves* when using self-directed IRA funding (as mentioned earlier, there are lots of rules, so do your research!), but there is great upside potential to deferred taxes if you have a trustworthy crew to work with.

CHAPTER TWENTY-FIVE

JACK BOSCH

Buying Land at Pennies on the Dollar

Jack Bosch was born and raised in Germany, so it's no big surprise that he does things differently from every other investor in this book. When he was fresh out of college in Mannheim, he immigrated to the States for a software development MBA, met his wife, Michelle, and then landed a tech job in Phoenix, Arizona.

After quickly learning that he wasn't, in fact, a software guy, Jack began seeking other career paths. Real estate investing seemed like something he could explore as a side hustle, so he and Michelle began making offers on local properties that had unpaid taxes. Jack explains:

"We were initially going after all sorts of properties, but all the responses we got were from landowners. We offered almost nothing for these parcels and got several accepted, which we then flipped for ten to twenty times what we'd paid. After a few deals, we decided, 'Why even deal with houses, when land is so much simpler?' For the next seven years we didn't touch a house."

In the '90s, land was plentiful in Arizona. Jack and Michelle dove into developing a land-flipping model based on the idea that tons of people owned land they simply didn't want. Usually these undesired parcels were inherited or came as add-ons to a primary purchase, and the owners had to deal with upkeep and taxes.

Jack and Michelle found that such owners didn't seem to know (or care) about the best way to get rid of their property—they mostly just ignored its existence. Having written off the land as useless, they were often willing to let the properties go for 5 to 25 cents on the dollar.

Ken's Take To many readers, Jack's offers might seem ridiculously low, but for Jack, it was just a numbers game. Some percentage of these offers would get accepted. He figured sellers were likely open to selling at such a deep discount because they didn't have an emotional attachment to the property. That may seem unbelievable, but it's often just an out of sight, out of mind situation. More importantly, he'd had success and knew there had to be more opportunities out there.

Jack stuck with his software job just long enough to get his green card. With fifty land deals in the bag by the time he quit, he was ready to scale to full-time investing.

Today Jack still follows that same land-flipping model, though with a few upgrades to the finding and outreach processes. Since he can do almost all the necessary research and marketing online, he only needs one full-time salesperson and one full-time virtual assistant to help prepare listings. All other processes are outsourced or automated, enabling him to move more than a hundred deals a year.

In fact, he's turned more than 4,000 deals to date. After getting parcels under contract, he either wholesales at a 50 to 60 percent markup, purchases and flips at an 80 to 100 percent markup, or seller finances for returns well over 100 percent. It's just wholesaling and house flipping... without the houses!

Seller financing makes up about 80 percent of Jack's deals, and there's a good reason why. With added interest, he makes up to three times the profit of a traditional direct sale. I'll let him explain how:

> "Let's say we find a $40,000-value property that we put under contract for $5,000. We turn around and seller finance for $35,000 with $6,000 down. The buyer's down payment is more than what we paid for the property, and now we get $500 monthly for the next ten years. It's pure profit, and we ultimately collect about $70,000 total."

You might think the best part is that there are no toilets, termites, inspectors, mold, maintenance, repairs, surprises, or rehabs to deal with—but you'd be wrong. The actual best part? There's almost no competition. Plus, since he never has to see land or show it, he can do both the acquisition and the disposition 100 percent remotely.

Insider Info Jack says that most of the land deals he finds are just outside of a metropolitan area. As you would guess, land at pennies on the dollar is hard to locate in cities. However, once you target less densely populated areas, there are plenty of opportunities.

FINDING THE DEAL

Jack's team uses list-building websites to get ultra specific on the properties they want, starting off with parcels that fall into one of the following categories:

1. One- to five-acre lots on the outskirts of growing areas
2. Rural acreage in areas with nearby points of interest
3. Infill lots

From there, they winnow the results down to those that meet the following criteria: out-of-state owners, values between $10,000 and $100,000, and free-and-clear ownership. (Offering 5 to 25 percent of the property's market value would be a much tougher sell to someone who still has a mortgage.) Using such strict criteria to select prospects for direct mail follow-up means that the likelihood of finding a seller is boosted straight out of the gate.

After populating the resulting addresses into a direct mail website, Jack sends out a piece written as an approval letter. It affirms that he wants to buy the property but first he wants more information. Then he waits for the phone to ring.

Ken's Take Jack's well-tested mailer is actually the only piece of marketing his team needs. It's a genius way to show the property owner that they've already been "approved," which makes the owner more likely to call. Then, over the phone, Jack's team can develop a rapport with the owner and better assess and cater to their motivation to sell.

Given that land investing is one of the most overlooked niches in real estate, Jack's highly specific selection process means that his mailers average a 4 to 15 percent response rate. He says:

"Sellers are a dime a dozen. In the house-flipping arena, finding the seller is the hardest part. In our process, finding the seller is the easiest part."

One of Jack's time-tested mailers landed in the hands of a California-based man named Michael. He owned a property in Prescott, Arizona, that he'd been wanting to sell, but he hadn't found the time or energy to seek a buyer. With Jack's letter showing him the path to an easy sale, he picked up the phone.

Michael filled Jack in on the details: A few years earlier, he'd taken a road trip to Prescott with his mom, and during the ride she had a heart attack. Although she was quickly stabilized in a nearby hospital, she passed away six months later. In Michael's mind, the Arizona property was tied to the loss of his mother, and largely because of that, he just didn't want to deal with it anymore.

ASSESSMENT

With its temperate seasons and outdoorsy appeal, the city of Prescott was recently rated one of the top fifty retirement towns in America. Bars and restaurants are plentiful, nature is at your fingertips, and Phoenix is only two hours away. Jack was definitely interested.

Michael's parcel covered a beautiful hillside acre with fifty-mile views of the surrounding desert and mountains. Million-dollar homes and big, stately boulders dotted the surrounding land. With downtown Prescott just five minutes away, there was no doubting the parcel's curb appeal—building a home here would create an incredible asset in one of the prettiest western cities in America.

However, there was a big issue: The existing road stopped short one hundred feet from the bottom of the property line. There was an access point at the top of the parcel, but it was a dangerous drive and simply didn't make sense as the primary point of entry. If someone were to build on this lot, they would have to get an easement to create a sensible access point at the bottom of the hill.

The county had valued the property at $10,000 a year earlier, which in Arizona tends to represent two-thirds of actual market value, so the property was really worth about $15,000. Despite that, Jack's familiarity with the area led him to believe that market buyers might pay as high as $100,000—much higher than the county's valuation indicated.

He also knew that clearing up the access issue and getting an easement in place could push the value even higher than $100,000. With costs for an easement estimated at a maximum of $40,000, going through the process and expense could pay off in a big way. He wasn't sure how he would turn the deal, but he knew there was money to be made and drew up an offer.

THE BREAKDOWN

Land parcel, one acre
Prescott, Arizona
Market value between $15,000 and $100,000

OFFER AND FUNDING

As Jack points out, *"the profit is made when you buy,"* and with the easement issue clouding the property's true value, he treaded carefully. Based on the county's numbers, he cautiously offered 12.5 percent of the estimated market value. That's right—$1,875 flat.

Incredibly, Michael accepted. They began getting the paperwork in order, and when closing was just two weeks away, the county happened to send out the new year's tax appraisal. Michael unfolded the notice to see that they now valued his property at $60,000 (a 600 percent increase!), suggesting that they'd caught on to Jack's initial hunch of its true market value.

This new assessment would mean higher property taxes, but it also meant that Michael had a much better idea of how little $1,875 was compared with the land's true value. Jack braced himself for Michael's outrage, but it never came. Instead, Jack says:

"He just stuck the assessment notice in an envelope and sent it to us with a little handwritten note saying, 'Next time I am in town, you owe me dinner.' He really did just want to get rid of the property."

The thing is, Michael wasn't upset about Jack's strikingly low offer for $1,875. Even though he knew the value of the property, the psychological and emotional backstory outweighed the numbers. He just wanted the relief of moving on with as little legwork as possible.

TURNAROUND

Jack could have made the extra effort to clear up the easement issue and sell for more than $200,000, but he didn't bother. After factoring in the interest he hoped to make by reselling the property through owner financing, the extra profit just wasn't worth the trouble of dealing with the county for zoning, construction, and paperwork. For Jack, there's value in simplicity. Saving time can be just as important as earning dollars and cents.

"We didn't go to the effort—we never do. We just make offers low enough that we can pass the deal on to a buyer and leave enough money in it for them to make it profitable for themselves. We just buy and sell."

In those days, Jack was buying hundreds of parcels every few months and holding one big quarterly land auction to move inventory. Using radio, television, newspaper, and online advertising, his team could fill up a convention center with nearly 1,000 people and sell 250 properties in one day.

When that quarter's auction rolled around, the Prescott parcel— untouched after Jack's purchase—went for $86,000 after a bidding war. They worked out a seller-financing plan where the buyer put down $17,000 on a fifteen-year amortized loan at 12.9 percent interest. On top of that easy upfront $15,125 profit from the down payment alone, the monthly payments of $850 brought in an extra $10,000 per year.

AFTERMATH

As Jack likes to say, *"For house flippers, the challenge is finding the deal. For land flippers, the challenge is finding the right buyer."* Considering that he made an 800 percent profit through the down payment alone, it's tough to claim that he'd found the wrong buyer—but all the same, that buyer ended up defaulting after less than a year.

Ken's Take Jack's story got me wondering how common it is for people to foreclose on land deals. He says he encounters about a 3 to 5 percent foreclosure rate—which is only slightly higher than typical bank loan foreclosure rates—and his secret weapon for keeping that number low is asking enough for the down payment. His general rule is to ask for about 10 percent down, but if the property is priced under $10,000, he asks for more, saying, *"As long as you're getting at least $1,000 to $2,000, people rarely let that money go away."*

Jack had already netted about $25,000 up to that point, so the default wasn't much of a hit. Since they'd used a land contract, it took only four weeks and a meager $60 to foreclose. After that, he turned around and resold the parcel for another $80,000, with a $10,000 down payment and the same 12.9 percent interest rate. The first buyer's foreclosure actually allowed him to net even more on the parcel than he originally would have.

Insider Info A land contract is a fairly straightforward way of selling property to a buyer that doesn't want (or doesn't qualify for) traditional financing. As with an owner finance, the buyer makes payments directly to the seller. However, in a land contract, the seller keeps the property title until the buyer has made payment in full.

That second buyer has been paying ever since. Jack is still collecting, and once the loan is all paid off, he'll have earned north of $120,000 on that $1,875 investment. Talk about a deal!

TAKEAWAY

Find Your Niche

One reason I love real estate investing is that there are just so many creative ways to make money. Many of the people who really excel in this industry find a niche and devote all their time and focus to perfecting a specific model.

Jack definitely found his niche in land. Not all land either—he targets very specific parcels based on type, area, and ownership criteria. With that ultra-specific model, Jack's been able to scale to the point of doing hundreds of deals every year. In fact, at that scale, he can even hold large auctions and sell hundreds of properties in a day.

Keep It Simple

Entrepreneurs (including myself) are notoriously bad about being lured into other money-making opportunities. Such endeavors, no matter how promising, can easily distract from scaling a specific model. Jack's model wasn't rocket science, but it required focus and commitment. Doing the same type of deal over and over eventually led to a very sizable portfolio of income-producing notes.

Jack was disciplined about keeping the boundaries he'd set for his investment model. Yes, it would have been easy to chase additional revenue on land deals by obtaining easements, rezoning, or even building, but that wasn't his model. In the same way that a wholesaler doesn't take the time and risk to buy and renovate houses, Jack kept the machine running by never stopping the conveyor belt for outside projects.

There is nothing inherently wrong with taking on multiple projects. Some of the most successful investors I know do a little bit of everything. Jack, on the other hand, believed that the best way to scale his business was through simplicity, and you'd have a tough time proving him wrong.

Seller Financing at Scale Can Be Life-Changing

Seller financing is already a great strategy, but Jack supercharged his business and changed his lifestyle by focusing on a technique centered on low-priced land deals. He puts it this way:

"I started really seeing the power of seller financing once I was debt-free with no car, credit card, or student loan payments. I started

shifting to more and more seller-financing loans because they pro-vided a beautiful stability. If something dramatic were to happen, I could literally just take a year off and take care of it. Now, because of our business structure, we can take three months off in the summer and go travel as a family because we know we have cash flow coming in from all these different sources."

ACKNOWLEDGEMENTS

I'm not sure I remember the exact point in time when I decided to take *The Best Deal Ever* concept and turn it into a book, but I distinctly remember having a phone call with Brandon Turner, who encouraged me to pursue the idea. Of course, I don't remember Brandon providing any additional color about all of the work that goes into writing a book. In typical entrepreneur fashion, I thought, "Yeah, no problem. I'll just write a book...it'll be easy."

Suffice it to say, while rewarding, writing a book takes a LOT of work—just ask my kids (Naomi, Rocco, and Kayla). They can tell you about the endless evenings they were left to clean the kitchen after dinner as I headed off to my screened porch to stare at a computer screen for a few hours. Truth be told, I really am incredibly grateful for Anita and the kids, who always understood the need to steal time away in the evenings to work on this book. While sometimes disappointed at my lack of availability, there was always an underlying level of excitement and appreciation about "Dad's book." I hope and pray that this book will one day bless and inspire them to never settle for mediocre, but to step out of conformity and pursue their passions in life.

I'm also appreciative of my parents, Don and Ronna Corsini, who while not entrepreneurially inclined, never squashed my dreams of pursuing real estate as a full-time profession. In fact, through my dad's family, I have a rich heritage of Corsinis who found their way to America in the early 1900s and proceeded to thrive as independent business owners and real estate developers. I suppose I can attribute my love of all things real estate to my genetic inheritance!

Through fifteen years of running multiple businesses, I've leaned on many people to "work in the trenches" on a daily basis while I pursued podcasts, filming a television show, writing a book, etc. The bottom line is that I would not have been in a position to even write a book like this without the help of business partners like Dave Emrich, Jessica Stansel,

Nathan Beavers, Dennis Hurley, Scott Marineau, Laura Crowe, and Kevin Turner.

Of course, this book wouldn't even exist without the amazing stories that these featured real estate investors shared with me. I am extremely grateful for each of them and the amount of time they were willing to commit to this book to ensure the facts were correct and that we told their stories as accurately as possible.

Having never written a book, I learned that it's definitely not a solo effort. I want to personally thank and acknowledge the tremendous amount of work and creative coordination that went on between Meggan Kaiser and me. Her assistance in coordinating interviews, refining stories, fact-checking, and editing was invaluable in bringing this book to fruition.

I also want to thank all of the editors that worked on this book as well: Kaylee Pratt, Katie Miller, Wendy Dunning, Louise Collazo, and Katie Golownia. Thanks to Rodrigo Corral and his team for the cover design and Austin Golownia for the headshot illustrations.

I've been tremendously lucky to have had a relationship with BiggerPockets since 2011. Interestingly enough, I was contributing to The BiggerPockets Blog back when it was just Josh Dorkin working on the site by himself. It's been an amazing experience to watch his fledgling website turn into the media monster that it is today, and I'm thrilled to continue this relationship through weekly videos, blogs, and now books. I don't know any other platform that delivers the amount of quality content that BiggerPockets does—it's hands down the ultimate resource for real estate investors. At the end of the day, this book would not be a reality if not for their belief in me as an author and their support to bring this book to print.

But above all, I want to thank and acknowledge my savior, Jesus Christ, who not only saved me from my sins, but loves me unconditionally and gives me new strength every morning to honor him with my life (Phillipians 4:13).

MORE ABOUT THE INVESTORS

Ken Corsini

Ken has flipped more than 800 homes in Metro Atlanta since 2005. His company, Red Barn Homes, offers brokerage, construction, remodeling, and mortgage services, and it transacted on over 1,000 homes in one year alone.

Website: redbarnhomes.com
Blog: www.biggerpockets.com/blog/contributors/kencorsini
Shows: HGTV's *Flip or Flop Atlanta*; BiggerPocket's *Best Deal Ever* YouTube series
Instagram: @kencorsini
BiggerPockets Profile: https://www.biggerpockets.com/users/garp

Anson Young

Anson is a real estate agent and the owner of Anson Property Group, which is based in Denver, CO and specializes in distressed property purchases. As a full-time real estate investor for the past ten years, he has completed more than 120 wholesale deals and 95 flips.

Website: ansonpropertygroup.wordpress.com
Book: *Finding & Funding Great Deals*
Instagram: @younganson
BiggerPockets Profile: https://www.biggerpockets.com/users/Anson

Frank Rolfe

Frank Rolfe has been a commercial real estate investor for over 30 years, having owned and operated billboards, mobile home parks, RV parks,

self-storage, apartments, retail, duplex, office, and commercial properties during that time.

Website: www.creuniversity.com
BiggerPockets Profile: https://www.biggerpockets.com/users/mhps

Corey Peterson

Corey has managed and acquired over $65 million in real estate across
the country. He speaks around the country on this subject, including at
Harvard and Nasdaq, and he is frequently featured on FOX, CBS, ABC,
and NBC affiliates.

Podcast: *Multi-Family Legacy*
Book: *Why The Rich Get Richer: The Secrets to Cash-Flowing Apartments*
Website: kahunawealthbuilders.com
Instagram: @kahunacashflow
BiggerPockets Profile:
https://www.biggerpockets.com/users/Kahuna

Stacy Rossetti

Stacy Rossetti is the founder of the South Atlanta REIA, and her passion
is teaching others how to invest in real estate. She is a master at buying
storage facilities, renovating homes, and acquiring properties for passive
income.

Website: stacyrossetti.com
Social media: facebook.com/stacyteaches

Krystal and Dedric Polite

Krystal and Dedric Polite are the husband and wife team behind Be Polite
Properties, which focuses on selling residential homes in markets nationwide. They've been in the industry for over a decade and buy and sell
hundreds of properties annually.

Facebook: www.facebook.com/BePoliteProperties
Instagram: @bepoliteproperties
BiggerPockets Profile: https://www.biggerpockets.com/users/DedricP

Brandon Turner

Brandon is an author, entrepreneur, and active real estate investor with more than 500 rental units and dozens of rehabs under his belt. He's the Vice President of BiggerPockets and author of four successful real estate business books.

Podcast: *The BiggerPockets Podcast*
Books: *The Book on Rental Property Investing, Investing in Real Estate with No (and Low) Money Down, The Book on Managing Rental Properties, How to Invest in Real Estate*
Instagram: @beardybrandon
BiggerPockets Profile:
https://www.biggerpockets.com/users/brandonatbp

Ola Dantis

Ola Dantis is the Founder and CEO at dwellynn.com, a multifamily investment syndication firm with a focus on acquisitions, repositioning, development, and management of affordable multi-family residential properties. Ola has successfully sourced deals of more than 40 million dollars by working closely with sellers and with other apartment syndicators across the country.

Website: www.dwellynn.com
Podcast: *Dwellynn Show*
Social media: www.facebook.com/MeetOlaDantis
BiggerPockets Profile:
https://www.biggerpockets.com/users/OlaDantis

Anna Myers

Anna Myers serves as Vice President at Grocapitus, a commercial real estate investment company in the San Francisco Bay Area. Anna is a third-generation commercial real estate entrepreneur who applies her 25+ years of experience in technology and business to finding, analyzing, acquiring and asset managing commercial properties in key markets across the U.S.

Website: www.grocapitus.com
Shows: MultifamilyU weekly webinars

Social media: www.facebook.com/MultiFamilyMasters
BiggerPockets Profile: www.biggerpockets.com/users/AnnaMyers

Sean Conlon

Sean J. Conlon is an Irish-American businessman, real estate entrepreneur, investor, television personality, and philanthropist. He is currently chairman and founder of Conlon & Co, CONLON/Christie's International Real Estate, CONLON Commercial and Conlon Capital.

Website: www.seanconlon.com/
Shows: *The Deed*, an unscripted television series focused on real estate investing on CNBC
Social media: @realseanconlon

Lee Arnold

Lee Arnold created The Lee Arnold System of Real Estate Investing to teach clients how to translate workbook education and real estate theory into the real world of real estate investment success. He also founded Cogo Capital®, where real estate investors could go for unlimited funds for their non-owner occupied investments.

Website: www.leearnoldsystem.com
Social media: www.facebook.com/LeeArnoldSystem

Brett Snodgrass

Brett Snodgrass is CEO of Simple Wholesaling and has been a full-time real estate investor for 10+ years. He specializes in wholesaling, wholetailing, creative financing, and scaling a business from a one-man band to an amazing full team running 100s of deals per year.

Website: www.simplewholesaling.com
Social media: www.facebook.com/BrettESnodgrass

Nancy Wallace-Laabs

Nancy Wallace-Laabs has more than 15 years of real estate investing experience, owns several rental properties, and manages properties in the North Dallas-Fort Worth area. Nancy and her husband own KBN Homes, LLC, a real estate investment company that's making neighborhoods great again, one home at a time.

Website: www.kbnhomes.com
Social media: @kbnhomesllc

Anna Kelley

Anna personally owns and manages a multi-million-dollar rental property portfolio and has ownership in over 2,000 units as both an active and passive investor. She is a General Partner, Sponsor & Asset Manager for large multi-million-dollar multifamily real estate acquisitions, and through Zenith Capital Group, actively seeks out the best opportunities for her partners and investors.

Website: www.reimom.com/
Social media: www.facebook.com/annakelleyreimom

Glenn and Amber Schworm

Glenn and Amber Schworm have flipped more than 600 homes (and counting), produced $57 million (and counting) in revenue, and generated monthly cash flow from their rental properties. Through Home Flipping Workshop, they have coached and mentored thousands of people to help them transform their lives and succeed.

Website: www.vestorpro.com/
Podcast: *Real Estate of Mind Show*
Facebook: www.facebook.com/Glenn.Amber.Schworm
Instagram: @glenn_and_amber_schworm

Nick Aalerud

Nick Aalerud started AA Real Estate Enterprises as a real estate acquisition firm in 2005, with the goal of assisting distressed homeowners while providing safe, affordable living for prospective tenants and homebuyers. AARE has since completed over $70 million in closed real estate transactions, including more than 170 rehabs and rebuilds with multiple active projects currently in process, and manages over 50 rental units in New England, Pennsylvania, and Florida.

Website: www.aapremierproperties.com/

Social media: www.facebook.com/NickAA

Joe Lieber

Joe Lieber has bought and sold more than 700 houses since 2008, and he has been involved in the brokerage side, management, rehabs, landlording, wholesaling, and multifamily. In 2004, with the help of his wife and family, Joe opened Real Estate Quest, which later became JL Investment Group, a full service brokerage that specializes in investment properties. He currently owns over 150 units mostly on the Westside of Cleveland.

Website: www.clevelandinvestor.com/

Zeona McIntyre

Zeona has been an Airbnb host since 2012, and she has grown her offerings to consulting and co-hosting homes from Seattle to Spain. At 33 years old, she is an avid real estate investor that owns seven homes and manages fifteen others, all rented short-term.

Website: ZeonaMcIntyre.com
Instagram: @adventurousZ
BiggerPockets Profile: https://www.biggerpockets.com/users/Zeona

Liz Faircloth

Liz is co-founder of the DeRosa Group, which has vast experience repositioning single family homes, multifamily, apartment buildings, mixed-use, retail, and office space to bring the properties to their highest and best use. The company controls close to 700 units of residential and commercial assets throughout the east coast.

Shows: *The Real Estate InvestHER Show*
Website: www.therealestateinvesther.com
Social media: www.facebook.com/groups/therealestateinvesther
BiggerPockets Profile: https://www.biggerpockets.com/users/efaircloth

Shawn Wolfswinkel

Shawn Wolfswinkel is a real estate investor from Houston, TX who has been investing in Real Estate for over 20 years. His company has bought and sold over 1,600 homes, and he currently manages over 1,300 homes and works with over 843 investors in 7 different countries.

Website: www.htownrpm.com
Social media: www.facebook.com/
RealPropertyManagementPreferred
BiggerPockets Profile: https://www.biggerpockets.com/users/
Shawn_W

Felipe Mejia

Felipe is a real estate investor born and raised in Nashville, Tennessee, where he currently resides with his family and owns various rental properties. Felipe has a passion for guiding real estate rookies through the process of acquiring their first real estate purchases.

Shows: *BiggerPockets Real Estate Rookie Podcast*
Website: http://www.teamfelipe.com/
Social media: @felipemejiarei
BiggerPockets Profile: https://www.biggerpockets.com/users/
FelipeM8

Andresa Guidelli

Andresa is a developer who specializes in full-gut renovation projects, new construction, and is currently focusing on building medium to larger commercial developments. She is the founder of "Monarch: Short Term Rentals. Long Term Relationships," where she helps investors diversify their portfolio by entering the short-term rental arena.

Shows: *The Real Estate InvestHER Show*
Website: https://therealestateinvesther.com/
Instagram: @therealestateinvesther
BiggerPockets Profile: https://www.biggerpockets.com/users/
Guidelli

Cory Boatright

Cory has completed over 1,000 real estate transactions, owns over 430 apartment units, and sold over 100 million in real estate transactions, including 100+ unit multifamily, single-family houses, land, and private angel investments. His company and partners buy and sell over 100 properties per year in the Greater Oklahoma City Area. Today he coaches high achieving entrepreneurs and their teams in getting phenomenal results in their businesses.

Website: www.coryboatright.com
Shows: *Real Estate Investing Profits*
Social media: www.facebook.com/coryboatright/
BiggerPockets Profile: https://www.biggerpockets.com/users/coryboatright

Sterling White

Sterling White is a real estate investor by both trade and passion, and he serves as Principal of Sonder Investment Group. Sterling's mission when it comes to real estate is to help as many people as possible and give them the push they need to create their own path to success. To date, he has been involved with the buying and selling of 100+ single family homes.

Website: www.sterlingwhiteofficial.com/
Book: *From ZERO to 400 UNITS*
Instagram: @sterlingwhiteofficial
BiggerPockets Profile: https://www.biggerpockets.com/users/SterlingW

Melisa Clement

Melisa Clement provides design services, consulting, and vision for your new home build or renovation. With over 13 years of experience and an extensive background in fine art and design, every home she remodel is truly a work of art. She creates sanctuaries, not just pretty houses.

Website: melisaclementdesigns.com
Instagram: @melisaclementdesigns

Jack Bosch

Jack Bosch (a.k.a "The Land Guy") is an experienced business owner, entrepreneur, real estate investor, respected industry leader, speaker, educator, and perhaps most importantly a parent and husband. He's the author of the bestselling financial literacy book *Forever Cash* and the creator of the Land Profit Generator real estate without hassles system.

Book: *Forever Cash*
Shows: Land Profit Generator with Jack and Michelle Bosch
Website: www.jackbosch.com
Social media: www.facebook.com/jack.bosch/

More from
BiggerPockets Publishing

How to Invest in Real Estate

Two of the biggest names in the real estate world teamed up to create the most comprehensive manual ever written on getting started in the lucrative business of real estate investing. Joshua Dorkin and Brandon Turner give you an insider's look at the many different real estate niches and strategies so that you can find the one that works best for you, your resources, and your goals.

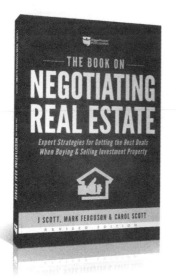

The Book on Negotiating Real Estate

When the real estate market gets hot, it's the investors who know the ins and outs of negotiating who will get the deal. J Scott, Mark Ferguson, and Carol Scott combine real-world experience with the science of negotiation in order to cover all aspects of the negotiation process and maximize your chances of reaching a profitable deal.

If you enjoyed this book, we hope you'll take a moment to check out some of the other great material BiggerPockets offers. BiggerPockets is the real estate investing social network, marketplace, and information hub, designed to help make you a smarter real estate investor through podcasts, books, blog posts, videos, forums, and more. Sign up today—it's free! **Visit www.BiggerPockets.com.**

Retire Early with Real Estate

Escape the 9-to-5 work grind, retire early, and do more with your life! This book provides practical methods for quickly and safely building wealth using the time-tested vehicle of real estate rentals. Experienced real estate investor and early retiree Chad Carson shares the investment strategies he used to create enough passive income to retire at 37. Learn from the more than twenty real estate investors and early retirees profiled in this book—retiring early is possible with a step-by-step strategy at hand!

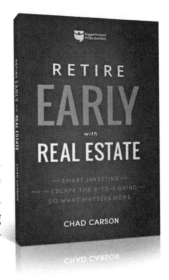

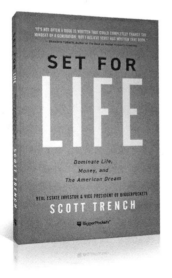

Set for Life: Dominate Life, Money, and the American Dream

Looking for a plan to achieve financial freedom in just five to ten years? *Set for Life* is a detailed fiscal plan targeted at the average income earner starting with few or no assets. It will walk you through three stages of finance, guiding you to your first $25,000 in tangible net worth, then to your first $100,000, and then to financial freedom. This book by Scott Trench will teach you how to build a lifestyle, career, and investment portfolio capable of supporting financial freedom to let you live the life of your dreams.